A Theology of Spiritual Exercises

A Theology of Spiritual Exercises

For a Sustainable Response
to the Call to Holiness and to the Apostolate

Douglas G. Bushman

Published by Douglas G. Bushman

Copyright © 2024 by Douglas G. Bushman
All rights reserved.

ISBN: 978-1-7349094-3-2

Except where otherwise noted, biblical quotations are taken from *The Holy Bible, Revised Standard Version; Second Catholic Edition* (San Francisco: Ignatius Press, 2006).

Excerpts from the English translation of the *Catechism of the Catholic Church* for use in the United States of America Copyright © 1994, United States Catholic Conference, Inc. – Libreria Editrice Vaticana. Used with Permission. English translation of the *Catechism of the Catholic Church*: Modifications from the Editio Typica copyright © 1997, United States Conference of Catholic Bishops—Libreria Editrice Vaticana.

Cover Art: *L'Angélus* by Jean-François Millet (1814–1875) from 1857 to 1859, Musée d'Orsay, Paris, France.

Contents

	Introduction	1
1	"What, then, shall we do?"	18
2	"I chose you and appointed you, that you should bear fruit."	40
3	Paschal Charity, the Soul of the Apostolate	66
4	Foundations for a Theology of Spiritual Exercises	92
5	A Sustainable Set of Spiritual Exercises	133
6	Complementary Exercises of Faith and Reason	187
	Conclusion	222

Introduction

This theology of spiritual exercises in the Christian life is intended to respond primarily to the interests of two groups. The first is those who find themselves asking what they must do to respond to the call of Jesus: "If anyone would come after me, let him deny himself and take up his cross and follow me" (Mk 8:34). It is a great grace to hear this call and to be disposed to act on it. But the call raises the question: What, precisely, must I do to deny myself in order to follow Jesus?

So it was in the gospels, when people responded to the exhortations of St. John the Baptist and the teaching of Jesus by asking: "What, then, shall we do?" These people clearly exhibited a serious commitment to faith: serious enough, in the case of those who put the question to the Baptist, to go out to him and to receive his baptism of repentance; serious enough, as in the case of the rich young man, to have observed the commandments since his earliest days.

The people who posed this question in the gospels, and, as we will see, in the Acts of the Apostles, realized that they were witnessing something new. God had prepared them for this, and their sense that every new gift from God entails a call for a new response led them to ask, "What, then, must we do?" Jesus answers the question in a variety of ways: "Be perfect as your heavenly Father is perfect." "Do what Abraham did." "Pick up your cross." "Bear fruit in order to glorify the Father." "Seek first the kingdom of God." "Forgive one another from your heart." "Just as I have loved you, you also should love one another."

These seemingly various ways of answering the question are fulfilled by following Jesus. For, He is the one who is perfect, did what Abraham did, carried His cross, bore fruit to the glory of the Father, established the kingdom, and forgave sinners. He did all of this by perfectly obeying His Father by loving us "to the end" (Jn 13:1). Thus, the way to act on Jesus's answers to the question, "What, then, must we do?" is to follow Him. But this raises the question: Where is Jesus, that I might follow Him? A theology of spiritual exercises is based on the answer to this question. Spiritual exercises are the wisdom of the saints about how to respond to the many ways that Jesus makes Himself present today so that men and women of today might follow Him.

The theology of spiritual exercises set forth here presupposes the desire to follow Jesus in order to attain the goal of the spiritual life. This goal will be designated by the biblical exhortation: "as he who called you is holy, be holy yourselves in all your conduct; since it is written, 'You shall be holy, for I am holy'" (1 Pt 1:15–16). Ever more perfect participation in God's own holiness is the goal of the spiritual life. Such a goal entails: faith that accepts what God has revealed in Christ about the human person's fulfillment or happiness; hope that strives for this happiness and turns to God for His aid in order to attain it and; charity that is the perfection and holiness of Christ's disciples and friends because God is love and "charity is the soul of holiness."[1] Interest in a theology of spiritual exercises is rooted in a desire for the goal of communion with God on earth, in view of communion with God in heaven. For, the desire for the goal is the only reason for embracing the means to that goal.

These reflections are also directed to those who play a role in guiding others along the paths of the pilgrimage of faith: clergy, catechists, parents, teachers, and spiritual directors. It is hoped that the theology of spiritual exercises set forth here, rudimentary as it may be, and the overview of particular spiritual exercises, basic as it may be, will be

---

[1] *Catechism of the Catholic Church* (hereafter *CCC*), 2nd ed. (Vatican City: Vatican Press, 1997), 826.

a helpful resource for them.

A theology of spiritual exercises might, at first glance, seem unnecessary. For, we are witnessing something of a Vesuvian eruption of publications, traditional as well as digital, on spirituality and the spiritual life. Has there ever been a time when so many courses on the spiritual life and degree programs unified by that theme have been made available and are attracting such great numbers? Moreover, Catholic as well as other Christian media—radio, television, podcasts, social media—are disseminating and facilitating the sharing of spirituality-related content to untold numbers.

Why, then, another book on the spiritual life from the perspective of the role of spiritual exercises? There are several answers to this question. First, and most important, is the encouragement received from former students and others who have found this material helpful. This theology of spiritual exercises draws from the experience of more than fifty years of receiving spiritual direction, more than forty years of serving as a spiritual director, primarily for lay men and women, and more than thirty years of teaching courses on Catholic spirituality. In my experience, God is generous, even lavish, in pouring out graces that bring people to become profoundly aware of His love for them. This gives rise to the question: What must I do to respond to God's love for me? In biblical terms: "What shall I render to the Lord for all his bounty to me?" (Ps 116:12).

The first response to this question surprises at first: Return to God and cling to Him so that He may love you further still. This causes the question to be asked again: But how do I do that? This theology of spiritual exercises makes available the answer to this question that many, according to their own testimony, have found valuable. Humble reverence[2] for their judgment and encouragement

---

[2] For Thomas Aquinas, "humility ... properly regards the reverence whereby man is subjected to God. Wherefore every man, in respect of that which is his own, ought to subject himself to every neighbor, in

is the source of hope that others may find herein an answer, even if only partial, to their question about how to respond to God's love.

Second, this book does not intend to offer *the* theology of spiritual exercises, which would attempt to be theologically erudite or exhaustive. Rather, it is offered as *a* theology of spiritual exercises. This is meant to convey that it is intended both to be a complement to other works on the spiritual life and spiritual exercises (often as a chapter within larger works on spirituality) and to be complemented by them. Even if this book repeats many things that have been presented elsewhere, there is a chance that one or another insight and one or another text educed as support will be the occasion for readers to advance in their understanding of the subject.

Third, several principal themes run throughout these reflections and unify them. These derive from Sacred Scripture and the tradition of Catholic theology and spirituality. The Second Vatican Council is an especially privileged source here. My years of theological service to the Church bears the marks of the historical period of the Church's life following the Council. I have taken seriously the challenge of adhering to what then Cardinal Wojtyła, later St. John Paul II, called the principle of integration. According to this principle, because the Holy Spirit guides the Church, throughout the Church's pilgrimage of faith there is an essential continuity in doctrine and in the Christian life based on that doctrine. For this reason, "we can rediscover and, as it were, re-read the magisterium of the last Council in the whole previous magisterium of the Church, while on the other we can rediscover and re-read the whole preceding magisterium in that of the last Council."[3]

---

respect of that which the latter has of God's" (*ST* II-II, Q. 161, a. 3). Throughout, *ST* is the abbreviation for *Summa theologiae*.

[3] Karol Wojtyła (John Paul II), *Sources of Renewal: The Implementation of Vatican II* (San Francisco: Harper and Row, 1980), 40. On

Vatican II and the prior tradition shed light on one another. The Council did not alter the wisdom of the saints regarding the vocation to holiness but rather penetrated it more deeply in order to make it resound for the Church of our age. It did not attempt to present a complete theology of Christian life and the multiple subjects it entails. It should be no surprise, then, that in this theology of spiritual exercises, major themes from the Council serve an architectonic purpose, while the saints' lives and writings illustrate them or, in christological terms, incarnate them. First among these principles is the mutual complementarity of theocentrism and anthropocentrism—God-centeredness and man-centeredness. Once God defines His purpose in creation and salvation history as communion with men, and especially when God becomes man in Jesus Christ, the two are inseparable. To emphasize one to the detriment of the other always results in a distortion of Christian faith and life.

This is also true for spiritual exercises. Having God's love for man, fully revealed in Jesus Christ, as their foundation, a theology of spiritual exercises must safeguard the proper balance of theocentrism and anthropocentrism, that is, the role of God and the role of man. By the faith that is operative in them, spiritual exercises reproduce the dynamism of God's search for man and man's search for God in salvation history.

> In Christ, religion is no longer a "blind search for God" (cf. Acts 17:27) but the *response of faith* to God who reveals himself. It is a response in which man speaks to God as his Creator and Father, a response made possible by that one Man who is also the consubstantial Word in whom God speaks to each individual person and by whom each individual person is

---

theocentrism and anthropocentrism, see John Paul II, *Dives in misericordia*, 1.

enabled to respond to God. What is more, in this Man all creation responds to God. Jesus Christ is the new beginning of everything. In him all things come into their own; they are taken up and given back to the Creator from whom they first came.

In Jesus Christ God not only speaks to man but also *seeks him out.* The Incarnation of the Son of God attests that God goes in search of man. Jesus speaks of this search as the finding of a lost sheep (cf. Lk 15:1–7). It is a search which *begins in the heart of God* and culminates in the Incarnation of the Word. If God goes in search of man, created in his own image and likeness, he does so because he loves him eternally in the Word, and wishes to raise him in Christ to the dignity of an adoptive son. God therefore goes in search of man who *is his special possession* in a way unlike any other creature. Man is God's possession by virtue of a choice made in love: God seeks man out, moved by his fatherly heart.[4]

The root of this mutual search is a mutual love, which the *Catechism* conveys by the metaphor of thirst. "God thirsts that we may thirst for Him." Prayer, the most fundamental spiritual exercise, "is the encounter of God's thirst with ours."[5] Faith in what God has revealed allows us to see things from His perspective, and with this we realize that God's search for us is first: "We love because He first loved us" (1 Jn 4:19). Prayer, like the faith that is active in it, is our response to God's initiative in revealing His love.[6]

---

[4] John Paul II, *Tertio millennio adveniente*, 6–7.

[5] *CCC*, 2560.

[6] On faith as response to God's initiative, see *CCC*, 166. On prayer as response to God's initiative, see *CCC*, 2567.

Introduction

Our prayer is participation in the prayer of the Eternal Son, Jesus Christ, true God and true man.[7] Spiritual exercises are events of encounter, in which these two searches and loves, of God and man, meet.

In actual practice, the christological theme of imitating Christ takes the form of the ecclesiological theme of imitating the saints and drawing from the fount of their wisdom. St. Paul puts it this way: "Be imitators of me, as I am of Christ" (1 Cor 11:1). Vatican II's teaching on the Communion of Saints[8] bears the marks of its pastoral solicitude to promote "an ever-increasing vigor to the Christian life of the faithful."[9] The Council's concern was to overcome a twofold split: between faith and daily life, and between liturgy and daily life. Both splits are the result of the devastating influence of secularism on increasing numbers of those baptized faithful who retain only a veneer of Christian faith and who live more and more "as if God did not even exist."[10]

To attain the goal of a new ardor of holiness, Vatican II wished to stir the memory of faith regarding the role of the saints in the Church's life. For, God "speaks to us in them."[11] It also clarified that: "The authentic veneration of the saints consists not so much in the multiplying of external acts, but rather in the greater intensity of our love, whereby, for our own greater good and that of the whole Church, we seek from the saints 'example in their way of life, fellowship in their communion, and aid by their

---

[7] *CCC*, 2616: Christ prays in us and we pray in Him. Our prayer is a participation in Christ's prayer. See *CCC*, 2635, 2637, 2716, 2780, 2842.

[8] See Vatican II, *Lumen gentium*, Chapter 7.

[9] Vatican II, *Sacrosanctum Concilium*, 1. This is a principal theme that runs through all of the Council's documents. The most elaborate development of the theme comes in Chapter 5 of *Lumen gentium*, on The Universal Call to Holiness in the Church.

[10] John Paul II often used this phrase to describe secularized Catholics. Both he and Benedict XVI also spoke of a "quiet apostasy" to describe the gradual alienation from the Church of many among the baptized.

[11] Vatican II, *Lumen gentium*, 50.

intercession.'"[12] The saints are not only examples of heroic virtue. By their lives and in their writings, they also bear witness to what we can and must do in order to open ourselves to the graces that God provides so that we can advance in greater perfection of the highest Christian virtue, charity. They also exhort us to practice the very spiritual exercises that they found beneficial, and many among them set forth elements of a theology of spiritual exercises. The theology of spiritual exercises presented here is an aspect of a pastoral theology of the Communion of Saints.

Fourth, this theology of spiritual exercises shows that examination of conscience and prayer are the two most fundamental spiritual exercises. The efficacy of other spiritual exercises depends on conscience and prayer. Without these, there is no authentic encounter with God, and spiritual exercises are exactly that: encounters with the God who defines Himself as love and ever eager to bless us with His grace. The whole point of spiritual exercises is simply to come into the presence of divine love in order to let God do what He does so well, that is, to love us. As is always the case, God takes the initiative, and spiritual exercises are our response. They are ways that we show hospitality to God and cooperate with Him in His approach of love.

This theology of spiritual exercises, then, incorporates a central theme of revelation and tradition, that is, the primacy of God's initiative of love and the corresponding response of receptivity on man's part. In this way, they closely follow Vatican II, especially the Constitution on Divine Revelation, and the *Catechism*. For the latter, the couplet of divine initiative and human response is a major structural theme. It is an essential element of the theme of dialogue, which the *Catechism* enlists in order to set forth

---

[12] Vatican II, *Lumen gentium*, 51. The text uses the traditional expression, "cult of the saints." I have substituted "veneration" for "cult" in order to avoid potential misunderstanding.

its teaching on revelation and faith, the liturgy, and prayer. Based on these, spiritual exercises are dialogical in character. They entail a dialogue between the God of love—fully revealed in Jesus Christ and the gift of the Holy Spirit—and those who, by faith, desire to live in the certainty of being loved.[13]

Vatican II took place at a time when faith in God's love was profoundly misunderstood as an affront to human dignity, responsibility, and engagement in the world. An increasingly secular culture promoted man as a self-realizing shaper of history, thus cutting him off from God. The Council provided a much-needed restatement of the truth about God's love in order to affirm two things. First, man is not wrong, but on the contrary is coming to grips with the reality of his own mystery, when he becomes aware of his deepest dynamism and desire to be a genuine actor, an authentic agent engaged in the struggle to make the world conform more fully to his surpassing dignity. Second, this dynamism and desire can only be fully realized by the love and grace of God that transforms man into being a genuine collaborator with God in the realization of His plan of love.[14]

These two assertions come together in St. John Paul II's summary of the purpose of Vatican II: "To 'make human life more human' is the Council's fundamental objective, closely linked to the desire to share in the divine life and in the mission of Christ."[15] For, "Christ ... fully reveals man to man himself and makes his supreme calling clear."[16]

---

[13] See *CCC*, 2778. See also, Benedict XVI: "this is faith: being loved by God and letting oneself be loved by God in Jesus Christ. Letting oneself be loved in this way is the light that helps us to bear our daily burden" (General Audience, February 16, 2011).

[14] The Council develops this in the Pastoral Constitution on the Church in the Modern World, *Gaudium et spes*.

[15] Wojtyła, *Sources of Renewal*, 279.

[16] Vatican II, *Gaudium et spes*, 22.

Where can people of faith find God's transforming love and grace? Above all, in the liturgy, and especially in the Eucharist. Participation in the Eucharist is the supreme spiritual exercise. All the other spiritual exercises prepare for and culminate in the Eucharist, and the Eucharist enriches them. For this reason, we can understand spiritual exercises in light of Vatican II's goal for liturgical renewal. For, the liturgy is the work of the risen Lord, Jesus Christ, who acts through the very love that He fully revealed in His paschal mystery. At the same time, the liturgy is our response of faith to this initiative of love. Vatican II intended that this response of faith should match, as much as possible, the totality of Christ's gift of Himself in love.

The Council described the faith-response to Christ's work in the liturgy as the full, conscious, and active participation in the liturgical action in which Christ actuates His paschal love for us. The term, "active receptivity,"[17] incisively conveys this duality of the primacy of Christ's initiative of love and man's response and cooperation. The Virgin Mary's faith at the Annunciation illustrates this. She actively willed that God accomplish in her what His word announced, through the Archangel Gabriel. The virginal conception of Jesus is God's work, accomplished by overshadowing Mary with the Holy Spirit, but not without her consent so to be overshadowed. Mary's faith is the paradigm of the active receptivity of faith at work in every spiritual exercise. Full, conscious, and active participation in spiritual exercises enhances the full, conscious, and active participation in the Eucharist, and vice versa.

Finally, the theology of spiritual exercises presented here underscores the inseparability of love of God, love of self, and love of neighbor. The unity of these three loves underpins the unity of faith and life, since the revelation of

---

[17] John Paul II spoke of an "active passivity" in his *Ad limina* address to bishops of the United States, October 9, 1998, 3.

God's love in Jesus Christ is central to both. God is love and man, made in His image, is "the supreme creation of God's love, who in love alone will rediscover the meaning of his own life and destiny."[18] Judgments of conscience, which are the proximate rule for action, specify what must be done or avoided for a concrete act to correspond to these three loves. Faith allows believers to discover that love is the meaning of life. Judgments of conscience make that meaning actually come to life in concrete human acts. A properly informed Christian conscience assures that the revealed truth about love becomes a life of "truth in love" (Eph 4:15).[19]

Spiritual exercises are encounters with God's love, fully revealed in Jesus Christ, especially in His paschal mystery. For this reason, they promote the ongoing purification of conscience. A conscience purified from the dead works of sin is the great gift that Christ imparts through Baptism (Heb 9:14; 10:20–22; 1 Pt 3:21). In God's plan, the function of conscience is to make judgments regarding what it means to love God, self, and neighbor in concrete human acts. A life that is fully meaningful and integrated is the fruit of cooperation with God in the purification of conscience for the sake of a holy life, which is the perfection of Christian love.

The second unity that is a principal focus of this theology of spiritual exercises is the unity of the call to holiness and the call to the apostolate. Spiritual exercises are encounters with God's love. They are transformative

---

[18] John Paul II, Message for 7th World Day of the Sick, February 11, 1999, 8 (dated December 8, 1998).

[19] St. Thomas comments on this verse: "put true doctrine into practice since it is not enough simply to hear or teach the truth, it must be acted on as well. Thus the Apostle counsels Timothy: 'take heed to yourself and to doctrine; be earnest in them. For in doing this you shall both save yourself and them that hear you' (1 Tim 4:16). 'Be doers of the word and not hearers only (Jas 1:22) since doers shall be justified' (Rom 2:13)" (Aquinas, *Commentary on St. Paul's Letter to the Ephesians*, Ch. 4, lect. 5, [Marietti, 222]).

because God's love is transformative. Spiritual exercises are ways of cooperating with God in being renewed in the image of His Son, Jesus Christ. This ongoing renewal deepens participation in Christ's relation to His Father (love of God) and in the mission that He received from the Father (love of neighbor).

Spiritual exercises, then, have a missionary dimension, because by its very nature Christian love is missionary. Vatican II emphasized that mission (or apostolate, ministry, service) is not something added onto holiness, as if one could be holy without engagement in mission. Mission is holiness in action. The holy God, who is love, reveals Himself through the missions of the Son and the Holy Spirit. For this reason, communion with God in holiness necessarily entails mission. While the mission to love one's neighbor raises practical questions of prudence regarding how best to love, no accumulation of such practical wisdom can compensate for a defect in holiness. This is precisely where spiritual exercises come in. Spiritual exercises are ordered directly to the encounter with God's love. Because His love is transformative, they bear the fruit of a renewed commitment to love one's neighbor as oneself, that is, to the mission of bearing witness to God's love through serving others. This is why this theology of spiritual exercises incorporates another theme of Vatican II, which is a very rich theme of the Catholic tradition, namely, the primacy of being over having and doing.[20]

The great interest in the spiritual life, mentioned above, must be counted among the most impressive and edifying signs of the times. How could it be attributed to anything other than the work of the Holy Spirit, working in the hearts of countless men and women? It is to be expected that the same Holy Spirit will provide for the need for a sound theology of the spiritual life, spiritual direction, and

---

[20] See Vatican II, *Gaudium et spes*, 35.

a theology of spiritual exercises. This work of the Holy Spirit should be understood in relation to Vatican II. For, the Council insisted that the renewal of the Church is first and foremost the renewal of Christian life, a personal renewal into deeper and deeper holiness through ongoing conversion. St. Paul VI and St. John Paul II told us that the Council's teaching on the universal call to holiness recapitulates its message and purpose.[21] Believing that the Holy Spirit was at work guiding the Council in this renewed emphasis on holiness, it is to be expected that the same Holy Spirit is guiding the Church in implementing the Council, even as He both inspired the Sacred Scriptures and enlightens the minds of those who read them.

In more general terms, the same Holy Spirit who provides objective gifts of sanctification—Scripture, sacraments, charisms, magisterium—also provides personal graces so that the objective gifts can bear fruit in the lives of people of faith. This reproduces how the Spirit acted in salvation history. He guided God's chosen people by purifying their hope that God would accomplish all that He promised with the coming of the Messiah, and He Himself is the holy Anointing of Jesus, the Christ, who fulfills God's promises.

Spiritual exercises operate according to the same twofold activity of the Holy Spirit. He excites in Christ's disciples and friends an irresistible desire to grow in holiness, and He provides the means by which He fulfills this desire. This is why the theology of spiritual exercises exposited here draws from the saints, and thus from the Scriptures and Tradition from which they drew and to which their lives bear witness as a synthesis of love of God, love of self, and love of neighbor. In the saints, we see the Holy Spirit's twofold activity of making Christ present objectively and working personally in the hearts of

---

[21] See Paul VI, Apostolic Letter, given Motu proprio, *Sanctitas clarior*, March 19, 1969, and John Paul II, *Christifideles laici*, 16.

those who desire to respond to His call to follow Him in the holiness of His way of life. Spiritual exercises are the ways in which Christ's disciples and friends cooperate with this twofold action of the Holy Spirit by imitating the saints and taking their wisdom as God's answer to the question, "What, then, must I do?"

The phrase "disciples and friends" has appeared three times in this introduction and will be used throughout this book. This intends to convey the implications of Jesus's words indicating that His paschal mystery will bring about a transition for the apostles from being His disciples to being His friends: "You are my friends if you do what I command you. No longer do I call you servants, for the servant does not know what his master is doing; but I have called you friends, for all that I have heard from my Father I have made known to you" (Jn 15:14–15). It is true that "servant" and "disciple" are not equivalent and that the Gospels and Acts of the Apostles refer to the apostles and others as disciples even after the resurrection and Pentecost. Nevertheless, it is one thing to be a disciple who follows Christ, is taught by Him, and even lives with Him prior to His passion, death, resurrection, and the outpouring of the Holy Spirit, on one hand, and after these, on the other hand. It is the difference between the way that the apostles responded to Jesus's initial call to follow Him (Mt 4:19; 8:22; 9:9) and the way that they followed Him when He renewed the call after His resurrection (Jn 21:19). It turns out that even though they had left everything of their former lives to follow Jesus (Mt 19:27), prior to His death and resurrection they were in fact "following Jesus at a distance" (Mt 26:58; Mk 14:54; Lk 22:54).

Every friend of Jesus is also a disciple, but not every disciple is a true friend of His. For Jesus, to be His friend entails two things: knowing all He reveals, which He has received from the Father, and doing what He commands. Both of these become possible only after the consummation of the Father's plan in Jesus's suffering, death, resurrection, and the outpouring of the Holy Spirit on Pentecost. This in no way diminishes the significance of the time of discipleship prior to the paschal mystery. In fact, it magnifies its importance. For, without the formation that Jesus provided, the apostles would not have recovered from having denied Him, either in word and deed, as Peter, or in deed alone.[22] No one becomes a friend of Jesus without first having been a disciple.

Spiritual exercises are ordered to the ongoing conversion from those ways in which disciples of Jesus still follow Him at a distance into the friendship that is characterized by following Him into and through the paschal mystery. For, conversion is the law of the spiritual life. It is correlative to the active receptivity of God's mercy, which Jesus fully revealed in His paschal mystery. This is why the themes of God's mercy and conversion figure so prominently in this theology of spiritual exercises.

Readers must avoid drawing two corollaries from the preceding. The first concerns the very common use in spiritual and theological writings of the term "disciple." Authors who use that term rightly use it in the same way that the Acts of the Apostles refers to the first believers in Christ as His disciples. As was said, friends of Jesus do not cease to be His disciples. So, readers of this book should not read the distinction being made here into the writings of others.

Second, it should not be thought that the discipleship

---

[22] Significantly, the Gospels record the other apostles professing their readiness to die with Jesus, as Peter did: "And so said all the disciples" (Mt 26:35; Mk 14:31). We know that none of the apostles died with Him *then*. Only *later*, transformed by the power of the Holy Spirit and we know not how many celebrations of the Eucharist, they would die with Him as His martyrs. Thus, like the Parable of the Prodigal Son, Jesus's words to Peter, "Where I am going you cannot follow me *now*; but you shall follow *afterward*" (Jn 13:36), can be understood as applying to those ways in which a disciple does not yet follow Jesus into and through His paschal mystery.

and friendship duality entails mutual exclusivity. For, the two coexist in the lives of those who follow Jesus. In reality, anyone who heeds the call to follow Christ is by that very fact His friend. For, no one can do so without the grace of the Holy Spirit and without some knowledge of His paschal mystery. During the time of their discipleship, the apostles were most certainly Jesus's friends. And, yet, He reserves these words, "You are my friends," until the end of His mission. It is as if He said: Henceforth, following your fall and conversion and empowerment by the Holy Spirit, you will be fully and perfectly my friends.

It is a question, then, of realizing that in some ways those who become Jesus's friends through personal appropriation of and responsibility for the graces of Baptism still follow Him at a distance and are thus still, perhaps only in some respects, more disciples than friends. The Parable of the Prodigal Son can be read in the same way. Someone who has refused to cooperate with the graces leading to Baptism or who has renounced the graces of Baptism through a mortal sin that remains unrepented may well totally identify with the prodigal son after he had turned away from his father and made off for a distant land. But those who take seriously the call to follow Jesus are not living the totality of their lives in a distant land. Rather, there are certain aspects of their lives that remain in a distant land or have not completed the pilgrimage of return to the father's house.

The use of the expression, "disciple and friend," then, is meant to occasion the reader's awareness of the ways in which discipleship has not yet become friendship with Christ—ways that a disciple still follows Jesus at a distance, or still loiters in a distant land. May it be that this will contribute to this book being more than a source of information about the role of spiritual exercises in the lives of Christ's disciples and friends. May it be that it is also the occasion for moments of truth in the reader's conscience, that is, transforming encounters with Jesus Christ, who is the truth about God's merciful love. May it be that reading this book will bear the fruit not only of being better informed about spiritual exercises but also of advancements from discipleship to friendship with Jesus.

1.
"What then shall we do?" (Luke 3:10)

The theology of spiritual exercises presented here intends to be a response to the question asked by many who become aware of having received a grace of conversion: "So, now what do I do? Now that God has given more to me, what more does He expect in return?" The question spontaneously arises from the awareness of being the beneficiary of God's blessing: "What shall I return to the Lord for all his bounty to me?" (Ps 116:12).

God expects the question, and is greatly pleased by it. It gives Him glory, since it is a remarkable effect of His great love. In fact, God blesses us precisely so that we will ask the question, "What, then, shall I do?" as our first response to His blessing. For, He knows that having made us in His image, when we become aware of His having blessed us, we are moved to respond by blessing Him.[1] But we must know what it means to bless Him in return. Therefore, when He blesses us with His gifts, it is so that we will turn to Him to ask: "What is the proper response to having been loved by you, Lord?" The first thing we should ask for is that God should bless us even more. In this, St. Thomas Aquinas is a great model. When the Lord asked him what He could grant to him, St. Thomas responded: "Nothing but you, Lord." It is a great witness to His love that we should more ardently desire to receive it more and more.

Spiritual exercises operate according to this logic of responding to being loved by desiring to be loved even more. God's response to the question, "What, then, must I do?" is, then, twofold. First, He says, "Now that you have tasted my love, come back for more. For, I always have

---

[1] See *CCC*, 1078–1083.

more to give." Spiritual exercises are the ways in which we return to God to receive the "more" that He has to give. Second, He says, "Now that you have received my love, be my associate in bringing others to receive this love." Spiritual exercises are also foundational for collaborating with God in the mission to love others whom He desires to love through us. Because we cannot give what has not first been given and received, in order to be agents of divine love we must first receive that love.

The awareness of being a beneficiary of God's love is the foundation of the virtue of religion. This virtue is traditionally understood as a form of justice toward God. It is the response of those who recognize that because they have received everything from God they owe Him unreserved reverence, thanksgiving, obedience, and love. This is what it means to affirm that every human person is by nature religious.[2] Religion is the response of the image of God to the acts of God's love. Spiritual exercises, by which we submit to being loved by God, are acts of religion because it is a matter of justice that we relate to God based on the truth about who He is, and the truth is that "God is love" (1 Jn 4:8, 16). We relate to God justly, we fulfill all justice, when in response to His love for us we love Him with our whole heart, mind, soul, and strength.

The word "religion" makes many think first of institutions and organizations. In the case of Catholicism, and Christianity more generally, this is certainly not inaccurate. Indeed, like most religions, Catholicism entails a number of objective, institutional elements, such as sacred writings, liturgical rites, a hierarchical structure, settled procedures, and prescribed and proscribed activities. But it is inaccurate to think of the Catholic Church primarily in institutional terms. Perhaps reacting to the obvious and undeniable disconnect between the way that some Christians live and their beliefs and practices, it has

---

[2] See *CCC*, 44, 1807, and 2095.

become something of a trend for people to shun institutional religion and to say that they do not have a religion, but they do have a spirituality. They think of religion as some optional, man-made and thus imperfect and limited institution, and "spirituality" as some, often vague, personal relationship with God or transcendent higher power. The prevailing attitude is: Spirituality, that is, some kind of personal relationship with God?—Of course! Organized religion?—Of course not!

Even if it is not thoroughly thought out, this kind of rejection of religion actually affirms a fundamental truth about Catholicism. For Christ's apostolic Church, primacy goes to the interior and profoundly personal acts of religion. The Church's outward, visible, institutional aspects are meant both to enrich and to express the interior and deeply personal acts of religion.[3] For, as Vatican II asserted, "the exercise of religion, of its very nature, consists before all else in those internal, voluntary and free acts whereby man sets the course of his life directly toward God."[4] In the language of the Bible, faith and religion are a matter of the heart. This is what recent popes and the *Catechism* mean when they describe faith as a personal relationship with God.[5]

The prophets warned against the disconnect between the inward acts of religion and its outward acts. One of the more graphic images they employed was a call for the circumcision of the heart.[6] King David came to realize that the sacrifice that is acceptable to God is a broken, contrite heart (Ps 51:13). The prophets denounced those who

---

[3] See Vatican II, *Sacrosanctum Concilium*, 2 and *Lumen gentium*, 8.

[4] Vatican II, *Dignitatis humanae*, 3.

[5] See John Paul II, *Dominum et Vivificantem*, 34; Homily, February 7, 1993, 4; *CCC*, 299, 2558.

[6] See Dt 10:16; 30:6; Jer 4:4. St. Paul summarized: "For he is not a real Jew who is one outwardly, nor is true circumcision something external and physical. He is a Jew who is one inwardly, and real circumcision is a matter of the heart, spiritual and not literal" (Rom 2:29).

thought that they could appease God with outward sacrifices when they were mistreating the poor. Jesus received this tradition and fulfilled it by perfecting it. Twice he quoted the prophet Hosea: "I desire mercy, and not sacrifice" (Hos 6:6; Mt 9:13; 12:7). His every thought, word, and action was reverence, thanksgiving, obedience, and love for the Father. At the same time, His mission was ordered to calling us His friends. His final act, in which His whole life and mission culminated, was the offering of His life as the definitive sacrifice of love to the Father for us.

To affirm the primacy of the internal, spiritual, and interpersonal in religion is not to affirm that religion—man's response to God's generosity—is only this and that faith can do without certain exterior, visible, and institutional elements of religion. Primacy or priority does not eliminate that which is secondary. Rather, that which is secondary can only be understood by reason of its relation to what is primary. Outward acts of religion, including the bodily and institutional acts that are involved in spiritual exercises, express the interior acts. Regarding sacrifices, St. Augustine put it this way: "every sacrifice that is offered exteriorly is a sign of an interior sacrifice in which one offers one's soul to God."[7]

St. Thomas Aquinas explained that the relation between the interior and exterior, invisible and visible, personal and institutional elements of religion is rooted in and reflects man's nature as composed of soul and body.[8] He also taught that, just as the soul is superior to the body yet depends on it, the interior acts by which we know and love God are primary while depending in a certain way on exterior acts that accompany them.[9] This is clear in the

---

[7] Augustine, *City of God*, 10.5.

[8] "It would seem most fitting that by visible things the invisible things of God should be made known" (Aquinas, *ST* III, Q. 1, a. 1). Also, the divine missions, which in themselves are invisible, are fittingly made known to man through visible missions (see *ST* I, Q. 43, a. 7).

[9] See Aquinas, *ST* II-II, Q. 81, a. 7. See also *ST* I-II, Q. 106, aa. 1, 2; Q.

celebration of the sacraments, which presume interior acts of faith.[10] It is clear, most fundamentally, in the observable actions of Jesus Christ.

From the outset, following Christ entails "a conversion that passes from the heart to deeds and then to the Christian's whole life."[11]

> Jesus' call to conversion and penance, like that of the prophets before him, does not aim first at outward works, "sackcloth and ashes," fasting and mortification, but at the *conversion of the heart, interior conversion.* Without this, such penances remain sterile and false; however, interior conversion urges expression in visible signs, gestures and works of penance.[12]

With the preceding, we have identified one of the fundamental truths about spiritual exercises, namely, that in their essence they consist of interior acts of knowing and loving God. There are also secondary elements that accompany these interior acts and are ordered to them, like bodily positions conducive to prayer, a book upon which to meditate, the act of traveling to a church or shrine in order to pray or to celebrate the sacraments, and the visible elements of the sacraments.

But there is more. It is clear that many people come to a point at which they put the question to God, "What, then, must I do?" yet do not follow through on God's response. They are like the rich young man in the Gospel, who, having heard Jesus's full response to his question, "Teacher, what good deed must I do to have eternal life?"

108, a. 1. In words attributed to St. Francis Xavier: "it is not the actual physical exertion that counts towards one's progress, nor the nature of the task, but by the spirit of faith with which it is undertaken."

[10] See *CCC*, 1122–1126.

[11] John Paul II, *Reconciliatio et paenitentia*, 4.

[12] *CCC*, 1430.

(Mt 19:16), "went away sorrowful" (Mt 19:22). He was hoping for a different answer. He did not anticipate that Christ's response would be so demanding.

The case of the rich young man drives home the confrontational character of God's word. Because human receptivity has been distorted by sin, God's word cannot fail to result in a confrontation that demands conversion. Jesus is God's Word. His every word is a sign to be opposed and contradicted (Lk 2:34) by the presuppositions of minds that have been formed apart from God's word. We see, then, that being honest with oneself is crucial when asking the question, "What, then, must I do?"

But, what does it mean to be honest with oneself? This question places at center stage the one thing without which spiritual exercises cannot produce any fruit. As will be discussed later, it is the issue of how the nature of God's love and the freedom and responsibility inherent in human dignity combine to make it necessary that men cooperate with God in His acts of loving them. In the end, am I prepared to embrace the violence of conversion by confronting opposition and contradiction within me, and to resolve them by "taking sides with God's truth against myself?"[13] Honesty with oneself is, essentially, to be humble by acknowledging the rights of God's truth to shape how we view ourselves, God, and the world.

We must pause here, in order to elaborate on this most fundamental disposition without which spiritual exercises are but a masquerade. St. Augustine describes conversion as "severity against oneself." It is an act of judging oneself in light of God's truth in order "to avoid being judged by God." The realism with which he understands faith as participation in God's truth leads him to conclude that by that same faith we participate in God's judgment. "So let those who find themselves in such case take their seats on

---

[13] Hans Urs von Balthasar, *Prayer*, trans. A. V. Littledale (New York: Sheed and Ward, 1961), 183.

the bench of their minds against themselves …. Let them put themselves in the dock before themselves, to avoid this happening to them later on."[14]

The *Catechism* captures the eschatological dimension of Augustine's words and ties it to the Sacrament of Penance and Reconciliation: "In this sacrament, the sinner, placing himself before the merciful judgment of God, anticipates in a certain way the judgment to which he will be subjected at the end of his earthly life. For it is now, in this life, that we are offered the choice between life and death, and it is only by the road of conversion that we can enter the Kingdom, from which one is excluded by grave sin."[15]

Humility in the truth and humility for the truth: this is the foundation of the spiritual edifice. Every person who is honest with himself will agree with St. Paul: "I do not understand my own actions. For I do not do what I want, but I do the very thing I hate" (Rom 7:15). The reason why God's word is received with opposition and contradiction, which must be resolved through conversion, is because of the interior opposition and contradiction that the honest man discovers within himself. The honest man discovers that his capacity and thus his vocation to love—even to love himself—are distorted, wounded, and weakened. The very inability to understand his own behavior indicates that man is not his creator and master, for how can the maker not know what he makes? The truth about man and his dependence upon God is ultimately rooted in the truth that God reveals about Himself. Man's search for truth constitutes the most profoundly personal, interior dimension of man's own mystery.

The question of honesty in the search for truth leads to the question: Am I prepared for an answer that does not

---

[14] Augustine, Sermon, 351, 7, in *The Works of St. Augustine. A Translation for the 21st Century. Sermons III/10, 341–400 On Various Subjects*, trans. Edmund Hill (Hyde Park, NY: New City Press, 1995), 125–26.

[15] *CCC*, 1470.

correspond in all respects to what I might expect? The story of the rich young man, who turned away from Jesus because he was not ready to sell all that he owned in order to follow Him, forewarns us. As does the account of the zealous Israelites who came to Jeremiah to ask the prophet, in a matter of life and death, what they should do (Jer 42:3). They were, as it turns out, overly confident in their determination to abide by what Jeremiah would tell them: "May the Lord be a true and faithful witness against us if we do not act according to all the word with which the Lord your God sends you to us. Whether it is good or evil, we will obey the voice of the Lord our God to whom we are sending you, that it may be well with us when we obey the voice of the Lord our God" (Jer 42:5–6). When Jeremiah informed them of the Lord's answer, they rejected it (Jer 43:1–2). They had a preconceived idea of how a God of love and wisdom would answer their question. The obedience that they had thought they were ready to enact turned out to be conditional. So long as God's answer met their test of what is worthy of God, they were ready to obey.

Before putting the question to Jesus, "What, then, must I do?" it is wise to reflect on what happened to the rich young man and the Israelites at the time of Jeremiah. One might well ponder Isaiah's words: "For my thoughts are not your thoughts, nor are your ways my ways" (Is 55:8). So, putting the question to Jesus entails putting a question to oneself: Do I really believe that He is the Son of God, whose wisdom is divine and who, because He loves me, will never be anything but truthful with me about what is best for me?[16] Each one must probe his own heart and conscience to put motives and understandings to the test. For, Jesus answers the question, "What, then, must I do?" in the same way that He answered the question of James

---

[16] This is the meaning of the formula that God "can neither deceive nor be deceived" (Vatican I, quoted in *CCC*, 156).

and John. They asked to sit, one on His right and the other on His left, in the glory of His kingdom. Aware that they did not understand that His kingdom will come only through His suffering and death, Jesus answered: "You do not know what you are asking. Are you able to drink the cup that I drink, or be baptized with the baptism that I am baptized with?" (Mk 10:38)?

The lesson learned from the Israelites who approached Jeremiah, the rich young man, and James and John, exposes just one of the great fallacies of the preference for a personal, that is, private form of religion or spirituality that is independent of any institutional aspect. In the end, there is no real dialogue between the person of private religion and God. He usurps the place of God by answering his questions for himself. By imposing upon God his own way of thinking, according to which He simply could not entangle Himself with a human institution, this person has set himself up as the final arbiter of what God can and cannot say and do. How likely is it that his answer to his own question will include the most difficult and demanding aspects of Christ's answer to the rich young man, and James and John? Unlike God, we can both be deceived and deceive—even ourselves!

It is a redeeming quality—literally!—therefore, that the Catholic Church precedes us. The Church comes before us. The Church's doctrine, sacraments, and hierarchical structure have been determined independently from us— and by a Higher Power of Wisdom and Love, Jesus Christ. We do not shape the Church, her doctrine, and the witness of the saints according to our own preferences. Christ's institution of the Church is the foundation for the objective assurance that we are not deceiving ourselves and that our life of ongoing conversion is what God intends it to be. How else can we be confident that we are truly dying to ourselves rather than following our own plan for life?

Neither God nor Christ nor His Church nor His saints will fashion their response to the question, "What, then, must I do?" in order to satisfy our superficial desires and understanding of God's ways. For, they love us too much to do so.[17] The saints, in fact, show us that fidelity to Christ takes the form of fidelity to His Church. This is why faith and humility are the conditions for membership to the Church. Faith: that "Christ ... the one Mediator and the unique way of salvation....affirmed the necessity of faith and baptism and thereby affirmed also the necessity of the Church."[18] Faith: that He is present in His Church and that to say "Yes" to His call to follow Him is to enter and to remain in His Church. Humility: to submit to God by submitting to what Christ has established.[19]

While there are numerous elements of the Church that God Himself has established—sacred doctrine, sacraments, hierarchical-apostolic structure—this theology of spiritual exercises takes the lives and writings of the saints as the proximate norm of the spiritual life. In the saints, we perceive the transformative impact of the truth of doctrine, the grace of the sacraments, and the humility of submission to divinely established authority. Saints are proof that the Church is the efficacious "sacrament of Christ's action at work in her through the mission of the Holy Spirit."[20] Saints are proof of "the presence and action of the life-giving Spirit,"[21] Who abundantly imparts charisms of holiness,[22] which apostolic authority has recognized as

---

[17] This is the principle that the *CCC* invokes to explain why God does not answer certain prayers: "God cannot answer us, for he desires our well-being, our life" (*CCC*, 2737).

[18] Vatican II, *Lumen gentium*, 14.

[19] "[H]umility ... properly regards the reverence whereby man is subjected to God. Wherefore every man, in respect of that which is his own, ought to subject himself to every neighbor, in respect of that which the latter has of God's" (Aquinas, *ST* II-II, Q. 161, a. 3).

[20] *CCC,* 1118.

[21] John Paul II, *Dominum et Vivificantem*, 64.

[22] On the charisms of holiness, see Congregation for the Doctrine of the Faith, Letter to the bishops of the Catholic Church on the relationship between hierarchical and charismatic gifts for the life and the mission of

authentic and worthy of imitation.[23] With this we see that the Church's apostolic authority is not above these charisms but is ordered to serving them.[24]

The saints teach us that to entrust oneself to Jesus Christ and to accept His answer to the question, "What, then, must I do?" entails leaving behind previous conceptions and former way of life. Most radically, it means entrusting oneself wholly to God, even to the point of accepting His definition of human fulfillment and happiness as *my* fulfillment and happiness. It also entails, as we have seen, entrusting oneself to Christ's Church because this is what He determined to be the concrete way of entrusting oneself to Him. Christ calls His disciples and friends to embrace the path to holiness as He has revealed it—He Himself is the way (Jn 14:6).—and as the saints have done. We give glory to Christ by turning to those whom He has sent to us as models, teachers, guides, and accompanying friends. This means taking the wisdom of the saints regarding religion and spiritual exercises as the sure norm for our lives.

Jesus knows better than anyone the full truth about man. He knows "what is in man" (Jn 2:25). This is one way that St. John conveys that Jesus is divine. For, "the Lord looks on the heart" (1 Sam 16:7); only God "knows the secrets of the heart" (Ps 44:21). We encounter God in our hearts.[25] He is there, awaiting us.[26] Only Jesus Christ can accompany us into our consciences, where we are alone with Him.[27] Jesus "must always be for us the closest onlooker, the one who sees all our actions and is aware of

---

the Church, *Iuvenescit Ecclesia*, June 14, 2016.

[23] "Among these gifts the grace of the apostles is surpassing, for the Spirit himself makes even those with spiritual gifts subject to their authority (cf. 1 Cor 14)" (Vatican II, *Lumen gentium*, 7).

[24] See Vatican II, *Lumen gentium*, 43, 45; *Perfectae caritatis*, 1.

[25] See *CCC*, 2563.

[26] See Vatican II, *Gaudium et spes*, 14.

[27] See Vatican II, *Gaudium et spes*, 16.

all the verdicts which our consciences pass on them."[28] For, Jesus is God, and God is love, and conscience is all about love. Only Jesus and the Holy Spirit can convince us about sin (Jn 16:8–9), which is the rejection of God's love, and about the power of God's mercy. All spiritual exercises have this heart-conscience encounter with God as their foundation. Which is to say that the essential content of all spiritual exercises is the paschal mystery of Jesus Christ, in which He definitively reveals the depths of the evil of sin and the deeper depths of God's mercy.[29]

It is not at all surprising, therefore, that Jesus should reveal that we are made to respond to God's generous love. He does this in two ways. First, He pronounces what amounts to a universal principle: "From everyone to whom much has been given, much will be required; and from the one to whom much has been entrusted, even more will be demanded" (Lk 12:48). Our very existence is evidence of having been loved by God, our Creator. It is the foundation for the virtue of religion, as we have seen. And we have received even more through the gift of redemption in Christ. Second, Jesus shows us what this means by the example of His life. For, this principle applies first of all to Him. He lives it to perfection because to no one has God given more: "in Him all the fullness of God was pleased to dwell" (Col 1:19). In return for the gift that the Father makes of Himself, Jesus's entire life is a gift of Himself to the Father by doing the will of the Father who sent Him, and from whom He has received everything.

Indeed, Jesus's words about more being demanded of the one who receives more must be taken with utmost seriousness. We should, however, be alert to the fact that Jesus could pronounce them because He lived them. He delights in revealing that He obeys the Father in everything: "My food is to do the will of him who sent me

---

[28] John Paul II, Meditation on the 8th Station of the Cross, Good Friday, 2003.

[29] See John Paul II, *Dominum et Vivificantem*, 31–32.

and to accomplish his work" (Jn 4:34); "I seek not my own will but the will of him who sent me" (Jn 5:30); "I have come down from heaven, not to do my own will but the will of him who sent me" (Jn 6:38). For good reason does St. Paul teach that Jesus saves and justifies us by His obedience (Rom 5:19). Jesus obeys the Father because He loves Him: "I do as the Father has commanded me, so that the world may know that I love the Father" (Jn 14:31).

Loving obedience is the interior dimension of Jesus's life. At the same time, it has an exterior and quite visible dimension. The spiritual exercises in Jesus's life include prayer, participation in the liturgy of the synagogue, and His observance of the Jewish festivals: Passover (Jn 2:13, 23; 6:4; 12:1); Tabernacles (Jn 7:2); Hanukkah (Jn 10:22). These practices express His interior life of constant awareness that "The Father loves the Son and has given all things into his hand" (Jn 3:35). Jesus translates this awareness into a life of perfect fulfillment of the mission that the Father entrusted to Him. This is why the Father is His constant point of reference: "the Son can do nothing on his own, but only what he sees the Father doing; for whatever the Father does, the Son does likewise" (Jn 5:19).

Jesus pours His entire self into everything that He does. He holds nothing back, as if He had another life to live apart from doing His Father's will. This indicates that when Jesus says that more is demanded of one to whom more is given, the "more" that is demanded should not be understood as more activities done for God. The "more" that God desires is not, first of all, more spiritual exercises or apostolic activities, but rather *more love*: doing all things with more love for the Father and for the Father's glory. For, unlike with Jesus, sin causes us to withhold the total gift of ourselves to the Father. Sin makes us cling to something as if it were our possession. The call to holiness through ongoing conversion entails renouncing every kind of holding back and clinging so that, like Jesus, we have no other life than that of doing the Father's will. In this way, we participate in His spirituality, "that the Father may be glorified in the Son" (Jn 14:13).

With this, perhaps the most important thing about spiritual exercises has been said. It would be easy to say that they are not ends but means. Yet, it is more accurate to say that they are various ways of exercising the Christian virtues of faith, hope, and charity. These are called theological virtues because they have God as their object. By these virtues we know and love God and ourselves as He knows and loves Himself and us. If any actions qualify as ends, as being done for their own sake, certainly acts of faith, hope, and charity supremely qualify. For, by these virtues we not only encounter God. We participate in His life of knowing and loving.

Precisely because in their essence spiritual exercises are acts of faith, hope, and charity, they bear the fruit of deepening the experience of being loved by God. This is a transformative experience. When by the theological virtues we cooperate with God in loving us, He expands our capacity to love—the essential "even more" that is required from those who are given more. This is the biblical dilation of the heart,[30] which is the true measure of all spiritual exercises. For, love is the only fitting response to the one who first loved us: "We love because he first loved us" (1 Jn 4:19). As St. John of the Cross puts it: "Now, loving is my only exercise."[31]

The purpose of spiritual exercises is to promote an ever more perfect participation in the "eternal exchange of love"[32] that constitutes the very being of God. And because

---

[30] See Ps 119:32; Prov 21:4; Is 60:5; 2 Cor 6:11.

[31] John of the Cross, *The Spiritual Canticle*, 19, first redaction, as quoted by Antonio Royo and Jordan Aumann, *The Theology of Christian Perfection* (Dubuque, IA: The Priory Press, 1962), 177. Kavanaugh and Rodriguez (*Collected Works of St. John of the Cross* [Washington, D.C.: ICS Publications, 3rd edition, 2017,]) translate the stanza: "Now I occupy my soul / and all my energy in his service; / I no longer tend the herd, / nor have I any other work / now that my every act is love."

[32] *CCC*, 221.

the divine life of love reveals itself in missions of love, spiritual exercises also perfect our communion with Christ by fulfilling the mission that He entrusts to us. It is precisely at times in the pilgrimage of faith when a disciple and friend of Christ might think that it would be good to increase the number, frequency, and duration of spiritual exercises, and to expand missionary activity, that it is important to remember that the *one thing that God desires above all else is more love*.

Because spiritual exercises are ordered to this increase of love, they are a vital element of the answer to the question that has been posed: "Now that I am aware of having been loved more and given more, what more is expected of me?" In a slightly different form, this question appears several times in the New Testament. In response to the preaching of St. John the Baptist, first the crowds as a whole, then tax collectors, and finally soldiers ask, "What shall we do?" (Lk 3:10, 12, 14). This becomes something of a pattern, or theme, in St. Luke's Gospel and Acts of the Apostles.[33] One of the rulers also asks Jesus, "What must I do to inherit eternal life?" (Lk 18:18). Again, on the day of Pentecost, reacting to Peter's preaching about Christ's death and resurrection and the outpouring of the Holy Spirit, the crowd asked, "What shall we do?" (Acts 2:37). And after he witnessed Paul and Silas having been set free from their chains, the jailor asked, "What must I do to be saved?" (Acts 16:30).

St. Paul, too, realizing that the Lord's appearance to him initiated a new beginning for his life, asked: "What shall I do, Lord?" (Acts 22:10). We know that the answer to this question entailed the mission to proclaim the mystery of Christ among the Gentiles (Acts 9:15; 22:21). We also know St. Paul's teaching about the primacy of love. Good works accomplished through charisms count

---

[33] The theme is also present in John's Gospel: "What must we do, to be doing the works of God?" (Jn 6:28).

for nothing without love (1 Cor 13:1–3). What doing the Father's will and acting on Jesus's words are in His terse words against those who boast of great acts done in His name (Mt 7:21–24), love is for St. Paul. There will always be a mission to accomplish, but it must flow from communion in love and can never take precedence over it.

The pattern is clear. When people become aware that they are in the presence of God, this question spontaneously arises: "What, then, must we do?" They may become aware of God's presence when it is mediated by someone sent to speak on His behalf, as in the case of John the Baptist, or the apostles. Or, it could be the result of a miracle, which points to God's power at work. Whatever the external cause, the result is an interior moment of truth when a person perceives having been "cut to the heart" (Acts 2:37) by God Himself, and that God is asking something of that person. "What, then, must we do?" is the proper response to God's presence because only He can give a definitive answer to this question.

Because "God is love" (1 Jn 4:8, 16), the question about what one must do really boils down to this: Now that I am aware that God is present, what must I do, how should I respond, in order to open myself to receive His love? What is expected of me, now that God has given my life a new beginning? What does this new and hopeful future, which is God's gift to me, require of me? What is my mission, that is, my vocation? What must I do in order to hear those blessed words of Jesus directed to me: "Well done, good and faithful servant; you have been faithful over a little, I will set you over much; enter into the joy of your master" (Mt 25:21, 23)?

The history of God's initiatives of love is the history of covenants. The first, creation, is paradigmatic. It begins with God's initiative of love and its purpose is to make it possible for others—images of God, angels and men—to experience the fulfillment and joy of God's love. "God made the world so that there could be a space where He might communicate His love, and from which the response of love might come back to him."[34] How could Adam and Eve know how to respond if God had not given them the one commandment, forbidding them to eat of the tree of the knowledge of good and evil? What God was saying through this commandment is essentially this: It is my prerogative to determine good and evil, that is, the truth about love.[35] So long as you abide by this commandment, you will be good stewards of the gift of life and love.[36]

Those who heard John the Baptist, Jesus, and the apostles, realized that their mission was to reveal a radically new initiative of God's love, which naturally demanded a radically new response that could not be deduced from prior revelation. This realization is the motive for the question, "What, then, shall we do?" In contrast, the servants in the parable of the talents know very well what to do when their

---

[34] Benedict XVI, Homily, April 23, 2011. Similarly, and published at about the same time: "The cosmos was created, not that there be manifold things in heaven and earth, but that there be space for the 'covenant,' for the loving 'yes' between God and his human respondent" (Joseph Ratzinger – Pope Benedict XVI, *Jesus of Nazareth. Holy Week: From the Entrance into Jerusalem to the Resurrection*, trans. Philip J. Whitmore [San Francisco: Ignatius Press, 2011], 78).

[35] Knowledge of good and evil is necessary for a king to fulfill his mission of governing God's people. This is why God is pleased when Solomon prays for an understanding heart to know how to judge the chosen people based on the truth about good and evil (1 Kings 3:9; see 2 Sam 14:17). The definitive kingly act will occur when Jesus returns to judge and to separate the good from the bad, the sheep from the goats (Mt 25:31–46). And we know that the criterion of His judgment is anything but abstract: "as you did it to one of the least of these my brethren, you did it to me.... as you did it not to one of the least of these, you did it not to me" (Mt 25:40, 46).

[36] The bible links obedience to God's commandments and life. "but of the tree of the knowledge of good and evil you shall not eat, for in the day that you eat of it you shall surely die" (Gen 2:17); "If you obey the commandments of the Lord your God ... then you shall live and multiply, and the Lord your God will bless you ...." (Dt 30:16). See also: Neh 9:29; Ezek 20:21. For St. Paul, the mystery of sin consists in the fact that "The very commandment that promised life proved to be death to me. For sin, finding opportunity in the commandment, deceived me and by it killed me" (Rom 7:10–11).

master entrusts them with a portion of his wealth. From Moses to the time of Jesus, the standard answer to, "What, then, shall we do?" was: observe all the precepts of the law of Moses. When Jesus proposed this to the rich young man, he responded: "All these I have observed; what do I still lack?" (Mt 19:20). Perhaps this question arose from the insight that religion cannot be reduced to obeying commandments, that there must be something profoundly interpersonal about it—even friendship with God Himself. Perhaps this is why Mark records that "Jesus, looking upon him loved him" (Mk 10:21).

Faith cannot be reduced to keeping commandments, even if God is the commandment-Giver. Love is the "something more" that the young man senses he still lacks: the total gift of oneself to God in response to the total gift that He makes of Himself to us in Jesus Christ. Jesus's answer to the young man, and to everyone who puts the question to Him, corresponds to the intuition that religion must be about friendship with God: "Follow me."

We know that for the rich young man, this total gift necessitated divesting himself of all that he owned. This is not because possessions, or even great possessions, are in themselves an obstacle to the gift of oneself to God. It is because typically people do not become wealthy by accident. Rather, they set their minds on it, making it a priority, even *the* priority in their lives. This seems to be the case for the rich young man. His identity, the very meaning of his life, was so caught up in his wealth that when Jesus issued the invitation to follow Him, "he went away sorrowful; for he had great possessions" (Mt 19:22). Ironically, he was not ready for what the friendship with God that he sought demanded.

The call to follow Jesus entails a radical alteration of the definition of happiness. To follow Him, we must divest ourselves of whatever we think is the essential meaning of our lives and believe that following Him is that meaning, our very happiness. This is the biblical conversion, or *metanoia*, which entails "revising the reasons behind one's actions in light of the Gospel"[37] by "allow[ing] God to enter into the criteria of one's life."[38] It is the radical renewal of the mind (Rom 12:2; Eph 4:23) so as to "have the mind of Christ" (1 Cor 2:16).

The account of the rich young man holds valuable lessons for all who aspire to accept Jesus's invitation to follow Him. Everyone is called to take love to be the essential meaning of life, the definition of happiness. This means that Christ's disciples and friends are called to examine the reasons behind their actions and to change their mind (*metanoia*) by converting into God's definition of happiness, which is love. And love does not depend on wealth. Traditionally the account of the rich young man has been taken as a foundation for the evangelical counsel of poverty, expressed in the lives of consecrated men and women. Nevertheless, the underlying principle regarding detachment from possessions for the sake of living in the primacy of love applies to all of Christ's disciples and friends. An important spiritual exercise, the asceticism of self-denial, entails ordering one's life accordingly. More will be said about this later.

In the end, spiritual exercises are "what we must do" in order to respond to God's love, to receive more of His love, and to live a life of love. Their entire purpose is to place us in the presence of the God of love, who has definitively revealed His love in Jesus Christ. When a lawyer asked Him, "What shall I do to inherit eternal life?" (Lk 10:25), Jesus responded by asking him about his understanding of the Law of Moses. The man replied: "You shall love the Lord your God with all your heart, and with all your soul, and with all your strength, and with all your mind; and your neighbor as yourself" (Lk 10:27).

---

[37] John Paul II, *Ecclesia in America*, 26.

[38] Joseph Cardinal Ratzinger, Address to Catechists and Religion Teachers on the Occasion of the Jubilee of Catechists, December 10, 2000.

Upon hearing this, Jesus said to him: "You have answered right; do this, and you will live" (Lk 10:28). Spiritual exercises are ordered to this living—to life in the fulfillment these two commandments of love.

Who is able to reassure us about what we must do in order *to live in love* if it is not the one who is Life itself and Love itself? Jesus is the living God; He is life (Jn 11:25; 14:6); He is love (1 Jn 4:8, 16). Jesus fulfilled the mission entrusted to Him by the Father, and He defines that mission in terms of life, truth, and love. Life: "I came that they may have life, and have it abundantly" (Jn 10:10). Truth: "For this I was born, and for this I came into the world, to testify to the truth" (Jn 18:37). Love: "those who love me will be loved by my Father" (Jn 14:21). The truth that Jesus reveals is God's own life of love. This is the truth about love that makes us free (Jn 8:32).

In this light, Jesus also identifies the most fundamental of all spiritual exercises: "Truly, truly, I say to you, unless you eat the flesh of the Son of Man and drink his blood, you have no *life* in you" (Jn 6:53). "As the *living* Father sent me, and I *live* because of the Father, so whoever feeds on me, he also will *live* because of me" (Jn 6:57). In one way or another, all spiritual exercises lead to or flow from the preeminent spiritual exercise of receiving the body and blood of Jesus Christ, that is, His love outpoured, in the Eucharist. To the one who takes up and practices the spiritual exercises of the saints, Jesus says: "Do this, and you will live" (Lk 10:28).

This theology of spiritual exercises, then, intends to set forth God's own answer to the question, "What, then, must I do?" which spontaneously arises as a result of the awareness of having been loved by God. God's answer comes to us through the saints, whether they be those who lived and cooperated with God during the economy of revelation—like Moses, the prophets, Mary, Joseph, and the apostles—or following Pentecost, during the history of the Church. *Spiritual exercises are the practice of the wisdom of the saints about how to respond to the many ways in which God makes himself present in order to pour out His love.* To know the ways that God is present and how to respond to His presence constitutes the point on which all the secrets of the interior life converge:

> If I have a great desire to hear the lectures of a master, but if I do not know in what country or in what city he lives, the first thing I need to do is to search for him. And once I have found him, it is indispensable to know the language he speaks so that I may enter into communication with him. The same thing occurs in the interior life. All its secrets consist in this: to know how to find God and to know how to enter into communication with Him.[39]

God makes Himself present in numerous ways,[40] so that we might find Him—so that we may never be without Him—especially in His revealed word, in the Church's liturgy and sacraments, and in the Church's teaching. A complete list of the ways that God is present would include: creation; charisms; the duties of one's vocation; sacramentals. The saints have much to tell us about how best to respond to these ways that God is present, and a treatise on the spiritual life that would attempt to be complete would include all of this wisdom. This theology of spiritual exercises does not attempt to be comprehensive.

Further, as an introductory theology of spiritual exercises and a brief overview of eleven spiritual exercises, this summary of the wisdom of the saints will not address many questions that, though important, are best left to the more developed treatment that they receive, both in the

---

[39] Luis Martinez, *Secrets of the Interior Life*, trans. H. J. Beutler (St. Louis: B. Herder Book Co., 1949), 97.

[40] See Vatican II, *Sacrosanctum Concilium*, 7 and Paul VI, *Mysterium fidei*, 35–38.

classics of spirituality and in theological treatises. The motivated reader will easily find reliable sources on the theological realities that accompany prayer, examination of conscience, celebration of the sacraments, and other spiritual exercises.

2.
"I chose you and appointed you that you should go and bear fruit." (John 15:16)

As events of intentional encounter that develop the bond of communion with God, spiritual exercises constitute an essential element of our response of faith to God's twofold call: to holiness and to the apostolate. The two calls or vocations are distinguishable but not separable. They are two aspects of one vocation, which can be viewed either vertically as communion with God in Christ by the gift of the Holy Spirit, or horizontally as communion that entails a mission of service to others. In reality, the active apostolate is holiness in action, that is, charity in action serving others.

The call to holiness and the call to the apostolate are united even as the two commandments of love are united. Christ's commandment for the new covenant is: "that you love one another: just as I have loved you, you also are to love one another" (Jn 13:34). The apostolate is the fruit of being loved by Christ, and spiritual exercises are ways of encountering His love. The more we receive from God, the more we have to give to others.

Jesus conveys the same order or movement from communion with Him to active service of others by comparing His disciples to branches attached to Him, the vine. The final point of reference here is the glory of the Father. To bear fruit is proof of being a disciple and friend of Jesus Christ, proof of being attached to Him. Just as His mission glorifies the Father, so His disciples and friends also glorify the Father—precisely by bearing fruit: "By this my Father is glorified, that you bear much fruit, and so prove to be my disciples" (Jn 15:8). To accomplish this, one must remain attached to the fruit-producing Vine, Christ himself. "I am the vine; you are the branches.

Whoever abides in me and I in him, he it is that bears much fruit, for apart from me you can do nothing" (Jn 15:5).

Spiritual exercises are the ways that Christ's disciples and friends remain attached to Him and deepen their attachment. They are like the vascular tissue through which the Vine's life-sustaining and fruit-producing nutrients flow into the branches. While attachment to Christ and bearing fruit can be distinguished, they cannot be separated. Consequently, the absence of fruit indicates that a person is not in communion with Jesus. In the words of St. John Paul II: "Bearing fruit is an essential demand of life in Christ and life in the Church. The person who does not bear fruit does not remain in communion: 'Each branch of mine that bears no fruit, he [My Father] takes away'" (Jn 15:2).[1]

Not infrequently, when people are called to some form of apostolate, or service, they immediately become aware of being unprepared. Whether the call is to the most common of all missions, namely, to marriage and family, or to serve on a parish council or as a catechist, or to engage in works of mercy, they think, and rightly so, that they need instruction, or formation. Mary's question at the Annunciation conveys this sense of confronting a mission that one is unable to fulfill by oneself: "How will this be? "(Lk 1:34). The same question, "What, then, shall I do?" expresses the sense of dependence on God and that there is a right way to respond to the call that only God can make known.

The answer is twofold. The first element derives from what has already been discussed, and consists of the principles that are common to all who are committed generously to respond to the universal call to holiness.[2] This is the spiritual formation that the Church prescribes for all of her members[3] and which constitutes the answer to

---

[1] John Paul II, *Christifideles laici*, 32.

[2] See Vatican II, *Lumen gentium*, chapter 5.

[3] When listed, doctrinal or theological formation typically precedes spiritual formation, and pastoral formation follows. Spiritual formation is ordered to conversion into deeper experience of the realities made

the first posing of the question, "What, then, shall I do?" The set of sustainable spiritual exercises is the answer to this question. Since the saints are recognized as exemplars of the right response, their wisdom gives us confidence to imitate the ways that they lived the answer to the question: "What must I do to respond in the proper way to God's love and His desire to give more of that love to me?"

The second element consists of principles that are specific to a particular apostolate and its corresponding spirituality. What one needs to know and to do in order to embrace the vocation to marriage and family or the vocation to ordained ministry are quite different. Here the more elaborate version of the question is: "What must I do to respond in the proper way to God's call to be an active associate of Christ in the continuation of His mission in this particular vocation?" In the case of marriage and ordained ministry, the answer is: Be well formed in order to receive and to cooperate with the graces of the sacraments of Matrimony and Holy Orders. For other vocations, one responds by actively participating in being formed for them, for example, through the novitiate for religious and through a program of formation for catechists, extraordinary ministers of Holy Communion, etc.

These two calls to which people respond with the question, "What, then, must I do?" correspond to a verse in the Gospel of St. Mark in which numerous saints have discovered a biblical paradigm for their own experience of being a disciple and friend of Jesus Christ: "And he appointed twelve, that they might *be with him*, and he might *send them out* to preach" (Mk 3:14 NAS). Observe, first, that the way Jesus relates to the apostles extends to them the way that He relates to the Father. For, Jesus knows Himself as being one with the Father, and He extends that to us: "Holy Father, keep them in your name, which you have given me, that they may be one, even as

---

known through doctrine. Then, conversion bears the fruit of active participation in the Church's mission.

we are one" (Jn 17:11). Jesus also knows Himself as being sent by the Father, and He extends that to us as well: "As the Father has sent me, even so I send you" (Jn 20:21).

Observe, second, that Jesus takes the initiative. From among those who were attracted to Him because of His miracles and teaching, Jesus selected twelve, who will be known as apostles. The word, "apostle," means "one who is sent." But observe, also, that before being sent, Jesus invites them to be with Him. Thus, we have two initiatives of Jesus that become a unified reality in the lives of the apostles. First, "so that they might be with Him": this is the call to holiness, to receive His love, to remain attached to the Vine. Second, "so that he might send them out to preach": this is the call to ministry or apostolate, to active service, to a particular vocation, to a particular way of being fruitful in order to glorify the Father. As always, the initiative is His: "You did not choose me, but I chose you and appointed you that you should go and bear fruit" (Jn 15:16).

Jesus's initiative is twofold, as we have seen. He sends us as His friends and associates in His mission to bear fruit. But before this He calls us to be with Him, in order to share in His life of communion with the Father. The order is always the same: "to be with Him" always precedes "being sent by Him," even as He was with the Father before being sent by Him.

The focus of this theology of spiritual exercises is on how to respond to Jesus's first initiative, that is, His call to be with Him. A theology of the apostolate, or a pastoral theology, corresponds to His second initiative, which is to commission His disciples and friends to bear fruit. The logic by which these two initiatives are inseparably linked is the logic of love. For, the love by which we love Him with our whole heart, mind, soul, and strength is the same love by which we love our neighbors as ourselves and as He has loved us.[4] A theology of spiritual exercises

---

[4] On the unity of the virtue of charity and its two objects, God and man,

considers this love in relation to the call to holiness, while pastoral theology considers the same love as the soul of the apostolate. For this reason, a theology of the apostolate is the natural complement to a theology of spiritual exercises.

Let us return, then, to what Jesus said about remaining attached to Him, the Vine, as the condition for bearing fruit in ministry, apostolate, and acts of service. The first fruit that Jesus has in mind is His disciples' and friends' life of Christian virtue. The first way to glorify God is through cooperating with the graces ordered to one's own transformation. For, the glory of God is the new and abundant life that is Christ's gift to those who believe in Him. The transformation caused by Christ's merciful love demonstrates that His love is effective, or "performative," as Benedict XVI put it.[5] This is evident, visibly, in Jesus's miracles of healing to restore the infirm and diseased to full health. It is evident, spiritually, in the re-orientation of life brought about by faith that heeds the call to follow Jesus.

St. Peter exemplifies this transformation. The change is manifest, first, when he left everything to follow Jesus (Mt 4:19–20; 19:27). It is clear again in his conversion from having denied the Lord in order to save his own life, only to end up dying a martyr in order to be faithful in loving Jesus "to the end," even as Jesus had loved him "to the end" (1 Jn 13:1). We see it in the change in the apostles from huddling out of fear behind locked doors (Jn 20:19) to boldly witnessing to Christ despite persecution (Acts 4:13, 29, 31). We see it in St. Mary of Magdala, St. Paul, St. Augustine, St. Francis of Assisi, St. Ignatius of Loyola, and many more. We can even see it in ourselves, if we compare our current set of values and way of life to our former way of living, or if we think of what we would be were it not for God's grace.

Among the many discernable signs of transformed life

---

see Aquinas, *ST* II-II, Q. 25.

[5] See Benedict XVI, *Spe salvi*, 2, 4, 10; *Verbum Domini*, 53, 56.

of Christ's disciples and friends (Gal 5:22–23), Jesus places a special emphasis on love and the unity that it brings. Love is the new commandment of the new covenant (Jn 13:34). Love among His disciples and friends, then, is the great indication of the efficacy of Christ's redemptive love: "By this all men will know that you are my disciples, if you have love for one another" (Jn 13:35). Let us take the testimony of three saints as expert commentary on this.

> If a person wants to know experimentally [*experiri*] whether God dwells in him ... then let him scrutinize the depths of his heart. Let him examine whether he fights pride with humility, and envy with a proper interior goodwill. Let him ask to what extent he avoids falling prey to flattering words, and rejoices over the success of others. Let him ask whether he refuses to return evil for evil and prefers to forget wrongs done to him ... In short, let him see whether he finds charity, the mother of all virtues, in the most intimate recesses of his heart ... to such an extent that he wishes for his enemies the same good he wishes for himself. If a person finds these dispositions in himself, then he need not doubt that God guides him and dwells in him. And his response to God will be all the greater if he boasts in the Lord rather than in himself.[6]

> The work of the Holy Spirit in man is to place in him the desire of charity, as shown by the words of St. Paul: "The charity of God has been poured into our hearts through the Holy Spirit that has been given to us" (Rom 5:5). The Apostle John indeed speaks of charity when he says that we

---

[6] Leo the Great, *Sermon* 38, 3; PL 54, 262 (as quoted by Stanislas Lyonnet, "The Novel Aspect of the Gospel," in *Foundations of Mission Theology* [Maryknoll, NY: Orbis Books, 1972], 19).

> must examine our hearts in the presence of God: "If our own hearts do not condemn us" (1 Jn 3:21), that is, if our hearts bear witness that that fraternal charity is the source of all that is good in our deeds... If indeed there is charity in you, you have the Holy Spirit within you.
>
> How, then, can we know that we have received the Holy Spirit? Let each examine his own heart! If he loves his brother the Holy Spirit dwells within him... Examine your heart, and if you love your brother, be at rest. This love cannot be present without the Holy Spirit being present, since St. Paul exclaims: "charity has been poured into our hearts through the Holy Spirit that has been given to us."[7]

> [T]he soul can know clearly whether or not she loves God purely. If she loves him her heart or love will not be set on herself or her own satisfaction and gain, but on pleasing God and giving him honor and glory. Whether the heart has been truly stolen by God will be evident in either of these two signs: if it has longings for God or if it finds no satisfaction in anything but him.[8]

Jesus stakes a great deal on our witness to the efficacy of His love, when He says, "The works that I do in my Father's name, they bear witness about me" (Jn 10:25); "believe the works, so that you may know and understand that the Father is in me and I am in the Father" (Jn 10:38); and, "believe me for the sake of the works themselves" (Jn 14:11). The works to which He is referring are, first of all,

---

[7] Augustine, *Homilies on the First Epistle of St. John*, Homily 6 on 1 Jn 3:19–4:3, nn. 9–10.

[8] John of the Cross, *The Spiritual Canticle*, Stanza 9, 5, 6.

the seven great signs, the miracles that St. John records: changing water into wine (Jn 2:1–12); healing the royal official's son (Jn 4:46–54); healing the man who had been ill for thirty-eight years (Jn 5:1–11); feeding the five thousand (Jn 6:1–15); walking on water (Jn 6:16–21; healing the man born blind (Jn 9); raising Lazarus to life (Jn 11).

These works have astonishing effects, which constitute His glory. Jesus performs these displays of divine power for the sake of those who benefit from them and to lead His disciples to faith. Jesus's work is inseparable from its impact in the lives of those whom He heals and in those who witness it and come to faith. This is the second aspect of Jesus's work. St. John draws special attention to the raising of Lazarus. Many Jews came to believe in Jesus because of Lazarus's witness to His power over death (Jn 12:9–11). Lazarus himself, then, restored to life, is a work of Jesus that leads to faith in Him. Every disciple and friend of Christ is similarly called to be a work of Christ that bears witness to His saving love simply by living the new life that He imparts.

In light of the preceding, we can see that Jesus's teaching deserves to be counted among His works. For, it, too had a profound impact on the people who heard Him. That impact is called faith. This is evident in Jesus's dialogue with the Samaritan woman at the well. Not only did He lead her to believe in Him. Following her long dialogue with Him—her being with Him—she becomes an evangelizer and proclaims Jesus to her neighbors (Jn 4:28–30)—she is sent by Him. What a transformation! "[W]hoever receives new life from encountering Jesus cannot but proclaim truth and hope to others. The sinner who was converted becomes a messenger of salvation and leads the whole city to Jesus."[9] The woman who habitually went to the well at the hottest time of the day in order to

---

[9] 13th Ordinary General Assembly of the Synod of Bishops, The New Evangelization for the Transmission of the Christian Faith, Message to the People of God, October 26, 2012, 1.

avoid contact with her neighbors no longer fears what they might think of her and boldly goes out to invite them to come to meet Jesus.[10]

So, when Jesus links faith in Him to His works, He is drawing attention to how His mission brings about integral human healing and fulfills the aspirations of all who place their hope in God's intervention of love. If we were, so to speak, to bundle up all of Christ's works we would see that they come together to form His Church. The Church, the assembly of all those who believe in Him, is Christ's greatest work. He calls the Church His glory when He says: "I am glorified in them" (Jn 17:10). The "them" He is speaking about are his great works *and* their effect or impact on those for whom He has exercised His saving power. Faith in Him is His greatest work! Man fully alive by faith in Jesus Christ, this is the glory of God.[11] The Church is the fruit that He commissions His disciples and friends to build up for the glory of the Father. This is how we should understand that "the Church is the goal of all things."[12] This is also how we should understand that the Blessed Virgin Mary is the personification of the Church. There is more of God's glory to see in her than in any other creature.

The first mission of every disciple and friend of Christ, then, is to be with Christ to be transformed by Him in the school of His discipleship. It is to remain attached to Him in order to receive from His vitality the graces that sustain new life in Him. The second mission is to bear fruit by being a sign, like Lazarus, that points to His transforming love. It is to bear witness to the transforming power of His love. This witness has the effect of leading others to Christ and thereby of building up His Church. The two missions are the same new life in Christ considered from two perspectives. The first constitutes a disciple's and friend's

---

[10] Notice the same movement from a motivation of fear to avoid people to a bold and fearless proclamation, as we have already seen in the apostles.

[11] See John Paul II, *Dominum et Vivificantem*, 59.

[12] *CCC*, 760.

relation to Christ by being with Him in order to receive from Him. The second points to a disciple's and friend's relation to Christ being sent by Him as a witness to His love to others who, perceiving this new life and its relation to Christ, are moved to desire it for themselves.

This twofold relationality, which is evident in the role of Lazarus in people coming to believe in Jesus, pertains to the new life of His disciples and friends. Jesus has displayed the power of His love by raising up those who believe in Him from the spiritual death of self-centeredness to the life of love of God and love of neighbor. This transformation is evident in many ways, for example, in Christian unity, mutual service, love for the poor, and worship of Jesus Christ in praise, adoration, and thanksgiving, especially in His Church's liturgy. These are indicators, or signs, of a new orientation of love that pours itself out for all the poor in need of being loved—even for those who reject it (enemies). As St. John Paul II put it: "the witness of a holy life is the most convincing affirmation of the Gospel."[13] It is the "wordless witness"[14] of holiness. "Holiness, a message that convinces without the need for words, is the living reflection of the face of Christ."[15] And, among the conspicuous indications of a holy life, transformed by faith in Jesus Christ, the works of mercy shown to the poor and unloved have always had a compelling impact on those who observe them.

> The evangelical witness which the world finds most appealing is that of concern for people, and of charity toward the poor, the weak and those who suffer. The complete generosity underlying this attitude and these actions stands in marked contrast to human selfishness. It raises precise

---

[13] John Paul II, *Ad limina* address to the bishops of Scotland, October 29, 1992, 3.

[14] Paul VI, *Evangelii nuntiandi*, 21.

[15] John Paul II, *Novo millennio ineunte*, 8.

questions which lead to God and to the Gospel.[16]

Such love for the poor points to the Eucharist, as an effect points to its cause: "*The Eucharist commits us to the poor.*"[17] It is a work of Christ because it is the result of the greatest of all of His works, namely, the definitive revelation of God's love in His passion, death, and resurrection. Love for the poor is also the way that we fulfill the new commandment of the new covenant: to love others *as Christ has loved us, in our poverty.*

Christ's great work, by which He is glorified, is identical with the fruit that His disciples and friends are commissioned to produce for the glory of the Father. Essentially, His great work is to bring about the conversion of sinners into more and more perfect love, a resurrection from the death of sin to a new life of love that attains its summit in love for the poor and laying down one's life for one's friends. Christ's great work, which is His glory because it is the Father's glory, is the participation of His disciples and friends in His mission to reveal the love of God through perfect obedience to the Father's will. This love reaches its apex by consenting to the role of suffering in God's plan of love and in Christ's mission, and thus in the disciple's and friend's own life.[18] For, the primary form of mission is witness to the fulness of life in Christ,[19] and

---

[16] John Paul II, *Redemptoris missio*, 42. "Since the works of charity and mercy express the most striking testimony of the Christian life, apostolic formation should lead also to the performance of these works so that the faithful may learn from childhood on to have compassion for their brethren and to be generous in helping those in need" (Vatican II, *Apostolicam actuositatem*, 31).

[17] *CCC*, 1397.

[18] "unless a grain of wheat falls into the earth and dies, it remains alone; but if it dies, it bears much fruit" (Jn 12:24).

[19] See Benedict XVI, Apostolic Exhortation *Ecclesia in medio oriente*, 66: "Christian witness, the primary form of mission, is part of the Church's deepest vocation, in fidelity to the mandate received from the Lord

this witness is all the more transparent and compelling when a disciple and friend of Christ remains faithful in trusting and loving God under the most extreme conditions of deprivation. This reveals authentic love of God for His own sake and not just for His gifts.

Just as Christ's works of saving love point to His identity as the eternal Son sent by the Father, so the works of His disciples and friends in behalf of the poor, the suffering, and the unloved point to their identity as His friends, to whom He entrusts the mission of continuing to bear witness to God's love.

Once again, then, we see the inseparability of the vertical and horizontal dimensions of Christian life, of "being with" Christ and "being sent" by Him, the call to holiness and the call to mission. Insofar as they are ordered to communion with Christ—or, remaining attached the Christ the Vine—spiritual exercises directly concern "being with" Christ. Precisely for this reason the same spiritual exercises are related to the mission of bearing fruit or "being sent" by Christ. This happens in three ways. First, by increasing love for Christ, spiritual exercises bear the fruit of love for those whom He loves, especially the poor and unloved. Second, insofar as spiritual exercises themselves are visible to others—such as celebrating the sacraments and pilgrimage—they are endowed with the power of witness and thereby constitute an element of "being sent" by Him. Third, they bear the fruit of daily living the new life of love through exercising all the Christian virtues in fidelity to the duties of one's vocation.

St. John Paul often emphasized this third dimension of spiritual exercises when he taught that mission flows from holiness. The fruits of mission, or active apostolate (being sent), derive from holiness, that is, being with Christ, or remaining attached to Christ the Vine.

Jesus: 'You shall be my witnesses in Jerusalem and in all Judea and Samaria and to the end of the earth' (Acts 1:8)." See also Vatican II, *Ad gentes*, 11–12, 20, 21.

The call to mission derives, of its nature, from the call to holiness. A missionary is really such only if he commits himself to the way of holiness: "Holiness must be called a fundamental presupposition and an irreplaceable condition for everyone in fulfilling the mission of salvation in the Church."[20]

The *universal call to holiness* is closely linked to the *universal call to mission*. Every member of the faithful is called to holiness and to mission. This was the earnest desire of the Council, which hoped to be able "to enlighten all people with the brightness of Christ, which gleams over the face of the Church, by preaching the Gospel to every creature."[21] The Church's missionary spirituality is a journey toward holiness.

The renewed impulse to the mission *ad gentes* demands holy missionaries. It is not enough to update pastoral techniques, organize and coordinate ecclesial resources, or delve more deeply into the biblical and theological foundations of faith. What is needed is the encouragement of a new "ardor for holiness" among missionaries and throughout the Christian community, especially among those who work most closely with missionaries.[22]

In every case it is clear that there can be no true proclamation of the Gospel unless Christians

---

[20] John Paul II, *Christifideles laici*, 17.

[21] Vatican II, *Lumen gentium*, 1.

[22] John Paul II, *Redemptoris missio*, 90. This passage ends with a footnote: "Cf. John Paul II, Address at CELAM Meeting, Port-au-Prince, March 9, 1983: *AAS* 75 (1983): 771–779; Homily for the Opening of the 'Novena of Years' promoted by CELAM, Santo Domingo, October 12, 1984."

also offer the witness of lives in harmony with the message they preach: "The first form of witness is the very life of the missionary, of the Christian family, and of the ecclesial community, which reveal a new way of living... Everyone in the Church, striving to imitate the Divine Master, can and must bear this kind of witness; in many cases it is the only possible way of being a missionary."[23]

Spiritual exercises are *directly* ordered to holiness, to being with Christ and abiding in the Vine, Jesus Christ. *Secondarily*, they are ordered to mission or apostolate. Only when they are practiced as ends in themselves, for the sake of being with Christ, do they also bear the fruit of being sent by Christ. For, Christ entrusts participation in His mission to those whom He loves and calls His friends. To respond to His love for us by returning to Him in hope of deepening friendship with Him is always primary. This is evident in the love of spouses, who in expressing their love for one another also cooperate in bringing new life into the world. In their union, we see how profoundly "being with" and "bearing fruit" are united.

St. Thomas Aquinas confirms that the perfection of human salvation consists in loving God in response to experiencing His love for us.[24] In fact, the goal of the entire history of salvation, which culminates in the Incarnation of the eternal Son of God and His paschal mystery, is to elicit love for Him from those who are otherwise turned away by sin. For, as St. Thomas puts it:

---

[23] John Paul II, *Ecclesia in Asia*, 42, quoting *Redemptoris missio*, 42.

[24] "Among means to an end that one is the more suitable whereby the various concurring means employed are themselves helpful to such end. But in this that man was delivered by Christ's Passion, many other things besides deliverance from sin concurred for man's salvation. In the first place, man knows thereby how much God loves him, and is thereby stirred to love Him in return, and herein lies the perfection of human salvation" (Aquinas, *ST* III, Q. 46, a. 3).

"Nothing so induces us to love someone as the experience of his love for us."[25] With this we see that spiritual exercises are ordered to eliciting such acts of love insofar as they are a response to God's love fully revealed in the paschal mystery of Jesus Christ.

Spiritual exercises, then, entail both receptivity and activity, being loved and loving in return. During a given spiritual exercise, awareness of one or the other may predominate. Nevertheless, both are present, for they are inseparable. Similarly, since communion with Christ consists in participating in His truth and in His love, awareness of one or another of these may predominate at any given moment; a person may be more aware of the union of minds or of the union of wills. Should awareness of one or another predominate for a period, we can speak of a discernable season of grace. So long as a person does not intentionally force a preference for one or the other, both are present, for they too are inseparable.

The preceding has shown that in the Church, mission and apostolate are a participation in Christ's life and mission. Just as His mission flows from communion with the Father, our mission flows from communion with Him. Christ fulfilled his mission by living His communion with the Father in our midst. He thereby revealed the full truth about God and about man, the truth that God is love and that man, made in his image and likeness, is made for this very love.[26] Similarly, Christ's disciples and friends fulfill their mission by living in communion with Him in the midst of their familial, societal, communal, and cultural realities, thereby bearing witness to the truth about God and about man.

In light of the preceding, faith in Jesus Christ is also faith in His work of love. It must be, then, more than a notional assent to the fact that God is love. It must also be

---

[25] Aquinas, *Summa contra gentiles*, IV, 54, 5.

[26] See Vatican II, *Gaudium et spes*, 22 and 24.

consent to be loved and thus transformed by God's love. In this way, faith consents to taking one's place among Christ's works and to being a member of His Church, which is the sum of all of His individual works. Because God's love is transformative, it draws man into communion with Him and with Christ and His mission. The great question regarding spiritual exercises, the entire value of which is that they direct our response to the presence of this transforming love, is: Am I ready to be transformed according to the wisdom of God, which entails accepting the place of suffering and death in His plan of love? Am I ready for the dark nights of purification? Do I realize that the condition for receiving the "more that God has to give" is to put to death the sin that turns me away from His love? Or, am I like Peter, who professed to love Jesus so much that he thought himself ready to go to prison and to die for Jesus, and yet shortly after the Last Supper denied Him and followed Him at a distance?[27]

It comes down to a humble self-questioning: "Am I prepared for *God's answer* to the question, 'What, then, must I do?'" For, to say that the goal of spiritual exercises is to deepen communion with God in Christ is to say that their purpose is to foster conversion into a more perfect love for Him, which is always a deepening of baptismal death to self and to sin. As the *Catechism* reminds us: "Reading Sacred Scripture, praying the Liturgy of the Hours and the Our Father—every sincere act of worship or devotion revives the spirit of conversion and repentance within us and contributes to the forgiveness of our sins."[28] This is true of every spiritual exercise.

Just as our vocation is one with two aspects (holiness and mission), so too our participation in Christ's mission

---

[27] "Lord, I am ready to go with you to prison and to death!" (Lk 22:33). "Even if I must die with you, I will not deny you!" (Mt 26:35). Matthew relates that this was the mindset of all of the disciples present at the Last Supper: "And so said all the disciples" (Mt 26:35).

[28] *CCC*, 1437.

has two dimensions, which correspond to the Lord's commandment: "You shall your neighbor as yourself" (Mt 19:19). The first mission for every disciple and friend of Jesus Christ is fully, consciously, and actively to embrace the baptismal call to holiness. The focus of the first dimension, then, is oneself as loved by God. It entails opening oneself up to God's love, consenting to being loved by God. But this first mission entails a second mission, namely, to cooperate with Christ, in the Holy Spirit, in bringing the Good News of God's love to others. The focus of the second dimension, then, is one's neighbor as loved by God. Here we see the order between love of self and love of neighbor. Love of self corresponds to being with Christ, and love of neighbor corresponds to being sent by Him. The positive formulation of the Golden Rule as the command to love one's neighbor as oneself is the foundation for all mission, apostolate, ministry, and service in the Church.

These two missions are necessarily connected because whenever God loves a person (first mission), He envisions loving someone else with and through that person (second mission). The reason is that God's grace is a participation in His life, and as St. Augustine so incisively informs us, we do not really possess God for the truth of Who He is unless we actively work to share Him with others.[29] This is rooted in the very nature of love, which, as St. Augustine insightfully wrote:

> nor when it is given is it lost, but it is rather multiplied by giving it.... And since it cannot be given unless it is possessed, so neither can it be possessed unless it is given; nay, at the very time when it is given by a man it increases in that man, and, according to the number of

---

[29] "For a possession which is not diminished by being shared with others, if it is possessed and not shared, is not yet possessed as it ought to be possessed" (Augustine, *On Christian Doctrine*, I, 1).

persons to whom it is given, the amount of it which is gained becomes greater.[30]

St. Paul goes so far as to assert that this one commandment, "you shall love your neighbor as yourself" (Lev 19:18), sums up all of the commandments.[31] With this, he demonstrates his continuity with Jesus, who sums up the law and the prophets with the Golden Rule: "So whatever you wish that men would do to you, do so to them; for this is the law and the prophets" (Mt 7:12). St. Thomas elaborates: "insofar as we love our neighbor as ourselves ... we wish to fulfill our neighbor's will *as though it were ours*."[32] This means: "I love my neighbor as myself in the same way that I love myself, when I will him a good for his sake, and not because it is useful or pleasant for me."[33] Since suffering for the sake of clinging to the supreme good, which is God Himself, even to the point of martyrdom, is the irrefutable sign of love of self, this is also the measure of love for neighbor. And with this we understand Jesus's words: "Greater love has no man than this, that a man lay down his life for his friends" (Jn 15:13).[34]

Loving one's neighbor as oneself clarifies the link between the first purpose of spiritual exercises, namely, to

---

[30] Augustine, Letter 192 to Cælestine, 1.

[31] "The commandments, 'You shall not commit adultery; You shall not murder; You shall not steal; You shall not covet'; and any other commandment, are summed up in this word, 'Love your neighbor as yourself'" (Rom 13:9). See also: Mt 19:19; 22:39; Mk 12:31; Lk 10:27; Gal 5:14; Jas 2:8.

[32] Aquinas, *ST* II-II, Q. 29, a. 3, emphasis added.

[33] Aquinas, *Commentary on St. Paul's Letter to the Galatians*, Ch. 5, lect. 3 (Marietti, 305).

[34] Since this theology of spiritual exercises emphasizes the role of conscience, it is apropos to point out that St. Thomas further elaborates on the relation of love of self to love of neighbor in terms of conscience. This is because dictates of conscience are dictates about what love requires. See Aquinas, *Commentary on St. Paul's First Letter to Timothy*, Ch. 1, lect. 2 (Marietti 15–16).

augment communion with Christ, and their second purpose, which is the mission of service to others. The missionary motivation is precisely to do whatever is possible so that others can have the same experience of Christ's merciful love that first transformed the life of the missionary. This is evident in the mission of the Samaritan woman, who exclaimed to her neighbors: "Come, see a man who told me all that I ever did. Can this be the Christ?" (Jn 4:29). Similarly, a formerly blind man, miraculously healed by Jesus, knows by experience that there is hope for others who are blind, and his love for them moves him to bring them to Jesus. It is the same for a leper whom Jesus healed. The Christian mission is in behalf of all who are spiritually blind and leprous as a result of sin—as was the disciple and friend of Christ before encountering Him.

The Christian experience is to receive the gift of the Holy Spirit for the forgiveness of sins: "Repent, and be baptized every one of you in the name of Jesus Christ for the forgiveness of your sins; and you shall receive the gift of the Holy Spirit" (Acts 2:38). To receive the Holy Spirit for the forgiveness of sins means to be transformed from the state of alienation from the Father's love, like the prodigal son before he returned home, to living in the joy of being a beloved son or daughter of God: "you have received the spirit of sonship. When we cry, 'Abba! Father!' it is the Spirit himself bearing witness with our spirit that we are children of God" (Rom 8:15–16).

Everyone who has not encountered Christ's mercy for the forgiveness of sins is like the lepers and the blind, whose experience of suffering contradicts their aspiration to enjoy life in its fulness. Apart from Christ's mercy, everyone is condemned to live in a state of fundamental conflict with himself because he is in conflict with the truth about the love for which he is made. St. Thomas points to what this state of internal conflict with oneself means when he states that remorse of conscience is a punishment on oneself by oneself.[35] The gift of a conscience purified by the blood of Christ[36] is absolutely necessary for the transformation of the life of Christ's disciples and friends. It is the very foundation of that transformation, which is from the non-love of sin to a life of love. And, the truth about love passes into every act by way of the judgment of conscience. And, as we have seen, life according to the new commandment of love (Jn 13:34) is the life that Christ imparts to us. In fact, it is because Baptism imparts this new life of love that it also necessarily confers the gift of a purified conscience.[37] This is a moral healing every bit as real and life-transforming as being healed of blindness or leprosy, or raised from death.

The internal state of conflict, or irreconcilability with oneself, cannot fail to affect a person's relationships with God and others. We see this in Adam and Eve's attempt to clothe themselves in God's presence, and even to hide from Him. We see it in the cry of Job: "Let me alone" (Job 7:16).[38] Sin is an act of disobeying a divine commandment, but its root cause is doubt about God's love.[39] If God's chief concern is to safeguard His divine prerogatives,[40] then man is simply being logical when he disobeys His commandment. For, on this supposition, the commandment is meant to serve God, not man, and man rightly rebels at the thought of being used—even by God. The sinner who disobeys God's commandment has already turned away from God and is acting on believing the lie that He did not give the commandment out of love. At the moment of turning away from God, the sinner can no longer hear those

---

[35] Aquinas, *ST* I-II, Q. 87, a. 1.

[36] See Heb 9:9, 14; 10:2.

[37] See Heb 10:20–22 and 1 Pt 3:21.

[38] On this, see the insights of Dominique Barthélemy in *God and His Image. An Outline of Biblical Theology*, trans. Dom Aldhelm Dean (San Francisco: Ignatius Press, 2007), 1–42.

[39] See John Paul II, *Dominum et Vivificantem*, 37–39.

[40] See *CCC*, 399.

most consoling words of God's affirmation of man's goodness (Gen 1:31), and thus of His love that imparts this goodness. Sin, then, entails doubting God's love as the foundation of one's goodness. But then the sinner is condemned to look for some other foundation, and there is none to be found.

Christ's mission to reveal God's love liberates mankind from doubt about being loved by Him. This doubt being the root cause of sin, it is thus also the root cause of the affliction of remorse of conscience. The only truth that can set us free (Jn 8:32) from this interior state of conflict and affliction is the truth that "God is love" (1 Jn 4:8, 16). This is why the Letter to the Hebrews describes redemption in Christ as the purification of conscience (Heb 9:14).

The love of God that Christ reveals is not any kind of love. It must be merciful love, which is always ready to forgive and to reconcile. God's mercy liberates us from slavery to the idea that He does not love us so that we can live in the freedom and joy that come with the "certainty of being loved"[41] by Him. A conscience burdened by sin so blinds a person that he is no longer able to see what God sees, that is, the fundamental goodness of his dignity as image of God. For, "Only He [Christ] 'knows what is in every man' (Jn 2:25): He knows man's weakness, but he also and above all knows his dignity."[42] This is the whole meaning of Jesus's mission to love us "to the end" (Jn 13:1).

To share in this knowledge by faith is to believe that God could love a sinner, which is precisely the foundation of Christian faith, hope, joy, and peace. "Believing in the crucified Son means 'seeing the Father' (cf. Jn 14:9), means believing that love is present in the world and that this love is more powerful than any kind of evil in which individuals, humanity, or the world are involved. Believing

---

[41] *CCC*, 2778.

[42] John Paul II, Letter to the Youth of World, *Dilecti amici*, 1985, 7.

in this love means believing in mercy."[43] This logic of mercy is the only logic that trumps the logic of sin, which St. Peter expressed when he said to Jesus: "Depart from me, for I am a sinful man" (Lk 5:8). These words incisively express that interior conflict between what man is made for and what he can hope for apart from the revelation of God's mercy in Jesus Christ. It is illogical, so the sinner thinks, for God, Who is love, to approach someone who has doubted and rejected His love. But Christ died in order definitively to reveal God's mercy and its logic: "God shows his love for us in that while we were yet weak ... sinners ... enemies, Christ died for us" (Rom 5:6, 8, 10). Everyone who has encountered this mercy knows by experience that it is the only foundation for a meaningful, joyful life, free from the interior irreconcilability of unpardoned sin. In keeping with the Golden Rule, this experience of God's mercy becomes the good that Christ's disciples and friends desire for all whom they love.

In his book on prayer and conscience, Paul Hinnebusch discusses the movement from love of self (first mission) to love of others (second mission) in terms of self-esteem.

> Because the primary responsibility for one's salvation and fulfillment falls upon self, the love of self is even more basic than the love of neighbor. Indeed, it is so basic that it is presupposed to both love of God and of neighbor; it is so fundamental that it does not even need to be expressed explicitly in the two greatest commandments (Mk 12:30–31). Neither God nor neighbor can be loved without a healthy self-esteem. On the other hand, one can rightly love self only by loving both God and neighbor.[44]

---

[43] John Paul II, *Dives in misericordia*, 7.

[44] Paul Hinnebusch, *Prayer, the Search for Authenticity* (New York: Sheed and Ward, 1969), 40.

Here, "self-esteem," is not something a person can acquire for himself. Hinnebusch understands it to be "authentic self-love," which is "a *sense* of one's intrinsic self-worth." It corresponds to and comes with experiencing God's look of approving and affirming love, expressed in His seeing that all that He had created is very good (Gen 1:31) and in the Father's words to the Son: "in you I am well pleased" (Lk 3:22 DRA).

This sense of one's goodness can only come from another. "We can love ourselves," asserts Cardinal Ratzinger, "only if we have first been loved by someone else.... It is only when life has been accepted and is perceived as accepted that it becomes also acceptable."[45] This is a constant in Joseph Ratzinger's vivid description of man's interior conflict of irreconcilability with himself.

> Only if God accepts me, and I become convinced of this, do I know definitively: it is good that I exist. It is good to be a human being. If ever man's sense of being accepted and loved by God is lost, then there is no longer any answer to the question whether to be a human being is good at all. Doubt concerning human existence becomes more and more insurmountable. Where doubt over God becomes prevalent, then doubt over humanity follows inevitably. We see today how widely this doubt is spreading. We see it in the joylessness, in the inner sadness, that can be read on so many human faces today. Only faith gives me the conviction: it is good that I exist.[46]

---

[45] Joseph Ratzinger, *Principles of Catholic Theology. Building Stones for a Fundamental Theology*, trans. Sister Mary Frances McCarthy (San Francisco: Ignatius Press, 1987), 80.

[46] Benedict XVI, Christmas Message to the Roman Curia, December 22, 2011.

Self-love is authentic, then, when by faith a person comes to see himself as loved by God and thus comes to see in himself the goodness that God sees. It is authentic when it is a response to God's love and gives rise to a desire to please God and to elicit from Him the same look of approving and affirming love that He first expressed when He surveyed His creation and declared "it was very good" (Gen 1:31), and when He said to Jesus, "in you I am well pleased" (Mk 1:11; Lk 3:22). In Hinnebusch's words: "For the command of God that we have self-esteem is a command to appreciate *His* love for us and measure true to the dignity this love has given us in creating and redeeming us, calling us to participate in His own life as sons in His Son."[47]

Authentic self-esteem, or love of self, is a corollary of having come to "know and believe the love God has for us" (1 Jn 4:16). This means that we look at ourselves from God's perspective, which St. John Paul II expressed this way: "How precious must man be in the eyes of the Creator, if he 'gained so great a Redeemer,'[48] and if God 'gave his only Son' in order that man 'should not perish but have eternal life' (Jn 3:16)."[49] If the Jews, observing Christ's tearful anguish over the death of Lazarus, could infer, "See how he loved him!" (Jn 11:36), how much more can a Christian say, when contemplating His suffering and death, say, "See how much He loved *me*!" This is precisely the language of St. Paul, who writes of Christ as "the Son of God, who *loved me* and gave himself *for me*" (Gal 2:20).

Authentic self-esteem, then, is the fruit of experiencing God's esteem for man. John Paul II called this God's amazement at man. His insight is that every act of love presupposes an act of the mind concerning the goodness of what is loved. Love begins with being amazed by another's beauty and goodness. So, since we know that God loves us,

---

[47] Hinnebusch, *Prayer*, 42.

[48] *Exsultet* at the Easter Vigil.

[49] John Paul II, *Redemptor hominis*, 10.

we also know that He sees something good, even beautiful and precious, in us. And what is this if not our capacity—the very capacity that He has placed in us—to receive His love and the good that He desires to impart to us. Jesus experienced the Father's love, and thus His own goodness at His Baptism, when He heard the Father say: "You are my beloved Son; in you I am well pleased" (Lk 3:22). Since He, too, is subject to the commandment to love others *as oneself*, He desires that we experience the Father's love as He did.

Spiritual exercises are ways by which we open ourselves to this love that Jesus reveals. We must not imagine that we experience the Father's look of amazement and affirming love alongside of Jesus, as if the Father could love us with a distinct love. Rather, all of the Father's love is lavished on the Son, so that the only way for us to experience it is by being one with the Him. Jesus desires to draw us into His experience of the Father's amazement and love for Him. For, "Christ enables us to live in Him all that He Himself lived, and He lives it in us."[50] In spiritual exercises, we cooperate with Jesus's love for us, bringing to them the desire to share in His experience of the Father's amazement and love. And this becomes participation in His mission, which is also something that He receives from the Father and desires to share with us. In this light, we see that the motive for mission is to love others as Jesus has loved us (Jn 13:34). Which is the same as to say that we love others as we love ourselves.

Not only is love of others is rooted in love of self, it can also enrich love of self. St. Augustine has told us that we do not possess a good thing that can be shared unless we actually share it. In sharing such a good we do not lose it; rather, it increases in us and in those with whom it is shared. This is the first way that love of others increases

---

[50] *CCC*, 521.

our love for the good that we share, namely, God, and thus also love of self. Furthermore, love of others can lead to a more perfect love of self. This happens when a person loves himself for the sake of others. For example, a husband and father is motivated to embrace a healthy diet and exercise regime, which is good for his health, because of his love for his wife and children. The same principle holds true for spiritual life, spiritual health, and spiritual exercises. Once a husband and father realizes that his own spiritual health affects his mission to love his wife and children, this love for them becomes an additional motive to be faithful to spiritual exercises.

This does not reduce being with Christ to a means to the end of fruitful apostolic work. No, we love Christ because He loved us first. It is simply a fact that failures in love for others drives home the realization that one's love of Jesus is not as strong as it ought to be, since it is the source of love of others. Failures in loving others indicate that in some ways I am not attached to the Vine; for I were, His love would flow through me. The missionary motive, then, becomes the occasion for a deeper conversion, the fruit of which is a more perfect love of self for the sake of making a more perfect gift of oneself, first to God and then to others. This confirms both the inseparability of the three loves—of God, of self, of neighbor—and the two missions—to self and to others.

The next chapter focuses on the nature of the merciful love of Christ that moves us from the first mission of love of self to the second mission of love of others.

3.
Paschal Charity, the Soul of the Apostolate

In its official texts, Vatican II quotes St. Paul's declaration that "the love of Christ impels us" (2 Cor 5:14 NAB) only once.[1] Nevertheless, the Council's very first "document" invokes it as the foundation of its purpose and authentic spirit. The Message to Humanity, made public on October 20, 1962, declares: "faith, hope, and the love of Christ impel us to serve our brothers, thereby patterning ourselves after the example of the Divine Teacher, who 'came not to be served but to serve' (Mt 20:28). Hence, the Church too was not born to dominate but to serve."[2]

To be a disciple and friend of Christ is not only to imitate Him by doing what He did, but to share in His motive of love. Thus, those participating in Vatican II disclosed their interior motivation: "As we undertake our work, therefore, we would emphasize whatever concerns the dignity of man, whatever contributes to a genuine community of peoples. 'Christ's love impels us' (2 Cor 5:14), for 'he who sees his brother in need and closes his heart against him, how does the love of God abide in him?' (1 Jn 3:17)."[3]

Christ's love, or charity, is the interior, driving force of all missionary and apostolic activity. Solicitude *to reinvigorate the Church's mission in the world as the fruit of authentic holiness* defined Vatican II as a pastoral council. Thus, for good reason, on two occasions the

---

[1] See Vatican II, *Apostolicam actuositatem*, 6.

[2] Vatican II, Message to Humanity, in Walter Abbott, ed., *The Documents of Vatican II* (New York: Guild Press, 1966), 3–7.

[3] Vatican II, Message to Humanity.

Council called charity "the soul of the apostolate":

> The lay apostolate, however, is a participation in the salvific mission of the Church itself. Through their Baptism and Confirmation all are commissioned to that apostolate by the Lord Himself. Moreover, by the sacraments, especially holy Eucharist, that charity toward God and man which is the soul of the apostolate is communicated and nourished.[4]

> The laity derive the right and duty to the apostolate from their union with Christ the head; incorporated into Christ's Mystical Body through Baptism and strengthened by the power of the Holy Spirit through Confirmation, they are assigned to the apostolate by the Lord Himself. They are consecrated for the royal priesthood and the holy people (cf. 1 Pt 2:4–10) not only that they may offer spiritual sacrifices in everything they do but also that they may witness to Christ throughout the world. The sacraments, however, especially the most holy Eucharist, communicate and nourish that charity which is the soul of the entire apostolate (cf. *Lumen gentium*, 33; cf. also *Lumen gentium*, 10).[5]

The link between the charity that is the soul of the apostolate and the sacraments of initiation (in the above text) indicates that mission and apostolate are rooted in personal participation in the paschal charity of Christ. This "love of Christ impels us" (2 Cor 5:14) to bear witness to God's love, which He fully revealed in the paschal mystery. It is a love so strong that through, with, and in

---

[4] Vatican II, *Lumen gentium*, 33.
[5] Vatican II, *Apostolicam actuositatem*, 3.

Christ, it can love "to the end" (Jn 13:1) and suffer for those who are being served through mission and apostolate. Only such a charity can allow an apostle to continue to love, even "to the end," when love is rejected.

Mercy is the name for this paschal charity of Christ. To reveal God's mercy "is, in Christ's own consciousness, the fundamental touchstone of His mission as the Messiah."[6] "Mercy constitutes the fundamental content of the messianic message of Christ and the constitutive power of his mission."[7] Jesus, "in a certain sense, is mercy." He is "the incarnation of mercy."[8] Since Christ entrusted the continuation of His mission to the Church of His disciples and friends, and since His mission of mercy flows from His very being as mercy, every baptized person is called to be mercy and to bring divine mercy into the world.

The prayer that is popularly attributed to St. Francis of Assisi well describes this mission of mercy. "Lord, make me a channel of Your peace, that where there is hatred, wrong, discord, error, doubt, despair, shadows, sadness ... I may bring love, the spirit of forgiveness, harmony, truth, faith, hope, light, joy." This is charity, to make present a good that is absent. Because of sin, which is the rejection of God's love,[9] there is a deficit of goodness and truth in people's lives. This is what is traditionally called the just punishment for sin. Life is experienced as being "subjected to futility" (Rom 8:20) and as groaning to be set free from this futility (Rom 8:21).

God alone is able to overcome this futility. He does so by "overcoming evil with good" (Rom 12:21). He is the fullness of the truth and goodness without which life is futility. The mission of Jesus, in whom "the whole fullness of deity dwells bodily" (Col 2:9), is to make God's fullness

---

[6] John Paul II, *Dives in misericordia*, 3.

[7] John Paul II, *Dives in misericordia*, 6.

[8] John Paul II, *Dives in misericordia*, 2.

[9] "Sin sets itself against God's love for us and turns our hearts away from it" (*CCC*, 1850).

present and thereby to inject truth and love where they are absent. He continues this mission through His disciples and friends, who by believing in Him are "filled with all the fullness of God" (Eph 3:19). His mission to "overcome evil with good" becomes their mission because He thinks of them as His friends. This is to say that Christians are called to carry out the mission of mercy in order to fill the void of truth and goodness by making Christ, Who is truth and goodness, present.

Given this centrality of mercy and of the paschal mystery, we see that the development of the spiritual life is, essentially, advancement toward a more perfect experience and knowledge of God's mercy. This experiential knowledge then becomes the source of the mission to love others. As the *Catechism* reminds us: "From this loving knowledge of Christ springs the desire to proclaim him, to 'evangelize,' and to lead others to the 'yes' of faith in Jesus Christ. But at the same time the need to know this faith better makes itself felt."[10] This better knowledge of faith entails a deeper understanding of the centrality of the paschal mystery in God's plan of love. In this way, it brings a profound realization of the fact that if Christ's love for us reaches its summit in the paschal mystery then it is from our participation in the paschal mystery that we are able to love others *as Christ has loved us*: "A new commandment I give to you, that you love one another; even as I have loved you, that you also love one another" (Jn 13:34). "The Eucharist must be the source and summit of the New Evangelization."[11]

---

[10] *CCC*, 429.

[11] 13th Ordinary General Assembly of the Synod of Bishops, The New Evangelization for the Transmission of the Christian Faith, Final Propositions, 34.

On *"the need to know this faith better"*

As discussed earlier, God always has more to give. He gives so that He can give even more. His giving has the happy effect of expanding our desire and our capacity to receive more. In this way, His grace creates in us a disposition of openness, of expectant anticipation, which corresponds to His desire to give more. We could say that every grace is the fulfillment of prior graces that prepared for it, and that it then becomes preparatory for future graces. The spiritual life, then, is Advent-like in structure, as every fulfillment of hope-filled expectation to encounter God's love gives rise to an increase in hope-filled expectation of encountering God's love—until the definitive fulfillment of heaven, beyond which there is nothing more for which to hope.

God's manner of giving always respects the dignity of our free will, which is conditioned by knowledge. We cannot desire what we do not know and cannot even imagine. This is why God has revealed His love to us, and thus what He desires for us and what we should desire as well. St. Paul puts it this way: "'What no eye has seen, nor ear heard, nor the heart of man conceived, what God has prepared for those who love him,' God has revealed to us through the Spirit. For the Spirit searches everything, even the depths of God.... Now we have received ... the Spirit which is from God, that we might understand the gifts bestowed on us by God" (1 Cor 2:9–10, 12).

God desires that we know the supreme value of the gifts He has bestowed on us. Only in this way can our desire for them be true and our consent to receive them be informed. Only in this way can we be one with Him by desiring and consenting to receive precisely what He desires to give. For, to know these gifts is to know His love, since this is His motive for giving. It is also to know oneself as loved, and thereby to live in "the certainty of being loved."[12] This dynamic is evident in the faith of the Virgin Mary at the Annunciation. With other devout Jews of her time, Mary lived in the certainty of having been loved while simultaneously she desired the "something more" what God had revealed and promised, namely, the coming of the Messiah for the "consolation of Israel" (Lk 2:25). Thanksgiving for the gifts God has already bestowed is the foundation for receiving the additional gifts He desires to bestow.[13]

God also wanted Mary to know her place in the fulfillment of the promise that He intended to fulfill. And so, Gabriel explained to her who her son will be and how she will conceive. Only then did she respond: "let it be to me according to your word" (Lk 1:38). God's promise regarding the definitive "something more" that He had always desired to give, namely, Himself, is fulfilled both *in* Mary and *through* her. These two prepositions, "in" and "through," convey, once again, the precedence of "being with" in "relation to being sent." Mary first receives Jesus into her own being and then brings Him into the world for others.

Mary's consent to all of this at the Annunciation is just the beginning of her pilgrimage of faith, which entails a constant growth in understanding the person and mission of Jesus. In her we see "a growth in the understanding of the realities and the words which have been handed down."[14] This is why she "kept all these things, pondering them in her heart" (Lk 2:19). Each new revelation confirms what she had already known and sheds new light upon it.[15] Mary

---

[12] *CCC*, 2778.

[13] "A person is not worthy to receive a blessing, if he does not express thanks for past blessings" (Aquinas, *Commentary on St. Paul's Letter to the Romans*, Ch. 1, lect. 5 [Marietti, 75]). "Through giving thanks for benefits received we merit to receive yet greater benefits" (Aquinas, *ST* II-II, Q. 83, a. 17, quoting a Collect Prayer).

[14] Vatican II, *Dei Verbum*, 8.

[15] John Paul II develops this theme in his encyclical on Mary's faith and mediation, *Redemptoris Mater*.

constantly grows in understanding God's plan and her place in it. Correspondingly, her love for God and for others continually grows.

We are all called to imitate Mary, the model of perfect faith, by similarly advancing in our understanding of God's plan of merciful love, which is fully revealed in Jesus Christ. The *Catechism* affirms this need to grow in our understanding of God's love, when it states:

> "Faith seeks understanding": it is intrinsic to faith that a believer desires to know better the One in whom he has put his faith, and to understand better what He has revealed; a more penetrating knowledge will in turn call forth a greater faith, increasingly set afire by love.[16]

This is the key for grasping the place of ongoing study of faith among the spiritual exercises. It explains why magisterial texts on formation—for deacons, priests, laity, catechists, consecrated, teachers—include theological or intellectual formation along with spiritual and pastoral formation. It is also why these texts stress that this formation be ongoing.

Growth in understanding faith, or "a more penetrating knowledge," can never be simply the acquisition of more information about God and His plan of love. This is because faith cannot be reduced to compiling a set of truths to which one assents. For, the center of God's plan, as we have seen, is the mercy by which He overcomes the sin that rejects His love. "The One in whom he has put his faith" is the One who laid down His life in order to reveal mercy for the forgiveness of sins and reconciliation to God. When Jesus says, "the truth will make you free" (Jn 8:32), He means: the truth that God is merciful love will set you free from the fear of having forever forfeited His love, a fear that accompanies

---

[16] *CCC*, 158.

having rejected that very love. This fear is the just punishment for sin. It is the logic of sin. Everyone is fated to be enslaved by this fear, for "all have sinned and fall short of the glory of God" (Rom 3:23). Only God's mercy can break the bonds of this enslavement.

God's mercy, with its effects in the transformed lives of those who believe in it, is the glory of God. During His time on earth, Jesus did more than to let the leprous, blind, and lame know that He loved them. He did not say, in effect: "Despite your ailment I still love you. I will not let your suffering come between us. You will always be accepted in my company." Without pronouncing the words, "I love you," He spoke love through His actions, loving them in deed and efficaciously restoring them to full health. Imagine going to a doctor who says: "I am so sorry. I have no skill to restore your health. But, you will always be my friend. I will not allow your illness to impede my friendship for you." We expect such words from our family and closest friends. From our doctor we hope to be treated and cured. We hope to be loved efficaciously, changed, transformed.

Jesus is the divine physician (Mt 9:12). His miracles of healing reveal that He has the power to heal. They point to a more profound healing, the healing of our souls, especially our consciences that are burdened with remorse and guilt. He has promised that He is always eager to grant our desire to be forgiven and reconciled to Him. Jesus's principal concern is with our relationship with the Father. This is the only reason for His concern about sin and the state of our conscience. "Like a physician who probes the wound before treating it, God, by his Word and by his Spirit, casts a living light on sin."[17] When Jesus says, "Your sins are forgiven" (Lk 5:20; 7:48), His words are just as efficacious as when He says, "Receive your sight" (Lk 18:42).

---

[17] *CCC*, 1848.

God reveals Himself and His plan of love, then, not only so that we have knowledge of it but so that we can knowingly cooperate with His love by receiving His gifts. This knowledge is necessary for the active passivity exemplified in Mary at the Annunciation. The relation of faith as *knowledge of the gift* to faith as *reception of the gift* is the foundation for Benedict XVI's assertion: "this is faith: being loved by God and letting oneself be loved by God in Jesus Christ. Letting oneself be loved in this way is the light that helps us to bear our daily burden."[18]

Faith is the person's response to divine revelation. Since the center of divine revelation is God's love,[19] faith must be a response to this love. It is a "Yes" with two elements: first, *assent to the truth about this gift of love* and what God desires for us; second, a *consent actually to be loved* in order *to receive His gift*. And, since it is the nature of love to make a gift of itself, St. John Paul II can assert: "Faith, in its deepest essence, is the *openness of the human heart to the gift*: to God's self-communication in the Holy Spirit."[20]

This is why the Mother of God professed her faith in a way that included a reference to herself. God's love is known by the effects of His grace in us. It is efficacious, it transforms us. The only way to be sure of God's love is to be sure of its effects. And so, Mary praises God by saying: "he who is mighty has done great things *for me*" (Lk 1:49). Mary professed her faith with the "for me" formulation because she knew that God's grace had transformed her to be a virgin mother and that through this transformation He was fulfilling His promise to send the Messiah. This is the way that the apostolic faith has always been professed, as in the Creed, when we say, "*For us* men and *for our* salvation he came down from heaven," and "*For our sake* he was crucified …".

---

[18] Benedict XVI, General Audience, February 16, 2011.
[19] *CCC*, 760.
[20] John Paul II, *Dominum et Vivificantem*, 51, emphasis added.

The "for me" formulation conveys the faith-awareness of having been loved by God. It conveys the truth about God's love that gives rise to hope for everyone who has come to realize that apart from the power of God there is no hope for a life of love. The witness of the Church's members' new way of living in love for one another and for the poor constitutes the evidence that God's love is efficacious, that it changes the human condition. In this way, the Church fulfills the mission to give glory to God: "the glory of God is the living man, yet man's life is the vision of God."[21] The human person, alive with the very love of God and love for others, particularly the poor, this is the glory of God.

Mary was not the only one to express her faith with the "for me" formulation. St. Paul does so as well: "the life I now live in the flesh I live by faith in the Son of God, who *loved me* and gave himself *for me*" (Gal 2:20). Benedict XVI calls this "a very personal profession of faith in which he opens his heart to readers of all times and reveals what was the most intimate drive of his life." He continues:

> All Paul's actions begin from this center. His faith is the experience of being loved by Jesus Christ in a very personal way. It is awareness of the fact that Christ did not face death for something anonymous but rather for love of him—of Paul—and that, as the Risen One, He still loves him; in other words, Christ gave himself for him. Paul's faith is being struck by the love of Jesus Christ, a love that overwhelms him to his depths and transforms him. His faith is not a theory, an opinion about God and the world. His faith is the impact of God's love in his heart. Thus, this same faith was love for Jesus Christ.[22]

---

[21] Cf. Irenaeus, *Adversus Haereses*, IV, 20, 7: *S. Chr.* 100/2, 648.

[22] Benedict XVI, Homily, June 28, 2008. See also his address to

Everyone who expresses faith and his relationship with God in this way thereby establishes the criteria for fulfilling the new commandment to love others as we have been loved by Christ (Jn 13:34). For, the "for me" formulation of faith expresses the awareness of having been efficaciously loved by Jesus Christ. In this way, being loved by Him, which happens when we are "with Him," leads to loving others in the same way, with mercy, which happens when we are "sent by Him." He can send us because we know Him in the biblical sense of to experience and to be one with Him in knowledge of God's mercy. When mercy becomes the meaning of our lives, we are ready to be sent by Him. And the "for me" formulation is precisely the expression of having received the gift of new life through God's mercy.

Professing faith in terms of having been loved by God in Christ was a bedrock principle for Benedict XVI. A verse from St. John's First Letter served as the unifying theme of his entire pontificate: "So we know and believe the love that God has for us. God is love" (1 Jn 4:16). The name of his first encyclical was taken from this verse. *Deus caritas est* is Latin for "God is love." Here is a sample of his exposition of the theme.

> Since God has first loved us (cf. 1 Jn 4:10), love is now no longer a mere 'command'; it is the response to the gift of love with which God draws near to us" (*Deus Caritas Est*, 1). Faith is this personal adherence—which involves all our faculties—to the revelation of God's gratuitous and "passionate" love for us, fully revealed in Jesus Christ. The encounter with God who is Love engages not only the heart but also the intellect: "Acknowledgement of the living God is one path towards love, and the 'yes' of our will to

---

participants in a course on the internal forum, March 16, 2007.

his will unites our intellect, will and sentiments in the all-embracing act of love. But this process is always open-ended; love is never 'finished' and complete" (*Deus Caritas Est*, 17). Hence, for all Christians, and especially for "charity workers", there is a need for faith, for "that encounter with God in Christ which awakens their love and opens their spirits to others. As a result, love of neighbor will no longer be for them a commandment imposed, so to speak, from without, but a consequence deriving from their faith, a faith which becomes active through love" (*Deus Caritas Est*, 31a). Christians are people who have been conquered by Christ's love and accordingly, under the influence of that love— "*Caritas Christi urget nos* [The love of Christ impels us.]" (2 Cor 5:14)—they are profoundly open to loving their neighbor in concrete ways (cf. *Deus Caritas Est*, 33). This attitude arises primarily from the consciousness of being loved, forgiven, and even served by the Lord, who bends down to wash the feet of the Apostles and offers himself on the Cross to draw humanity into God's love.[23]

These lines directly refute the overused and groundless objection that Christianity is a flight from reality and makes no difference in the world. Christians feel better about themselves and their faith may help them cope with life—so the objection goes—but it does not really change the human condition. To someone who so objects, one might ask if he knows anything at all about the millions of poor who were hungry, thirsty, homeless, diseased, without education, and neglected, and were attended to by Christian men and women who left their comfortable lives to come

---

[23] Benedict XVI, Message for Lent, 2013 (dated October 15, 2012).

to them in the name of Jesus Christ. One might ask Franciszek Gajowniczek if the faith of St. Maximilian Koble made any difference in his life, or Gianna Emanuela Molla if the faith of her mother, St. Gianna Molla, made any difference in her life. The very lives of Franciszek and Gianna Emanuela are testimonies to having been loved. Faith shapes history, especially for the neglected poor who need to be loved.

To say that the purpose of spiritual exercises is to foster and to reinforce a living faith that is able to express itself with the "for me" formulation is to say that they are meant to promote what St. Paul calls "the obedience of faith" (Rom 1:5:16:26). Faith is meant to penetrate into every act of free will. It does this by shining the light of divinely revealed truth on every judgment of conscience for every decision. Such faith makes Christian life a symphony of love. For, judgments of conscience concern what must be done and avoided for the sake of love. Thus, through conscience, the "for me" reality of faith is present in every action. When Christians are asked why they act as they do, their answer is simply: Because of what Jesus has done for me.

The "for me" way of professing faith corresponds to what is traditionally called the moral sense of Scripture.[24] Discovering this sense is the whole point of *lectio divina*. A person of faith certainly reads the Bible in order to ascertain what God has said. But faith does not stop there because faith is more than an intellectual assent to what God has revealed. Faith makes it possible to read the Bible for what it truly is, that is, God's word about His love—the very love that has transformed the believer's life and brought him to faith in the first place. Faith seeks to discover what God has to say to me, which is exactly what He has said to the saints.

---

[24] For a brief summary of the senses of Scripture, see *CCC*, 115–119.

Spiritual exercises keep faith alive, and faith keeps alive the question, "What, then, shall I do?" For, by faith a believer knows that love is the meaning of life, that every thought, word, and deed should be love. But this leads to the question: "What does it mean to love here and now, in this thought, in these words, and in this action? What, then, shall I do, here and now?" God answers this question through the judgment of conscience because faith shines the light of God's word on moments of truth in conscience. Thus it is that when faith consults God—His inspired word, His Church, His saints—it is with a view to the obedience of faith in love. "It is a question of acting truthfully in order to come into the light: 'Lord, what do you want me to do?'"25

Faith informs us about what God wants us to do. He wants us to love. For this reason, "a completely valid interpretation of words inspired by the Holy Spirit" begins by asking in prayer "for the love that alone enables one to understand the language of God, who 'is love' (1 Jn 4:8, 16)."26 To seek love is to seek God, and to seek God is to seek love. And, because we cannot love what we do not know, this entails seeking the truth about love. This is the true dynamic at work in all spiritual exercises.

Living, mature faith, then, does not seek to know God and His plan of love as some merely objective reality about which one can compile informational data. Faith seeks both to gain clearer insight into the meaning of doctrine and to ascertain its implications for one's life. Spirituality, in fact, is nothing more than the translation of the Creed into life.27 The obedience of faith in love always presupposes the consent of faith to be loved, and this consent presupposes

---

25 *CCC*, 2706.

26 John Paul II, Address on the occasion of the centenary of the encyclical *Providentissimus Deus* and the fiftieth anniversary of the encyclical *Divino afflante Spiritu*, April 23, 1993, 9.

27 "[T]here is no authentic spirituality that does not put dogma into action" (Henri de Lubac, *Theological Fragments* [San Francisco: Ignatius Press, 1989], 118).

assent to the meaning of God's love. For one who believes that God's love "constitutes ... *the apex of all* that has been revealed ... and that this truth illumines the whole content of divine revelation, and particularly the revealed reality *of the creation* and *of the Covenant,*"[28] doctrine is the sheet music that is meant to be played, to become performance in life. Spirituality is the symphonic performance resulting from the perfect playing of every note of doctrinal truth about God's love.

The Dignity and Vocation to Be Christ's Associates in Mission

The transformation brought about by God's efficacious love, discussed above, is ordered to participation in Christ's mission. When Jesus heals a leper, this is obviously a good thing for the leper. He knows that he has been loved, and he begins to relate to Jesus based on what He did *for him*. This former leper realizes that what Jesus has done *for him* He can also do *for other lepers*. His solidarity with other lepers is the foundation for him to experience the interior movement of *love for them*. How could he not go to them in order to bear witness to what Jesus did *for him*, and thereby bring them hope? "The love of Christ impels us" (2 Cor 5:14).

Certainly, Jesus knows all this, and, just as certainly, His love extends to all lepers. His strategy for His love to reach them includes the agency of the leper He had healed. For, He knows that it is a primordial dynamism of having been loved to extend that love to others. The point is that when God loves someone, He is always envisioning loving others with that person.[29] He desires that every disciple and

---

[28] John Paul II, General Audience, October 2, 1985, 1–2.

[29] This is essentially what Vatican II teaches about God's decision to enter into a special relationship with His chosen people. See *Dei Verbum*, 14, 3–4, *Lumen gentium*, 9, *Nostra aetate*, 4. Jesus Christ fulfills the vocation of Israel to be light to the nations (Is 42:6; 39:6; 60:3; Lk 2:32).

friend be "an associate in His compassion, His work of salvation."[30] Among all those who have cooperated with God in the mission of love, the Blessed Virgin Mary is the most perfect. "Because she was, by the design of divine Providence, the mother who nourished the divine Redeemer, Mary became 'an associate of unique nobility, and the Lord's humble handmaid,' who 'cooperated by her obedience, faith, hope and burning charity in the Savior's work of restoring supernatural life to souls.'"[31]

The examples of the healed leper and Mary reinforce the foundational principle of participation in the mission of Christ, namely, that one must first experience God's mercy before being able to bear witness to it and to bring it to others. In fact, showing mercy to others authenticates the encounter with God's mercy in Christ: "should not you have had mercy on your fellow servant, as I had mercy on you?" (Mt 18:33). With this we see that the first mission of holiness leads to the second mission of ministry and apostolate. Words of praise to God for His greatest attribute, which is mercy, and works of mercy towards those who are unloved are the fruit of having encountered His mercy. We also see that the second mission fulfills the commandments to love one's neighbor as oneself and to love others as Christ has loved us (Jn 13:34). To be with Jesus is to experience His mercy and to be transformed by it so that the disciple and friend is ready to be sent by Jesus as an associate in His mission of mercy.[32]

The preceding explains why instruction and training in the ways of divine mercy and of man's response through conversion constitutes an essential element of doctrinal, spiritual, and pastoral formation. For, the human dignity of Christ's disciples and friends requires that they knowingly

---

[30] *CCC*, 2575. See the theme in the *CCC* of God attuning hearts to his compassion or mercy.

[31] John Paul II, *Redemptoris Mater*, 22, quoting Vatican II, *Lumen gentium*, 61.

[32] See the discussion of Mk 3:14 in chapter two.

cooperate with Him. Doctrinal, spiritual, and pastoral formation are for the disciple and friend of Christ what nursing school and medical school are for nurses and doctors.

Having made human beings in His own image, God has also endowed all persons with "the dignity of acting on their own, of being causes and principles for each other, and thus of co-operating in the accomplishment of his plan."[33] Actually, this is true for all of creation, not just man. We need only think of the way that water cooperated with God at the time of the flood of Noah and the parting of the Red Sea at the time of the Exodus, and how it continues to cooperate with Him in the Sacrament of Baptism.[34] What makes man unique among the creatures cooperating with God is the way that He factors in his freedom.

> To human beings God even gives the power of freely sharing in his providence by entrusting them with the responsibility of "subduing" the earth and having dominion over it (cf. Gen 1:26–28). God thus enables men to be intelligent and free causes in order to complete the work of creation, to perfect its harmony for their own good and that of their neighbors. Though often unconscious collaborators with God's will, they can also enter deliberately into the divine plan by their actions, their prayers and their sufferings (cf. Col 1:24). They then fully become "God's fellow workers" and co-workers for his kingdom (1 Cor 3:9; 1 Thes 3:2; Col 4:11).[35]

To comment on this text at length is beyond the scope of this book. For, there are several kinds of cause. It is

---

[33] *CCC*, 306.

[34] See the Rite of Baptism.

[35] *CCC*, 307.

enough for our purposes to point out that throughout the Church's history, the saints bear witness to the reality that God works with and through holy men and women who exercise a genuine causality in imparting Christian faith and holiness to others. The clearest examples are the apostles and founders and reformers of religious orders, like St. Benedict, St. Francis of Assisi, and St. Teresa of Avila. For good reason, then, they are called fathers and mothers; for, like parents who effectively pass on life and faith to their children, they generate spiritual families. Many saints wrote books through which their causality—that is, their love—extends down through the centuries, shaping the spiritual lives of countless people of faith. Because the saints' causality does not end with their death, it is fitting to pray to them in order to obtain through their cooperation with God, their intercession, the graces that He desires for us.

The renewal of Vatican II and its extension in the New Evangelization are all about revitalizing this dignity of causality—that is, the dignity of love that is efficacious in the order of grace—in all of the faithful. The Council conveyed this when it taught that "the Church is 'the universal sacrament of salvation', simultaneously manifesting and actualizing the mystery of God's love for men,"[36] and that all of the baptized faithful participate in this mystery of the Church as sacrament of divine love. For, the holiness to which all are called entails communion with Christ in His life and His mission, being with Him and being sent by Him, abiding in Him as the Vine and producing fruit as branches. Charity, as we have seen, entails both love of God, on one hand, and love of self and of love of neighbor, on the other hand. Charity is the soul of the apostolate regarding love of self (first mission) and love of neighbor (second mission).[37]

---

[36] Vatican II, *Gaudium et spes*, 45.

[37] There can be no mission or apostolate directed to God regarding His

St. Thomas Aquinas, in fact, defined the worship of God precisely in these terms. "The purpose of divine worship is that man may give glory to God, and submit to Him in mind and body."[38] But since God is love and the proper act of love is to bestow gifts, "The worship of God is receiving and giving divine gifts."[39] This happens preeminently in the liturgy, especially Mass, when the faithful are "with God" and submit to His love by receiving His gifts of grace. Then, with the dismissal, they are "sent by God" to go and to share those gifts with others. The rhythm of Mass recapitulates and renews the rhythm of being with Christ in order to be sent by Him (Mk 3:14).

Spiritual exercises operate according to this same principle. In themselves, they are a time of being with Christ, to receive the divine gifts of grace in order to be conformed more and more fully to the image of Christ. At the same time, they bear the fruit of more perfect love of neighbor in the active giving of divine gifts. In this way, those spiritual exercises that are not explicitly liturgical nevertheless extend the pattern of the liturgy into daily life. They serve to make all of life a liturgy of worshipping God by receiving His gifts of grace and giving them to others.

Charity can never be content simply to desire the good

---

divinity. For, God is the font of all mission and missionary love. Nevertheless, the spirituality of consoling the Sacred Heart of Jesus conveys the understanding that acts of mercy and Christian virtue can be directed to Him in His suffering caused by sin. "Now if, because of our sins also which were as yet in the future, but were foreseen, the soul of Christ became sorrowful unto death, it cannot be doubted that then, too, already He derived somewhat of solace from our reparation, which was likewise foreseen ... in order that His Heart, oppressed with weariness and anguish, might find consolation. And so even now, in a wondrous yet true manner, we can and ought to console that Most Sacred Heart..." (Pius XI, *Miserentissimus Redemptor*, 13). In fact, Christ "became poor" (2 Cor 8:9) in order to elicit acts of mercy from us in His behalf. "God also reveals His mercy when He invites man to have 'mercy' on His only Son, the crucified one" (John Paul II, *Dives in misericordia*, 8).

38 Aquinas, *ST* II-II, 93, 2.
39 Aquinas, *ST* III, 63, 2.

of life in Christ for others. Like God's own love, our charity strives to be efficacious, or "performative."[40] Charity cannot rest until the one who is loved is actually transformed and enriched by faith and communion with Christ. Restated in terms of mercy, mercy cannot rest until evil is vanquished by good. In other words, it is the nature of charity to be missionary and efficacious.

Through pastoral formation for ministry and apostolate, the Church imparts the practical wisdom of Christ, the apostles, and the saints regarding what today we might call "best practices" ordered to the efficacious realization of the good that charity desires for others, namely, life in Christ. These principles, which guide and order acts of charity, constitute the art of Christian love. Seminaries and programs of formation transmit the wisdom of the art of Christian love to future priests and deacons. It is the same for initiatives to equip mothers and fathers with wisdom for effective parenting. Similarly, programs of formation for catechists and youth ministers entail instruction in methods for the efficacious communication the faith to various age groups. There are graduate degree and certificate programs for forming spiritual directors in the wisdom of the saints, that their service be efficacious. Countless books and recordings also impart the wisdom of the art of Christian love about how to sanctify suffering and to unite it to the suffering of Christ for the good of the Church and of the whole world.

All such formational programs for ministry or apostolate impart an education in practical wisdom that corresponds to charity's desire to be efficacious. In other words, they are at the service of actualizing the dignity of causality that pertains to all of Christ's disciples and friends. As suggested at the outset of this book, they should be seen as initiatives of the Holy Spirit to activate the many gifts that He bestows in this historical moment, which is to

---

[40] See Benedict XVI, *Spe salvi*, 2, 4, 10; *Verbum Domini*, 53, 56.

say, gifts that are ordered to the implementation of Vatican II's call to holiness and the New Evangelization.

The Essence of Christian Witness

Because God's love is efficacious, that is, transformative, the very life of Christ's disciples and friends, including their mission to others, bears witness to His love. To encounter Christ is to be called to follow Him. It is to receive a vocation that entails new relationships and new activities that identify a person as Christ's disciple and friend. Most conspicuous among these are participation in the liturgy and the new life of merciful love that manifests itself in mutual service, forgiveness and reconciliation, solicitude for the poor, and love for enemies. These actions point to the new definition of happiness—the beatitudes—that guides Christians' actions through the dictates of conscience. The Christian renewal of the mind (Rom 12:2; Eph 4:23) entails a reordering of life in the obedience of faith based on the priority of bearing witness to the truth about Christ's love to others. Once again, we perceive the precedence of the first mission of love of self in relation to the second mission of loving others.

Witness to Christ's love is the first and most fundamental element of participation in His mission. For, Christ's mission is to draw us into His mission—"As the Father has sent me, even so I send you" (Jn 20:21).—and He fulfilled His mission by bearing witness to the Father's love for Him and His unity with the Father. He constantly refers to Himself to being sent by the Father to establish the Kingdom of God.[41] Constantly He speaks about doing the Father's will.[42] His whole desire is that those He loves come to know the Father's love: "he who loves me will be loved by my Father" (Jn 14:21). His being loved by the Father is

---

[41] See Jn 4:34; 5:36–37; 6:44, 57; 6:16, 18, 42; 12:49; 14:24; 17:21, 25; 20:21.
[42] See Mt 6:10; 7:21; 12:50; 26:42; Jn 4:34; 5:30; 6:38; 8:28; 15:10; 17:4.

the measure of His love for us: "As the Father has loved me, so have I loved you" (Jn 15:9). Jesus fulfilled this mission by loving us "to the end" (Jn 13:1). Thereby He fulfilled His mission to be "the faithful and true witness" (Rev 3:14). His witness is so perfect and compelling that He can say: "I bear witness to myself" (Jn 8:18).

Like Jesus, then, His disciples and friends must be witnesses.

> The witness of a Christian life is the first and irreplaceable form of mission: Christ, whose mission we continue, is the "witness" par excellence (Rev 1:5; 3:14) and the model of all Christian witness. The Holy Spirit accompanies the Church along her way and associates her with the witness he gives to Christ (cf. Jn 15:26–27).[43]

One of the most succinct articulations of the Christian's participation in Christ's mission of mercy comes in Jesus's instruction to a man from whom he had driven out a legion of demons. Quite understandably, this man desired to become a disciple and friend of Jesus, to follow Him, and to be with Him. Having come to know how much Jesus loved him, the man was "thereby stirred to love Him in return"[44] and "begged him that he might be with him" (Mk 5:18). But Jesus had a different vision for his future. The former demoniac would indeed be with Jesus, but not as he had wished. He would be with Jesus by collaborating in

---

[43] John Paul II, *Redemptoris missio*, 42.

[44] "Among means to an end that one is the more suitable whereby the various concurring means employed are themselves helpful to such end. But in this that man was delivered by Christ's Passion, many other things besides deliverance from sin concurred for man's salvation. In the first place, man knows thereby how much God loves him, and is thereby stirred to love Him in return, and herein lies the perfection of human salvation; hence the Apostle says (Rom 5:8): "God commendeth His charity towards us; for when as yet we were sinners ... Christ died for us" (Aquinas, *ST* III, Q. 46, a. 3).

His mission.

The mission that Jesus entrusted to him was to be a witness among those closest to him. For, these would have knowledge of his condition prior to his encounter with Jesus: "'Go home to your friends, and tell them how much the Lord has *done for you*, and how he has had *mercy on you*.' And he went away and began to proclaim in the Decapolis how much *Jesus had done for him*" (Mk 5:19–20). This is equivalent to saying: "Go, and by your new life of liberation from demons, show people the transforming power of God's love. And by your words bear witness to the love of God that you encountered in Jesus of Nazareth."

As we have seen, these two simple words, "for me," convey the reality of having had a personal encounter with God's efficacious love in Jesus Christ. We have also seen that this is how the Virgin Mary (Lk 1:49) and St. Paul (Gal 2:20) professed their faith. St. Paul makes it clear that this is the fundamental truth for every Christian, for, when writing to the Ephesians, he uses precisely the same language: "Therefore be imitators of God, as beloved children, and walk in love, as Christ *loved us* and gave himself up *for us*" (Eph 5:1–2). This love of Christ is the model for the love of all Christians, for example, husbands: "Husbands, love your wives, as Christ *loved the Church* and gave himself up *for her*" (Eph 5:25).

This "for me" dimension of faith and witness confirms the order according to which loving oneself by receiving Christ's love (first mission) precedes love for one's neighbor (second mission). Moreover, the "for me" dimension points to the content of love of neighbor, namely, the mercy of God. Those who show mercy to others are already blessed because this is the great sign that they have received mercy. The mercy encountered in Christ is the measure of love for others. "A new commandment I give to you, that you love one another: even *as I have loved you*, that you also love one another. By this men will know that you are my disciples, if you have love for one another" (Jn 13:34–35).

St. Paul conveys that to be with Christ is not simply to be alongside Him, in His company. That is the way it was for the apostles prior to His death and resurrection, before the gift of the Holy Spirit on Pentecost. With the gift of the Holy Spirit, every disciple and friend can say: "It is no longer I who live, but Christ who lives in me" (Gal 2:20). Regarding the second mission of loving others, this can be rephrased: "It is no longer I who love, but Christ who loves in me." This harmonizes with the assertion that "the love of Christ impels us" (2 Cor 5:14) to love others as He has loved us. This is what the Second Vatican Council underscored by teaching that the Church is a sacrament, that is, a sign and instrument through which Christ continues His mission of mercy in the world.

The commandment to love others as we love ourselves (the Golden Rule) is the law of our very nature, putting into words the fundamental dynamism of what it means to be image of God. It is, in the words of St. Paul, written on the hearts of all men (Rom 2:15). For this reason, it is the law of Jesus's own life. Since He loves Himself by receiving the Father's love: "The Father loves the Son" (Jn 3:35; 5:20). He loves us by desiring for us this same experience of being loved by the Father: "As the Father has loved me, so have I loved you" (Jn 15:9). The goal of His mission is that others be loved by the Father as He is loved by the Father.

When Jesus speaks of the Father as the one who loves Him, whose love He has received, it is His version of the "for me" way in which we express our faith. For, "for me" conveys that one has been blessed and enriched by God's love. The "for me" dimension of Jesus's confession, then, is present in every statement that Jesus makes about being loved by the Father. It is present in the Father's first words to Him: "You are my beloved Son; in you I am well pleased" (Lk 3:22). It is present in the texts in the preceding paragraph. It is also present when He says: "For as the Father has life in himself, so he has granted the Son also to have life in himself" (Jn 5:26); "As the Father has loved me, so have I loved you" (Jn 15:9); "All that the Father has is mine" (Jn 16:15).

Knowing that Jesus is the fulness of revelation of God and that He defines His life and mission by the Father's love, we can perfectly understand that St. John would recapitulate the content of Christian faith with these words: "So we know and believe the love that God has for us. God is love...." (1 Jn 4:16). The love God has for us is first of all the Father's love for the Son. The Father does not love us with a love that would somehow be distinct from His love for the Son. The Father's love for us is the self-same love that He has for Jesus, the Son. It becomes ours by reason of our being taken into the Son's experience of being loved by the Father.

Just as Jesus is the witness to the Father's love for Him, so those whom He loves are witnesses through whom His love becomes known by others. "By this all men will know that you are my disciples, if you have love for one another" (Jn 13:35). Indeed, whoever sees Jesus in the truth of His being as Son thereby sees the Father, whose love for the Son becomes evident in Him and in His disciples. Renewed in Christ, the Church of His disciples and friends continues to elicit the Father's exclamation, first spoken to His Son: "In you I am well pleased." This is what it means to live in "the certainty of being loved."[45]

This is also what it means to say that "the Church is the goal of all things."[46] The Church is God's first intention, the unifying purpose of all that He has done. The Church, which the Church Fathers called the whole Christ, participates in Christ's mission to satisfy the Father's love.[47] The Church is the Father's new creation. Following it He can rest, as He did following the six days of creation,

---

[45] *CCC*, 2778.

[46] *CCC*, 760.

[47] "He it was, and he alone, who satisfied the Father's eternal love" (John Paul II, *Redemptor hominis*, 9).

because His love has been poured out according to the measure that satisfies it. The satisfaction of Father and of the Son is called the Holy Spirit, Who is Christ's gift to those who respond to His love for them by loving Him in return and continuing His mission.

Through its witness to Jesus Christ, the Church fulfills the mission to make God's love known and experienced. For, everyone is called to live in "the certainty of being loved" by God in Christ, which is to receive the gift of the Holy Spirit. Everyone is called to enter into Christ's experience of satisfying the Father's love and hearing the Father say: "In you I am well pleased." Christian witness, then, is not some activity in addition to living the Christian life. It is simply Christian life on display, lived in the midst of the world. For, Christ's mission is not something in addition to simply living His communion with the Father in our midst. He fulfills His mission by witnessing to this life of communion with the Father, lived among us so that by seeing Him we see the Father. The mission of Christ's disciples and friends, fulfilled in the power of the Holy Spirit, is to bear witness to the life of communion with Him. In this way, the first mission of being with Christ is present in the second mission of being sent by Him.

4.
Foundations for a Theology of Spiritual Exercises

Before considering a sustainable set of actual spiritual exercises and offering a few additional considerations, it will be helpful to review some of the main principles and considerations discussed above.

The truth about God as love, the truth about man as image of God and being made for love, and the truth about man's participation in the life and mission of Jesus Christ provide a secure foundation for spirituality and for all spiritual exercises. These foundational truths serve to counteract tendencies within a culture to focus on the individual, the pragmatic, and the "efficient": *doing* unanchored in *being*. The risk that being sent by Christ take precedence over being with Christ is real. A disciple may take an initiative, convinced that it is a response to Christ's call, when in reality it is his own. If his friendship with Christ is not sufficiently established, the initiative is premature. Finally, these principles undergird the inseparable unity of the faith that we profess and the life that we live. In essence, like spiritual exercises themselves, these principles serve to deepen awareness of being loved by the Father, to promote the dilation of the heart, and to expand the capacity to love—the essential "even more" that is required from those who are given more.

God always has more to give.

Spiritual exercises are premised on two things. First, God always has more to give, and He desires to give it. To receive this "more" is to be the beneficiary of a new divine mission.[1] And, since from the one to whom more is given more will be demanded (Lk 12:48), by their very nature as encounters with God's love, spiritual exercises necessarily entail the fruit of ongoing conversion. For, conversion is the fruit of encountering God's love. When by faith one comes to "know and believe the love that God has *for us*" (1 Jn 4:16) and also by faith knows where to find the God of love, the commitment to spiritual exercises is an inevitable necessity.

Saints like Ignatius of Loyola and Francis de Sales urge us to end a time of prayer with resolutions that, in effect, project the graces received during prayer into daily life. Resolutions anticipate the "something more" that is required of one to whom more has been given. The first and most fundamental resolution is to resolve to return to prayer the next day, or at the next time scheduled for prayer. Every return to God confirms the wise man's words about how the taste of true wisdom creates a desire for more: "Those who eat of me will hunger for more, and those who drink of me will thirst for more" (Sir 24:21). Every return to God, who awaits us in spiritual exercises, bears witness—first of all to the one who returns!—to the transforming love of Christ and the gift of faith by which receiving His love is the highest priority.

It gives God great glory simply to return to the places where we know He awaits us. Every such return is an encounter of God's thirst for us and our thirst for God:

> "If you knew the gift of God!" (Jn 4:10). The wonder of prayer is revealed beside the well where we come seeking water: there, Christ comes to meet every human being. It is he who first seeks us and asks us for a drink. Jesus thirsts; his asking arises from the depths of

---

[1] "The invisible mission takes place also as regards progress in virtue or increase of grace" (Aquinas, *ST* I, Q. 43, a. 6, ad 2).

God's desire for us. Whether we realize it or
not, prayer is the encounter of God's thirst with
ours. God thirsts that we may thirst for him.[2]

The commitment to keep a schedule of spiritual
exercises depends entirely on knowing the gift of God.
This is "to know" in the biblical sense of "to experience."
"'To know' a person is not only to know who he is and
what he is, but also to experience his presence and his
action on oneself."[3] To know God's love is to experience
having been enriched by that love and then to bear witness
to it with the "for me" formulation. Jesus defines eternal
life in terms of this kind of knowing: "this is eternal life,
that they may know you, the only true God, and Jesus
Christ whom you have sent" (Jn 17:3).

This kind of knowing is the condition for asking Jesus
to give precisely what He desires to give, namely, His love.
"If you knew the gift of God, and who it is that is saying to
you, 'Give me a drink,' you would have asked him and he
would have given you living water" (Jn 4:10). The living
water that Jesus desires to give is the saving truth that He
reveals, and the Holy Spirit, Who is the Spirit of truth. He
renews this mission with every new encounter with Him,
that is, with every spiritual exercise. For, Jesus assures us:
"you know him [the Spirit of truth], for he dwells with you,
and will be in you" (Jn 14:17).

As a result of their first encounter with Jesus, the
Samaritans, who had been introduced to Him by the
woman whom He met at the well, so very sensibly asked
Him to stay with them.[4] Similarly, the disciples from
Emmaus, with hearts set afire by the words of the

---

[2] *CCC*, 2560. This text ends with a reference to St. Augustine, *De diversis quaestionibus octoginta tribus* 64, 4.

[3] Jean-Hervé Nicolas, *Dieu Connu Comme Inconnu* (Paris: Desclée de Brouwer, 1966), 367.

[4] "So when the Samaritans came to him, they asked him to stay with them, and he stayed there two days" (Jn 4:40).

resurrected Jesus, pleaded, "Stay with us" (Lk 24:29). This is the spontaneous request that springs from knowing Jesus: knowing Him, that is, having been loved by Him, and the desire to be loved even more. These people—the woman at the well, her neighbors, and the disciples from Emmaus—had been touched by His love, and they realized that He had more to give.

Just as we thirst for Him and He thirsts for us, our desire that Jesus stay with us corresponds to His desire to stay with us. What He said to Zacchaeus, He says to all who seek Him: "I must stay at your house today" (Lk 19:5). The response of Jesus to our desire that He stay with us takes the form, first, of residing in our hearts, and, second, of assuring us that He awaits us in all the "places" to which there are corresponding spiritual exercises, and preeminently in the Eucharist. "He who eats my flesh and drinks my blood abides [stays] in me, and I in him" (Jn 6:56).

God awaits man's response.

The second premise of spiritual exercises is that while God's giving is rooted in His love, which is eternal and unchanging, the actual reception of what He gives is conditioned by our desire to receive. What happens in that moment between His offer and our response? He waits. St. Bernard eloquently expresses this patience of perfect love exhibited at the Annunciation, when "all creation—the angels, the patriarchs, the prophets, all the children of Israel—wait for her [Mary's] response."[5] Prior to Mary's consent to God's approach and offer of love, His people's hardness of heart had provoked Him to ask, on numerous occasions, "How long will this people not believe in me ... murmur against me ... love vain words and seek after lies

---

[5] Bernard of Clairvaux, Hom. 4, 8–9: *Opera omnia, Edit. Cisterc.* 4 (1966), 53–54.

... waver?"[6] Every divine "How long?" throughout salvation history finds its definitive answer in the Virgin Mary's *fiat* at the Annunciation.

Every spiritual exercise entails an act of faith that, like Mary's *fiat*, opens a person to God's approach of love, thereby answering His plea of love: "How long will you close yourself to my love?"

God's humble waiting for our response, His being reduced to having to ask, "How long?" is already a powerful affirmation of the freedom and dignity—and responsibility—that He bestows upon us. Strikingly, St. John Paul II and Benedict XVI convey the theology of God's waiting for our response by saying that He has circumscribed his own omnipotence by creating us with freedom.

> Yes, in a certain sense one could say that *confronted with our freedom, God decided to make Himself "impotent."* And one could say that God is paying for the great gift bestowed upon a being He created "in his own image, after his likeness" (cf. Gen 1:26). Before this gift, He remains consistent, and *places Himself before the judgment of man* ...[7]

> In reality, God, by creating free creatures, giving them freedom, has renounced a part of his power, empowering our freedom. In this way He loves and respects our free response of love to his call. Like a Father, God wants us to be his children and to live as such in his Son, in communion, in full intimacy with Him. His omnipotence is not expressed in violence, it is not expressed in the destruction of every adverse

---

[6] See Num 14:11, 27; Ps 4:2; Jer 31:22.
[7] John Paul II, *Crossing the Threshold of Hope* (New York: Alfred A. Knopf, 1994), 64–65.

power as we would like, but is expressed in love, in mercy, in forgiveness, in accepting our freedom and in the untiring call to conversion of heart, in an attitude that is only apparently weak—God seems weak, if we think of Jesus Christ who prays, who lets himself be killed. An apparently weak attitude, consisting of patience, gentleness and love, shows that this is the true way of being powerful! This is the power of God! And this power will win![8]

God's one and only tactic, then, is to reveal Himself, to make known His love, and to invite men to open themselves to seek it and to receive it as their greatest good. The calculation of His wisdom is that when people realize God has defined Himself as mercy, they will come to Him with desperate faith when they encounter evil and experience suffering—especially the interior suffering of remorse of conscience. For "God especially hears us when we are troubled: 'in my troubles I cried to the Lord, and he heard me' (Ps 120:1)."[9]

This is the premise that Isaiah and Jeremiah convey by contrasting the way that various animals so naturally comply with God's will to the way that those He has made in His image do not. "Even the stork in the heavens knows her times," and migrating birds "keep the time of their coming; but my people know not the ordinance of the Lord" (Jer 8:7). "The ox knows its owner, and the donkey its master's crib; but Israel does not know, my people do not understand" (Is 1:3). God's bewilderment over the irrationality of men in the face of the evidence of His love reaches its zenith in the Reproaches of Good Friday. God asks, in effect: "What have I left undone in showing my

---

[8] Benedict XVI, General Audience, January 30, 2013.
[9] Aquinas, *Commentary on the Gospel of St. John*, Ch. 17, lect. 1 (Marietti, 2180).

love for you, that you should have such contempt for me?"

Those who are committed to spiritual exercises are like the stork and other winged creatures of Jeremiah, and the ox and donkey of Isaiah. They obediently comply with the dynamism that God has imbedded in their human nature. They know that they are made to receive God's love, and they know where God has promised to be present in order to make His love accessible. They have the good sense to be diligent in performing their duty as jurors charged with weighing the case that God makes regarding His love for man and His closing argument known as the paschal mystery of Jesus Christ.

God makes His case to man.[10]

In contrast to other gods, the God of Israel revealed that jealousy is a trait of His love. Other gods do not make a claim to exclusive fidelity. Each is content with being included as one among multiple gods recognized and worshipped by a people. Israel's God is a loving husband whose expectation of exclusive fidelity is meant to keep His people from sin by giving themselves to other gods. "[W]hat God dreads more than anything is a heart that lets itself be satisfied with something other than Him."[11]

In the Old Testament, the Law expresses God's jealous love. Its purpose is to keep the people's focus on the only God who took an interest in them and liberated them from slavery in Egypt. This is the foundation that justifies His liturgical jealousy, that is, His command that He His chosen people worship Him alone. It is why the Ten Commandments begin with the assertion: "And God spoke all these words, saying: I am the Lord your God, who brought you out of the land of Egypt, out of the house of

---

[10] See Douglas Bushman, "Lessons for Lent from God's Argument about His Love," *Catholic World Report*, April 10, 2022.

[11] Barthélemy, *God and His Image*, 59.

bondage" (Ex 20:1–2). This is to say: I demonstrated my love for you by setting you free from slavery in Egypt. Now I expect you to trust me as I give you these commandments so that you will remain free.

With this we arrive at the definitive foundation for all spiritual exercises: "We love, because he first loved us" (1 Jn 4:19). In the Old Testament, the Law expresses God's jealous love. Its purpose is to preserve God's people from forgetting Him and becoming enticed by other gods, who did nothing for this people when they cried out for deliverance from slavery. By their inaction, these gods demonstrated their total indifference to the plight of this people. In contrast, by His marvelous deeds of liberation—ten plagues, parting of the sea, water from the rock, manna in the desert, the bronze serpent—God made the case for His love for them.

The ideal of Old Testament spirituality is to respond to God's initiative of liberating love with uninterrupted solicitude for faithful observance of the Law. Observing the Law is the one, all-embracing spiritual exercise of the faithful and holy Israelite—provided that this observance is rooted in seeing the link between God's liberating love and this observance. The motive for observing the Law is the fact that the Lawgiver has demonstrated His love for His people. "God has loved us first. The love of the One God is recalled in the first of the 'ten words.' The commandments then make explicit the response of love that man is called to give to his God."[12] Keeping the Law is the response of love on man's part to the initiative of love on God's part. It is based on God's argument regarding His love for His people.

In fact, seeing the relation between God's liberating love and the Law is the very condition for observing the Law. Based on this, when God and His messengers, the prophets, observe that the people fail to observe the Law, they conclude that they no longer perceive this link. Failure

---

[12] *CCC*, 2083.

to observe the Law must mean that the people have forgotten the saving acts that demonstrate God's love.[13] This is the reason for the constant exhortation to remember and not to forget.[14] The entire logic of the covenant, which begins with God's gratuitous initiative of love, is recapitulated when He pleads His case in the form of an indicting question: "What more was there to do for my vineyard that I have not done in it?" (Is 5:4).

That God's people could forget Him and His marvelous works of love so overturns every kind of right thinking that it overwhelms His heart, thrusting it into a state of discombobulation (Hos 11:8). The depths of God's love are revealed not only in His jealousy but also, and even more fully, in Hosea's insight that God cannot envision a future without His people in it. Hosea compares God to a husband whose love for his wife is so great that even when she is unfaithful to him he cannot stop loving her. He knows that by the calculation of justice he could repudiate his adulterous wife. He knows that this would protect him from any future wounds to his love for her. But Hosea's insight is that the husband whose heart has been wounded also realizes that such a repudiation would itself wound his love. "He cannot repudiate her without rendering judgment against himself. It is on this, on his personal, innermost bewilderment as lover, that the covenant's eternal and irrevocable character is based."[15]

Through Hosea, God reveals that He truly loves His people, and that it is impossible for Him to conceive of life apart from them.

---

[13] See Jer 2:32; 13:25; 18:15.

[14] The long list begins with exhortations of Moses. See Deut 4:9, 23; 5:15; 6:12; 8:11, 14, 19; Jdg 8:34; Ps 50:22; 78:7, 11–17, 42; 103:2; 106:7, 13, 21; 119:16, 61, 93, 109, 141, 153, 176, 137:5; Is 17:10; 51:13; 57:11; 65:11; Jer 2:32; 3:21; 13:25; 18:15; 23:27; Ezek 16:22, 43; 22:12; 23:35; Hos 2:13; 4:6; 8:14; 13:6.

[15] Joseph Ratzinger, *Daughter Zion. Meditations on the Church's Marian Belief*, trans. John M. McDermott (San Francisco: Ignatius Press, 1983), 22.

> How can I give you up, Ephraim? How can I hand you over, O Israel? How can I make you like Admah? How can I treat you like Zeboiim? My heart recoils within me; my compassion grows warm and tender. I will not execute my fierce anger; I will not again destroy Ephraim; for I am God and no mortal, the Holy One in your midst, and I will not come in wrath. (Hosea 11:8–9)

"God's passionate love for his people—for humanity—is at the same time a forgiving love. It is so great that it turns God against himself, his love against his justice."[16] As we have seen, God reveals Himself as mercy.

What Hosea reveals about God's anguished heart is definitively revealed in the agony of Jesus Christ. "The pierced Heart of the crucified Son is the literal fulfillment of [Hosea's] prophecy of the Heart of God."[17] We see the distressed heart of God when Jesus weeps over the death of His friend, Lazarus (Jn 11:35), and over the city of Jerusalem (Lk 19:41). We see it when the agony of His soul becomes so great that it causes His body to produce "sweat [that] became like great drops of blood" (Lk 22:44). And we hear of it in His own words: "My soul is very sorrowful, even to death" (Mt 26:38). By fulfilling the figure of the "man of sorrows" (Is 53:3), Jesus reveals how sin wounds the heart of God.

The graphic details of Jesus' passion are meant to stir hearts by the knowledge of how much He loves us. They are the final evidence that God presents in the case He makes about His love. The "for me" dimension of this knowledge reaches its summit when His disciples and friends realize that their sins are the cause of His suffering. In the unforgettable words of St. John Paul II: "Look at

---

[16] Benedict XVI, *Deus caritas est*, 10.

[17] Joseph Ratzinger, *Behold the Pierced One. An Approach to a Spiritual Christology*, trans. Graham Harrison (San Francisco: Ignatius Press, 1986), 64.

what you have done in this man to your God."[18] Faith knows Jesus as the one whom our own sins have pierced: "It is in discovering the greatness of God's love that our heart is shaken by the horror and weight of sin and begins to fear offending God by sin and being separated from him."[19] This is to know Jesus in the full truth of His mission of mercy.

In his meditations for the Stations of the Cross, St. Alphonsus Liguori expresses the same holy sentiment of personal responsibility for the suffering and death of Jesus: "My adorable Jesus, it was not Pilate; no, it was my sins that condemned You to die." "My beloved Jesus, it was not the weight of the cross but the weight of my sins which made You suffer so much." All spiritual exercises will bear the fruit of such self-accusation. In this way, we see their relationship to the Eucharist, from which all spiritual exercises flow and in which they culminate.

It does not follow from the preceding that this awareness of the cause-effect relation of one's sins to Christ's suffering predominates a person's consciousness during or following every spiritual exercise. It does mean that accusing oneself of being a sinner who has caused the heart of God to be grieved even to the death of Jesus Christ is a most precious fruit of faith that matures through spiritual exercises. For, only God knows how sin affects Him,[20] and He has revealed this in the paschal mystery of Jesus Christ *so that we might know it and participate in it*. For, by grace, this is what remorse of conscience is: participation in God's own suffering, in Jesus Christ, caused by sin.[21]

It remains true that our sins cannot detract from God's eternal perfection; neither can our virtues add anything to

---

[18] John Paul II, meditation on the second Station of the Cross, in *Sign of Contradiction*, 186. The *CCC* develops this theme in 598 and 1432.

[19] *CCC*, 1432. See Jn 19:37 and Zech 12:10.

[20] On this, John Paul II, *Dominum et Vivificantem*, 28–45.

[21] See John Paul II, *Dominum et Vivificantem*, 45.

His perfection. "If you have sinned, what do you accomplish against him? And if your transgressions are multiplied, what do you do to him? If you are righteous, what do you give to him; or what does he receive from your hand?" (Job 35:6–7). This means that the suffering and death of the Son of God are in every respect "for our sake and for our salvation." In the paschal mystery, "God proves His love for us" (Rom 5:8 NAB).[22] The whole purpose of God becoming a man and suffering as Jesus did is so that we can know how much God loves us and thereby be moved to love Him in return.[23]

By making the case regarding His love for us in this way, God effectively eliminates all competition for our faith. We have seen that no other god has any claim to credibility because no other god created Adam and Eve, liberated the Israelites enslaved in Egypt, or thought so highly of this people's dignity that when they sinned His pardon took the form of a purifying chastisement called the Exile, which was totally ordered to their true repentance return to Him, their one, only, and true Husband. Even so, no other god has shown such interest in human dignity, freedom, responsibility, conscience, and vocation to love so as to love us "to the end," that is, to the very extremities of a love that exhausts itself in the total gift of self in order to elicit the free response of faith and love from us. No other god has shown such interest in the moral rehabilitation of all men[24] and their dignity as causes, that

---

[22] ESV and RSV translate the verb as "to show," while NRS, NAB, and NJB translate it as "to prove." The NAS has "God demonstrates His own love." "To prove" and "to demonstrate" accord more closely to the theme of God making His case.

[23] This closely paraphrases Aquinas in *ST* III, Q. 46, a. 3.

[24] "The Church knows that the issue of morality is one which deeply touches every person; it involves all people, even those who do not know Christ and his Gospel or God himself. She knows that it is precisely *on the path of the moral life that the way of salvation is open to all.* The Second Vatican Council clearly recalled this when it stated that 'those who without any fault do not know anything about Christ or

is, their capacity to love as God loves. No other god is credible because no other god "is love" (1 Jn 4:8, 16).25 Jesus's passion, death, and resurrection constitute God's closing argument in the case He makes to support His claim to incomparable credibility. By faith in His testimony, we can to see that "It is right and just to entrust oneself wholly to God and to believe absolutely what he says. It would be futile and false to place such faith in a creature."26 Thus He refutes every indictment accusing Him of not even existing, or, if He exists, of not love enough to intervene to relieve his suffering, or, if He exists and loves, that He is powerless to change anything.

God's decision to make His case about His love for us derives from a prior decision to bring us to faith in a way that accords with the dignity of our freedom and responsibility, and our capacity to discern the truth and to love. To this end, He places himself before the tribunal of our judgment. God, the just judge, judges us based on our judgment about Him. He lays out His case about His mercy and rests His case with the question: "Have you understood all this?" (Mt 13:51). All this!—The truth about human dignity, freedom, conscience, and sin, and the truth about God's mercy fully revealed in Jesus Christ! God's revelation is accompanied by a rhetoric of confidence in the power of the truth about His love freely to attract those whom who has made in His image and for the truth. He

---

his Church, yet who search for God with a sincere heart and under the influence of grace, try to put into effect the will of God as known to them through the dictate of conscience ... can obtain eternal salvation'. The Council added: 'Nor does divine Providence deny the helps that are necessary for salvation to those who, through no fault of their own, have not yet attained to the express recognition of God, yet who strive, not without divine grace, to lead an upright life. For whatever goodness and truth is found in them is considered by the Church as a preparation for the Gospel and bestowed by him who enlightens everyone that they may in the end have life'" (John Paul II, *Veritatis splendor*, 3).

25 See Hans Urs von Balthasar, *Love Alone Is Credible*, trans. David Schindler (San Francisco: Ignatius Press, 2004).

26 *CCC*, 150.

knows that "truth cannot impose itself except by virtue of its own truth, as it makes its entrance into the mind at once quietly and with power."[27]

God's closing question comes to this: Does any account of history and of your personal story have the explanatory power contained in the case that I have made? Has anyone else so accurately and deeply revealed you to yourself? Is there any other narrative or philosophy or religion that is worthy of eliciting a profession of faith with the "for me" formulation? Is anything more profoundly "for you" than my love and mercy? Is there any other answer to the deepest and most vexing questions about the meaning and purpose of your life? Has any other god explained to you the nature of evil, suffering, and death, and demonstrated its power over them? Is there any other offer of eternal life that is stamped with the seal of a love that is willing to endure suffering and death *for you*?

Spiritual exercises keep faith alive, and lively, by keeping alive the dialogue of salvation that entails: first, man's questions to God about the meaning of life, especially in the context of suffering and especially moral suffering of conscience; second, God's response in the form of the case He makes about His wisdom, power, and mercy definitively revealed in Jesus Christ. Spiritual exercises reinforce the conviction of faith that the most intelligent way to fulfill the natural dynamism to love myself is by entrusting myself to God.[28] Knowing that our love has been disfigured, Jesus asks: "Do you want to be healed?" (Jn 5:6). He asks this, not to raise our hope only to disappoint us, but as one "with authority" (Lk 4:32, 36). Jesus, who is the resurrection (Jn 11:25), is alone capable of raising to new life the old hopes that have been buried for lack of faith in the one, true, and living God. The preeminent act of human reason is to entrust

---

[27] Vatican II, *Dignitatis humanae*, 1.

[28] Vatican II includes such self-entrustment to God in its description of faith in *Dei Verbum*, 5.

oneself to the God who has demonstrated His love for us by placing His wisdom and power at our service. Spiritual exercises are premised on this preeminent act of human reason, that is, faith.

Such self-entrustment to God entails the judgment that He knows me more perfectly than I know myself, that He loves me more perfectly than I am able to love myself, and that He possesses the power efficaciously to act on His knowledge and love in my behalf. In other words, God is entirely "for me." Such faith is the juror's acquiescence to the case God makes about His merciful love. And it is more than mere acquittal. It is being so completely won over by God's argument that one leaves the courtroom with a new understanding of the ground for all that exists—love is the definitive meaning of life. What began as a civic duty becomes a life-changing encounter with the truth that explains all things. The juror is transformed into being an active, full-time advocate for God. All of life becomes defined in terms of the dynamics of the trial, which faith relives intentionally in spiritual exercises. The former juror desires to relive, again and again, the whole process, not as if to remove any doubts that might remain, but to marvel anew at the coherence of the divine argument, to relive the unparalleled intellectual satisfaction in rediscovering, again and again, the "for me" dimension of God's argument about His love.

All spiritual exercises presuppose this surrender in faith to God's case regarding His love for us. In one way or another, they entail the retrial of God for the sake of renewing faith through cooperation with God's jealous love for us. This is how spiritual exercises keep faith alive and make it more and more vigorous. Freely to come to God where He has promised to be waiting for us is to agree with Him that it is foolish and vain to seek the satisfaction of our deepest desires in anything other than Him. To seek

Him where he can be found[29] is true wisdom: "The Lord looks down from heaven upon the children of men, to see if there are any who act wisely, who seek after God" (Ps 14:2; 53:2). In their essence, spiritual exercises are our response of love for God to His initiative of love for us: "We love, because He first loved us" (1 Jn 4:19). "For by loving us, God makes us love him."[30]

The self-entrustment of faith to God's love is the foundation for spiritual exercises because faith perceives the truth of God's closing argument: the suffering, crucifixion, and resurrection of Jesus Christ. Faith perceives the perfect correspondence between Jesus's words at the Last Supper and my search for an everlasting love that is more powerful than all evil and sin—than my sins. When faith hears Jesus say about His body that it is "given for you" and about His blood that it is "poured out for you" (Lk 22:19–20), it understands: given for me and poured out for me. And since the purpose of His sacrifice of love was to merit for us the very gift of love, the Holy Spirit, "Faith, in its deepest essence, is the openness of the human heart to the gift: to God's self-communication in the Holy Spirit."[31] Spiritual exercises renew the drama of the paschal mystery, from the Last Supper to the outpouring of the Holy Spirit on Pentecost. For, it is always through a new mission of the Holy Spirit that Jesus fulfills His love poured out for us and His promise, "I will come to you" (Jn 14:18, 28).

The preceding considerations of faith in terms of its "for me" dimension and focus on Christ's paschal mystery shed light on the all too common experience that despite faithfully practicing spiritual exercises, even for a long time, many people do not experience much actual progress in the spiritual life. While several factors might contribute

---

[29] "Seek the Lord while he may be found, call upon him while he is near" (Is 55:6).

[30] Aquinas, *Commentary on the Gospel of St. John*, Ch. 15, lect. 3 (Marietti, 2011–2012).

[31] John Paul II, *Dominum et Vivificantem*, 51.

to this, one is most certainly a misunderstanding of faith, its role in spiritual exercises, and the relation of spiritual exercises to the obedience of faith in daily life, and thus the role of conscience. The efficacy of spiritual exercises is determined by the two liturgical principles: first, that "the Church celebrates in the liturgy above all the Paschal mystery,"[32] and, second, that "the fruits of the sacraments also depend on the disposition of the one who receives them."[33] Christ's paschal mystery unifies all of the articles of faith that constitute the content of spiritual exercises, and their fruit will be all the greater when the articles of faith are viewed through the lens of faith's "for me" dimension, which corresponds to the "for you" dimension of revelation.

The challenge of spiritual exercises is the same as that of the liturgy: God has nothing new to say that He has not already revealed. Spiritual exercises are not for novelty seekers—unless by "novelty" one understands personal renewal through conversion into being a more perfect friend of Jesus Christ by participating more perfectly in His mission and its culminating act: His paschal mystery. Spiritual exercises are not so much about discovering new things about oneself and God. Even when this happens, and it commonly does, faith perceives that what appear to be new insights are really a deeper penetration into the one, all-embracing mystery of God's merciful love fully revealed in Jesus Christ. To practice spiritual exercises means to approach the God of love with the conviction of faith that He has more to give and the readiness to measure up to the more that will be demanded by it. Acts of such faith, along with acts of hope and charity, are the interior essence of spiritual exercises. The more perfect the acts of these Christian virtues, the greater the fruit that spiritual exercises will yield.

---

[32] *CCC*, 1067. See also *CCC*, 1076, 1085

[33] *CCC*, 1128. See also *CCC*, 1072, 1098, 1229, 1415.

The preceding assertion might lead a person to think that it is possible to ascertain that fruit, and thereby to gain some assurance regarding progress in faith, hope, and charity resulting from spiritual exercises. This is a misleading corollary, for more than one reason. First, while there are definite indicators of progress in these virtues, there are often long periods when the only sign that God permits a person to see is continuing fidelity to spiritual exercises. St. Teresa of Calcutta's well-known maxim be adapted here. Her actual words were: "God does not demand that I be successful. God demands that I be faithful." Adapted to the case at hand: "Success in spiritual growth does not require that I am aware of it. God demands that I be faithful to spiritual exercises and trust Him for the growth." The desire to see progress in the spiritual life can spawn the temptation to measure that progress by superficial and non-essential indicators. And this can impede rather than promote genuine growth in faith, hope, and charity.

Second, we are simply too close to ourselves to avoid the risk of seeing what we want to see and not seeing what we do not want to see. Third, it is imprudent to attempt to make a judgment about the quality of one's spiritual exercises based on a self-assessment of presumed fruit that is immediate. Perhaps there is some discernible awareness of greater devotion, a moving insight, or a holy resolution. But being satisfied with a premature discernment could result in being inattentive to some fruit or fruits that will come later, sometimes much later. How often does it happen that Christ's disciples and friends are unable to see the connection between a grace received, for example, during a retreat, and a purification that comes months or even years later—especially when that purification entails significant suffering?

It is certainly possible, even advisable, to attempt to identify the theological content or themes experienced during spiritual exercises. How else can one be a good steward of God's graces and be thankful for them? But what happens when for one reason or another a person is not conscious of such things? Such a person might assume that there is always some grace to be discovered and become overly concerned to find something for which to thank God and based on which to make some new resolution. But, is this "grace" a genuine gift from God, or is it merely the product of a person's own projection of his best but still immature understanding of God's ways? The experience of the saints teaches us that there are seasons of grace of various durations during which the only thing a person can do is to remain faithful to spiritual exercises and to do his best to transition to the daily duties of life with gratitude for the grace to have been faithful to those spiritual exercises. There can be times when what God is looking for is nothing more than the resolution, accompanied by humble petition for grace, to be faithful to those same spiritual exercises in the future.

Communion with God, the Goal of All Pastoral Activity

"The Church is both the means and the goal of God's plan."[34] God's plan of love is to restore men to communion with Him by vanquishing sin that separates them from sharing in His life. This communion constitutes the Church as the goal of God's plan. Christ has also endowed His Church with various means by which this communion is first imparted and then aided in developing. These means are God's word, sacraments, magisterium, charisms, and mutual support among the Church's members.

Christians of the early centuries conveyed this twofold dimension of the Church as goal and as means when they reflected on the words of the Apostles' Creed: "I believe in … the communion of saints." The *Catechism* elaborates: "The term 'communion of saints' therefore has two closely linked meanings: communion 'in holy things (*sancta*)' and

---

[34] *CCC*, 778.

'among holy persons (*sancti*)'."[35] "Holy persons" signifies those who have been made holy—that is, consecrated to God's service—by His grace and live by faith. This is the goal. "Holy things," on the other hand, refers to those instruments or means—God's word, the sacraments, apostolic authority, charisms, mutual service—through which God works to impart the grace that makes people become saints. With these two dimensions in mind, the *Catechism* recapitulates:

> *Sancta sanctis!* ("God's holy gifts for God's holy people") is proclaimed by the celebrant in most Eastern liturgies during the elevation of the holy Gifts before the distribution of communion. The faithful (*sancti*) are fed by Christ's holy body and blood (*sancta*) to grow in the communion of the Holy Spirit (*koinonia*) and to communicate it to the world.[36]

From what has been said, we can see that several terms are synonymous in signifying the Church as goal or end: holiness, perfection of charity (or love), and communion. When we think of the Church, we should think first and foremost of the interpersonal bond of communion in mutual self-giving with God, that is, participation God's own mystery of being "an eternal exchange of love."[37] The *Catechism* is emphatic about communion in love being the Church's deepest mystery.

> In the Church this communion of mankind with God by means of "the love [that] never ends" (1 Cor 13:8) is the goal that informs everything in the Church that is a sacramental means bound

---

[35] *CCC*, 948.
[36] *CCC*, 948.
[37] *CCC*, 221.

up with this world that passes. "[The Church's] structure is totally ordered to the holiness of Christ's members. And holiness is measured according to the 'great mystery' whereby the Bride responds with the gift of her love to the gift of the Bridegroom" (*Mulieris dignitatem*, 27). Mary precedes us all in the holiness which is the mystery of the Church as "the Bride without spot or wrinkle" (Eph 5:27). This is why "the Church's Marian dimension takes precedence over her Petrine dimension" (*Mulieris dignitatem*, 27).[38]

Some spiritual exercises, like retreats, reception of the sacraments, and spiritual direction, engage the charisms of others: the retreat master, an ordained minister, a spiritual director. Like all charisms, these have their place among the means to holiness. They are elements of the holy things (*sancta*) that are at the service of the communion of holy people (*sancti*) with God and one another. Charisms are entirely at the service of bringing people to faith (first conversion) and to growth in the life of faith (second conversion).[39] Nothing is more important for those who exercise charisms (pastoral agents) than to know what holiness is, what the means to holiness are, what the signs (fruits) of holiness are, and what the dynamics and stages of conversion are. How else can they cooperate with God in leading people to the conversion of faith and accompanying them along the way of ongoing conversion?

Furthermore, those who exercise charisms and those who benefit from them must have a proper understanding of what the Church means by insisting that *participation in the paschal mystery of Christ in the Eucharist is the goal of all mission and pastoral activity*:

---

[38] *CCC*, 773.
[39] On the second conversion, see *CCC*, 1428.

Pressing upon the Christian to be sure, are the need and the duty to battle against evil through manifold tribulations and even to suffer death. But, linked with the paschal mystery and patterned on the dying Christ, he will hasten forward to resurrection in the strength which comes from hope (cf. Phil 3:19; Rom 8:17).

All this holds true not only for Christians, but for all men of good will in whose hearts grace works in an unseen way (cf. *Lumen gentium*, 16). For, since Christ died for all men (cf. Rom 8:32), and since the ultimate vocation of man is in fact one, and divine, we ought to believe that the Holy Spirit, in a manner known only to God, offers to every man the possibility of being associated with this paschal mystery.[40]

The other sacraments, as well as with every ministry of the Church and every work of the apostolate, are tied together with the Eucharist and are directed toward it.[41] The Most Blessed Eucharist contains the entire spiritual boon of the Church,[42] that is, Christ himself, our Pasch and Living Bread, by the action of the Holy Spirit through his very flesh vital and vitalizing, giving life to men who are thus invited and encouraged to offer themselves, their labors and all created things, together with him. In this light, the Eucharist shows itself as the source and the apex of the whole work of preaching the Gospel.[43]

---

[40] Vatican II, *Gaudium et spes*, 22.

[41] "The Eucharist indeed is a quasi-consummation of the spiritual life and the goal of all the sacraments" (Aquinas, *ST* III, Q. 73, a. 3 c; cf. *ST* III, Q. 65, a. 3).

[42] Aquinas, *ST* III, Q. 65, a. 3 ad 1; Q. 79, a. 1 c., ad l.

[43] Vatican II, *Presbyterorum ordinis*, 2.

> The world still does not know it, but everyone is invited to the supper of the wedding of the Lamb (Rev 19:9). To be admitted to the feast, all that is required is the wedding garment of faith which comes from the hearing of his Word (cf. Rom 10:17). The Church tailors such a garment to fit each one with the whiteness of a garment bathed in the blood of the Lamb (Rev 7:14). We must not allow ourselves even a moment of rest, knowing that still not everyone has received an invitation to this Supper or knowing that others have forgotten it or have got lost along the way in the twists and turns of human living. This is what I spoke of when I said, "I dream of a 'missionary option,' that is, a missionary impulse capable of transforming everything, so that the Church's customs, ways of doing things, times and schedules, language and structures can be suitably channeled for the evangelization of today's world rather than for her self-preservation" (*Evangelii gaudium*, 27). I want this so that all can be seated at the Supper of the sacrifice of the Lamb and live from Him.[44]

The key to a proper understanding of such an emphasis on the Eucharist is to avoid isolating it from the rest of the Church's life and from other spiritual exercises. Christ never intended that the Eucharist carry the whole load of meeting all the needs for growth in faith, hope, and charity. The Eucharist bears the fruit that Christ intends when it is complemented by other spiritual exercises.

Forceful texts like the preceding, regarding the place of the Eucharist in a plan for a sustainable set of spiritual exercises, can and not infrequently does lead to an understandable but inexact conclusion in the practical

---

[44] Francis I, Apostolic Letter *Desiderio desideravi*, June 29, 2022, 5.

order. The final chapter of this book will address that issue.

Nemo dat quod non habet.

Spiritual exercises are activities in which a person cooperates with God in His acts of love. Since God is love, wherever He is present, He is loving. The conviction of faith that God is love and that He always has more to give is the indispensable foundation for all spiritual exercises. They are simply various ways that a person of faith consents to being loved by God.

When God loves us, He makes a gift of Himself, He pours more of Himself into us. In this way, as we have seen, spiritual exercises keep the "for me" dimension of faith alive, and this assures the dynamic nature of witness to God's love in daily life. Because God and His truth and His love are the highest of all goods and are meant to be shared with others, the fruit of spiritual exercises is always a renewal of the mission to bear witness to God's love. In this way, spiritual exercises greatly contribute to the observance of the commandments to love others as one has been loved by Christ (Jn 13:34) and to love others as oneself (Mt 22:39).

The classic principle that unites being loved so as to be transformed actively to love for others is: action flows from being (Latin: *operatio sequitur esse*). As the DNA that makes birds and fish and dogs and cats to be what they are and we perceive this in their characteristic behavior, so being loved by God and actively loving Him and others defines Christ's disciples and friends: "A new commandment I give to you, that you love one another; even as I have loved you, that you also love one another. By this all men will know that you are my disciples, if you have love for one another" (Jn 13:34–35). We understand, then, why St. John Paul could say that "love is the DNA of the children of God."⁴⁵ Making us in His image, God has made us for love: to receive His love and to bring it to others. Put another way: you cannot give what you do not possess (Latin: *nemo dat quod non habet*). Or, again, what you have received is meant to be shared with others. "You received without pay, give without pay" (Mt 10:8). There is no price that can be placed on love. Love, however, is ready to pay any price in order to be faithful to itself.⁴⁶

Spiritual Exercises: the Wisdom of the Saints

As has become apparent, spiritual exercises promote the increase of faith, hope, and charity, that is, holiness. Such increase comes about through conversion in response to a new encounter with God's love. Spiritual exercises are encounters with God's love, which comes to us through the joint mission of Christ and the Holy Spirit.⁴⁷ They are useful to the extent that they foster ongoing conversion,⁴⁸ which is the fruit of receiving more of God's love. Conversion is the essential dynamism of the spiritual life. Based on this, the following definition can be proposed:

> Spiritual exercises are enactments of the wisdom of the saints, who guide us in responding to the ways God is present in order to impart graces to

---

45 John Paul II, Message for World Day of Vocations, May 6, 2001, 2.

46 St. Paul refers to the suffering of Christ's redeeming love this way: "You were bought with a price" (1 Cor 6:20; 7:23). And St. Peter: "For you know that the price of your ransom from the futile way of life handed down from your ancestors was paid, not in anything perishable like silver or gold, but in precious blood as of a blameless and spotless lamb, Christ" (1 Pet 1:18–19 NJB).

47 See *CCC*, 689–690.

48 The increase in faith, hope, and charity that we seek in spiritual exercises is the fruit of the invisible missions of the Son and the Holy Spirit. See Aquinas, *ST* I, Q. 43, a. 6, ad 2. The continuation of these missions in the life of the Church and in the lives of people of faith correlates to the post-baptismal second conversion.

foster ongoing conversion that deepens communion with Him and invigorates the mission He entrusts to us.

It has also become apparent that the love God has revealed has the quality of being jealous. Now we can see that by reason of this divine jealousy He makes Himself present to us in a variety of complementary ways—so that our communion with Him be uninterrupted. Since God is love, and since the proper act of love is to bestow gifts that enrich the one who is loved, every distinct way that God is present is ordered to our reception of His gift of grace. To commit to practice spiritual exercises is like imitating bees who return to a source of nectar. Or, to take a biblical image, to seek God's love in spiritual exercises is like a deer seeking streams of living water (Ps 42:1).

In this way, spiritual exercises are an important element of the Church's vocation to give glory to God. It gives God glory to make spending time with Him a priority. For, this conveys that there is something good, something very good, that one finds in the practice of spiritual exercises. In this way, spiritual exercises contribute to the Church's mission to bear witness to Christ. For, they often entail a visible aspect, for example, when Catholics bear the mark of the cross on Ash Wednesday and make the Sign of the Cross. It is evident when they leave their homes to attend Mass, to celebrate the Sacrament of Penance and Reconciliation, and to participate in retreats and pilgrimages. It is evident in the prayers and devotions of Catholic families and communities. God's glory is evident, too, in all the acts of Christian virtue, such as peacemaking and charity for the poor and needy, which are the fruits of spiritual exercises.

The saints are our best guides. They constitute that "cloud of witnesses" (Heb 12:1) who inspire and instruct us by their examples. Many have described, at times under the counsel of obedience to a superior, their own spiritual itineraries, in which bear witness to the place of spiritual exercises in their lives. The *Life*, or autobiography, of St. Teresa of Avila, and *Story of a Soul* of St. Thérèse of Lisieux are examples of this. Many saints were bishops and pastors, theologians, or founders of religious orders, who wrote about the place of spiritual exercises in the life of those who desire to respond to Christ's call to follow Him and to be His friends. St. Francis de Sales' *Introduction to the Devout Life*, and the works of St. John of the Cross, are examples of this.

The discipline of regularly scheduled spiritual exercises, combined with the order resulting from the fulfillment of the duties of a person's vocation, creates an overall objective order in the life of a lay person that is comparable to the order of life resulting from fidelity to a rule of life and *horarium* for religious. This *objective* order is at the service of the *subjective* ordering of the soul by the Christian virtues. Its value is twofold. First, as already stated, it creates an objective schedule of "appointments"—spiritual exercises—for encountering God's love. Second, an overall objective order of life, in which virtuous activities of fidelity to the duties of one's vocation constitute the majority of the hours of each day, liberates a person from a great many sins and occasions of sin. To the extent that one's days are filled with the virtuous activities of spiritual exercises and fidelity to vocational duties, sin and the near occasion of sin are simply crowded out. This makes it possible to focus more intently on the subjective order of Christian virtue and the battle against interior sins and occasions of sin in order to bring about the purifications of the second conversion.

Allowing for the inevitable exceptions that will arise, especially for the lay faithful, and the need to adjust this objective order from time to time, a person's fidelity to God will be lived and measured in terms of fidelity to this order of spiritual exercises and fulfillment of vocational duties. This is obvious in the vocations that entail a new

Foundations for a Theology of Spiritual Exercises 119

state in life: marriage, ordained ministry, consecration by the evangelical counsels. From the moment the sacraments are celebrated or the vows professed, fidelity to all of the duties and circumstances that come with these vocations are the objective measure of fidelity to God.

The correlation between fidelity to God and fidelity to vocational duties and tasks invites us to see vocations as manifestations of God's jealous love. We have seen that God makes Himself present in various ways so that our communion with Him be uninterrupted. While spiritual exercises capitalize on several ways that He is present, by their nature they are events that last for only so long. They are at the service of preserving and enlivening a prior vocational consecration, which entails the entirety of a Christian's life being ordered by the tasks and duties corresponding to this consecration. In this way, fidelity to the objective order of life resulting from one's vocation—which includes a sustainable schedule of spiritual exercises—fulfills the function of the law in the Old Testament. The law served the twofold purpose of protecting the chosen people from influences that might become for them a temptation to sin by forgetting God, and directing the ways in which they worship God and relate among themselves, especially with regard to the orphan, the widow, the stranger, and the poor.[49]

This ordering of life is true for all vocations: the baptismal vocation to holiness and the various ecclesial vocations within which it is lived. Vocations entail a consecration by which Christ's friends live entirely for God by fulfilling the tasks and duties that come with their vocation. Baptism consecrates the whole person to God, not just some part or even the greater part. It is the same for Holy Orders, marriage, and consecrated life.[50] There are as

---

[49] On the function of the law in relation to God's jealousy and holiness, see Barthélemy in *God and His Image*, 154–169.

[50] Something analogous occurs through the profession of faith and oath of fidelity for those receiving ecclesiastical offices, and rites of institution or

many ways of living the call to holiness as there are personal vocations within the Church. The universal call to holiness is the call to the perfection of charity in every thought, word, and deed. God's jealous love is wounded by any act that is exempted from charity's dominion. For, God is love, and for this reason His jealousy is directed against all that is devoid of love. And since love takes direction from the truth of God's law, it comes to the same to say that His jealousy extends to every disobedience against His law. For, "Sin is lawlessness" (1 Jn 3:4). This means that the object of God's jealousy is sin. It is iniquity to remove from God something that by right belongs to Him. It is to profane His holiness and jealous love.

This is why God's law must reach into every single action, every single engagement of our free will. This happens when faith directs every decision. While faith provides the general principles of God's law, these must be concretized through judgments of the virtue of prudence, which presupposes the judgment of conscience. Such judgments entail an interaction between a person's freedom and the truth. By reason of the foundational covenant of creation, both of these—freedom and truth—are forever intertwined. By conferring faith, Baptism heals the ways in which the relation of freedom to truth are distorted by sin. By Baptism, Jesus consecrates His friends in the truth (Jn 17:17). This is a consecration of the totality of life. For, the vocation to live in the truth is all-embracing—there being no such thing as a human and Christian act being exempt from the truth. Living the truth in love (Eph 4:14; 1 Pt 1:22) is the new law of the new covenant.

Every decision of a friend of Christ, therefore, is an invitation from Him to renew the covenant of friendship with Him. Every decision of a friend of Christ is also constrained by God's jealousy, which is determined by the truth about God and the truth about man. But to be a friend

---

commissioning, for example, for extraordinary ministers of holy communion, catechists, acolytes and lectors, and parish council members.

of Christ is to participate in the divine jealousy, that is, to have internalized its motive and hierarchy of goods. This is why it is possible to take sides with the truth against oneself, as occurs in the examination of conscience that leads to the confession of sin. One of the fruits of spiritual exercises is to reinforce and to deepen this participation in and internalization of God's jealous love and law through an ever more complete death to self. In this way, Christ's disciples and friends make their entire lives a fragrant sacrifice of praise through the obedience of faith.

A few words regarding the universal vocation to suffering are in order here. To say that suffering is a vocation[51] means that it fits into God's plan of love and contributes to the perfection of our love. To say that it is universal means that it is an essential element of Christian life because this life is participation in the life and mission of Jesus Christ, who fulfilled the prophecy of Isaiah regarding the "man of sorrows, acquainted with grief" (Is 53:3). For some, it seems, suffering is the fundamental specification of the vocation to holiness. These have been called victim souls. For others, suffering is a vocation that is periodic, coming and going. It often comes as a surprise, with no warning. But by faith in God's revelation, no friend of Jesus Christ should be surprised by suffering. Because they keep faith alive and agile, spiritual exercises are the best preparation both for recognizing the call to suffer and for sanctifying suffering by responding to the way that God gives Himself to us in and through it. More on suffering will come in the final chapter.

To bring these general considerations to a conclusion, it should be observed that the goal of spiritual direction, in the early stages of the spiritual life, is to guide the directee in establishing a sustainable set of spiritual exercises. As the person progresses, the director will offer advice regarding the adjustment of these exercises to suit the

---

[51] On suffering as a vocation, see John Paul II, *Salvifici doloris*, 26.

person's vocation, state in life, circumstances, and seasons of grace. Finally, the director will assist the directee in responding to particular graces, especially those associated with the life of prayer and with mission, by discerning signs relating to progress in prayer and virtue, and to particular missions for the good of the Church.

The word, "sustainable" is selected here with the parable of the sower in mind. How many people, elated by the graces of an intense conversion and new way of life, embrace a set of spiritual exercises that will in a short time exhaust them and disappoint them? The early growth looks promising, but the roots are not deep enough. It is important to avoid translating the initial enthusiasm of conversion into a zealous but imprudent generosity that will lead to a crisis. The saints assure us that when God withdraws the consolations that accompanied an overly zealous regime of spiritual exercises for a time, the once enthusiastic disciple and friend will be crushed by the thought that his fervor has dissipated, or, even worse, that God is no longer pleased with him and has abandoned him.[52] Having taken the practice of spiritual exercises and the sense of satisfaction in doing them as signs of his love for God rather than as means through which God loves us, such a person will be tempted to think that he is backsliding, that his love for God has diminished, because he no longer derives consolations from doing his spiritual exercises, and even finds them wearisome.

The withdrawal of consolations can be a sign of what a friend of Christ is doing right, and of progress toward the maturity that is required to follow Jesus into the paschal mystery—that place where faith and fidelity are purified by the absence of consolations. The transition from a season of consolations to a season of despondency is meant to be

---

[52] "But what the sorrowing soul feels most is the conviction that God has rejected it, and with abhorrence cast it into darkness. The thought that God has abandoned it is a piteous and heavy affliction for the soul" (John of the Cross, *Dark Night* II, 6, 2).

educational and purifying. At such a time, a friend of Christ learns to refocus the eyes of faith in order to find Him present at a deeper level that had previously gone unnoticed precisely because of a certain enthrallment with consolations. For, God only "withdraws" from being present in one way in order to teach us to seek Him at a deeper, more spiritual level. "This is the lesson of the dark nights: we lose him at one level so that we may find him at another."[53] Peter, we know, lost Jesus on the level of His presence in teaching, working miracles, and discipling His followers. At first, he could not see His presence, as Messiah, in His arrest, condemnation, and crucifixion. But, by the mercy of God and the grace of repentance, he did come to see in Jesus's death and resurrection the fulfillment of all of God's promises. He came to see in His presence in the Eucharist the fulfillment of His promise always to be with His Church (Mt 28:20).

The friend of Jesus who experiences the withdrawal of consolations will learn, and not without some suffering, which is blessedly purifying, what David meant when he said to the Lord:

> As for me, I said in my prosperity, 'I shall never be moved.' By your favor, O Lord, you had established me as a strong mountain; [but when] you hid your face; I was dismayed. (Psalm 30:6–7)

These verses reveal the great lesson of humility learned by someone who is learning the ways of the Lord. St. Thomas Aquinas describes this as the purification of "the presumption of one who trusts in himself."[54] Applying this to the case at hand, the decision to embrace what turns out to be an unsustainable quantity of spiritual exercises was

---

[53] Hubert Van Zeller, *Spirituality Recharted* (Petersham, MA: St. Bede's Publications, 1985), 32.

[54] Aquinas, *Commentary on the Psalms*, 29 [30].

based on a zeal that has not yet been tempered by prudence. Instead, it was based on the person's assessment of his capacity for generosity in responding to God's love as it was supercharged by consolations. Prior to purifying conversions and deprived of the guidance of a wise spiritual director, a zealous disciple is left to rely on his own best judgment. This likens him to Peter, the disciple, who before acquiring that final degree of humility through his denials, repentance, and experience of Christ's mercy, contested with the Lord about the place of suffering and death in His mission (Mt 16:21–22). This is Peter, still lacking a clear understanding of the depths of the evil of sin, and of his own sin, overly confident in his love for Jesus, thinking that he is ready to die for Him (Mt 26:35).

The time of the consolations of Jesus's teaching and miracles and the swelling number of disciples was not enough to empower Peter to love Jesus "to the end" (Jn 13:1). Typically, it takes some time, as a result of a number of conversions along the way, before a disciple and friend of Jesus develops a deep enough humility and corresponding knowledge of the ways of grace so that he can follow Jesus into and through the paschal mystery and be able to say in truth with St. Paul: "I can do all things through him who strengthens me" (Phil 4:13).

All spiritual exercises are ordered to cooperation with God in the continual conversion for the sake of overcoming evil with good (Rom 12:21). The evil of sin is contempt for the word of the Lord (2 Sam 12:9) and for the Lord Himself (2 Sam 12:10). It is also contempt for oneself and for the way that God has made man for the truth. This is why sin entails an act of violence against one's very own conscience. In the language of the prophets, sin entails an act of deliberately forgetting the marvelous works of God precisely when one ought to remember them. The result is to remove a given decision from the perspective of faith and to act as though God had done nothing for His people. This is to put God to the test despite having seen His great works of liberating love (Ps 95:9).

In christological terms, sin entails denying Jesus, as Peter did: "I do not know the man" (Mt 26:72, 74). This is tantamount to saying: "He means nothing to me. He has had no impact on my life. I can live a meaningful life without Him. Right now, in this concrete act, He and all His miracles and teaching—it is as if they never happened." Gripped by fear for his life, Peter could not remember anything that had previously moved him to leave all things in order to follow Jesus (Mt 19:27). He could not even remember the words he had spoken just hours before: "Even if I must die with you, I will not deny you" (Mt 26:35); "Lord I am ready to go with you to prison and to death" (Jn 13:37).

It is precisely this failure to remember that makes Peter a powerful illustration of the drama of sin as forgetting all of the compelling evidence for God's existence, power, wisdom, and love. Peter personifies the warning of Moses directed to the Israelites who had witnessed the mighty deeds of God's liberating love for them: "Remember!"[55] "Do not forget!"[56] At the Last Supper, Jesus recapitulated Moses's exhortations, when He commanded: "Do this in remembrance of me" (Lk 22:19). Once again, the Eucharist shows itself to be the spiritual exercise par excellence. For, faith is the foundation of all spiritual exercises, and remembering in order to assent, to consent, and to obey is the characteristic act of faith. Jesus knew that the apostles would not remember Him in the breaking of the bread until after their experience of the mercy that would come to them from His cross, that is, from His body given up *for them* and His blood poured out *for them*, for the forgiveness of their sins (Mt 26:28). His mercy for their redemption is the *mysterium fidei*, the mystery of faith.

---

[55] See Dt 5:15; 16:3, 12; 24:9, 18, 22;25:17; 32:7.
[56] See Dt 4:9, 23; 6:12; 8:11, 19; 9:7; 25:19.

For Peter, the paschal mystery and his experience of God's mercy are the decisive transition into the possession of faith that cannot fail to remember. This was the final stage of his preparation to receive the gift of the Holy Spirit and thereby to have Jesus's suffering, death, and resurrection *for him* seared into his memory. In this way, Jeremiah's prophecy that God's law be written on His people's hearts (Jer 31:33) is fulfilled for Peter. This is the purification of consciences that constitutes the New Covenant of redemption in Christ.[57] Jesus's plan was to bring Peter and the apostles to the point that His words about friendship could be fulfilled in them: "I have called you friends" (Jn 15:15). For, a friend is another self (Ps 55:13). Friends are one on the profoundest level, that of the truth of conscience, and thus in their readiness for martyrdom. Accordingly, St. Thomas comments: "So, for one who is a friend of God, to suffer punishment and loss is no reason to fall away. Yet because the disciples had not yet received the Holy Spirit before the death of Christ, they did fall away during his passion: 'you will all fall away because of me this night' (Mt 26:31). But after the Holy Spirit came there was no falling away."[58]

That Jesus's words about friendship be fulfilled in us, we must reproduce the pattern observed in Peter and the other apostles. Spiritual exercises are ways that those who desire to be Christ's friends to the fullest—even to following Him into His paschal mystery—cooperate with the graces of the Holy Spirit. This is what it has meant to say, above, that spiritual exercises are ordered to ongoing conversion. The life-giving heart of spiritual exercises are Christ's paschal sacrifice of merciful love and the fruit of that sacrifice, the gift of the Holy Spirit. This alone can lead to living, not just knowing, the Eucharistic grace of

---

[57] See Heb 8–10, especially 9:9, 14; 10:2, 20–22; 1 Pt 3:21.

[58] Aquinas, *Commentary on the Gospel of St John*, Ch. 16, lect. 1 (Marietti, 2069).

making one's entire life a sacrifice acceptable to God.

The best way to begin spiritual exercises, then, is by reproducing the way that the Church begins the celebration of Mass, with the celebrant exhorting the assembly: "Brethren, let us acknowledge our sins and so prepare ourselves to celebrate the sacred mysteries." Every spiritual exercise is a celebration of the sacred mysteries—the paschal mystery—in the sanctuary of our hearts and consciences. Calling to mind our sins, we confess that we are not yet fully Christ's friends, that we still cling to consolations, that we still forget the evidence of His love, that we have not yet fully opened ourselves to receive the Holy Spirit. For, "The Giver is more precious than the gift."[59] We know that the Holy Spirit is our only hope that we no longer fall away. A sign of this is how close to Him Christ's friends feel during and shortly following a spiritual exercise. The exercise bears the fruit of renewed perspective, lively memory, and fervor in love of God. It is easier to overcome temptation and to avoid its near occasion shortly after completing a spiritual exercise precisely because the power of victory is the remembering of faith: "this is the victory that overcomes the world, our faith" (1 Jn 5:4).

The Holy Spirit is "the Church's living memory,"[60] and faith is our participation in this living memory. Jesus called the Holy Spirit "the Spirit of truth" (Jn 14:17). The Holy Spirit guides us into all truth (Jn 16:13), and for this reason He is also called the "light of consciences."[61] When judgments of conscience are truthful, they are a participation in the testimony of the Holy Spirit: "And the Spirit is the witness, because the Spirit is the truth" (1 Jn 5:7). The Spirit comes to us in every truthful confession of sin and act of faith and hope in God's mercy. His great gift

---

[59] *CCC*, 2604.

[60] *CCC*, 1099.

[61] John Paul II, *Dominum et Vivificantem*, 42, 45.

to us is "the gift of the truth of conscience and the gift of the certainty of redemption,"[62] which is essentially what it means to profess in faith that "Jesus is Lord" (1 Cor 12:3). Conversion into receiving the gift of the Holy Spirit was the path of Peter and the apostles, and there is no other path for the spiritual life.

Spiritual exercises always entail the faith "in its deepest essence, is the *openness of the human heart to the gift*: to God's self-communication in the Holy Spirit."[63] They are our efforts to cooperate with Christ in making us His friends by sending the Holy Spirit. For this, we must participate in His paschal mystery through remorse of conscience caused by sin. For, such remorse is participation in Christ's suffering, also caused by sin.[64] Remorse of conscience is the sacrifice of "a broken and contrite heart" that is "acceptable to God" and that He "will not despise" (Ps 51:17). This is why, in one way or another, every spiritual exercise flows from and leads to the Eucharist. Because the Eucharist is Christ's sacrifice for the forgiveness of sins, its celebration at Mass rightly begins with the humble confession of sin, as ought also our spiritual exercises.

When we remember our sins *in order to remember God's mercy* fully revealed in the paschal mystery, then, and only then, we "can do all things through him who strengthens us" (Phil 4:13). Because then, and only then, are we "clothed with power from on high" (Lk 24:49), the Holy Spirit, who makes us Jesus's friends and witnesses (Acts 1:8). As St. Paul puts it elsewhere: "for when I am weak, then I am strong" (2 Cor 12:10)—weak in the awareness of sin, strong in the power of the grace of the

---

[62] John Paul II, *Dominum et Vivificantem*, 31.

[63] John Paul II, *Dominum et Vivificantem*, 51, emphasis added.

[64] "When the Spirit of truth permits the human conscience *to share in that suffering* [of Christ], the suffering of the conscience becomes particularly profound, but also particularly salvific" (John Paul II, *Dominum et Vivificantem*, 45).

Holy Spirit. The Holy Spirit, who is "God's love ... poured into our hearts" (Rom 5:5), is our victory over the world and sin (1 Jn 5:4).

The preceding indicates that an analysis of sin contributes to how we should understand spiritual exercises, and why the Eucharist is the greatest of them. To sin is to disobey a divine commandment. Sin is disobedience rooted in doubt, or forgetfulness, regarding God's love.[65] Sin is an offense against God because it disregards the evidence that He has provided about His love.[66] Sin introduces a wedge between love of self and love of God, so that, as the result of a perverse reasoning, one rejects God's commandment in the name of loving oneself. So long as there remains doubt and forgetfulness about God's love, God responds to sin by showing that He is His people's Master (Jer 31:32). How much He prefers to write His law upon their hearts by showing them that He is their faithful husband!

Spiritual exercises are acts of faith[67] by which we strive to overcome sin by renewing the memory of all of God's mighty works of love—all of the evidence upon which He rests His case—the greatest of which is the suffering and death of Jesus Christ. The goal of spiritual exercises is that God's mighty works of love become more and more deeply etched in our memories and written on our hearts. Then, when a temptation comes, we will be strong by reciting our catechism—which is written upon our hearts, whether it be the catechism of the Garden of Eden, the catechism of the covenant of Sinai, the catechism

---

[65] See *CCC*, 399.

[66] This is the meaning of God's indictment of His people for sinning even though they had seen all of His works. See Ps 95:10 and Num 14:11.

[67] For a long period of the Church's life, when masters of the spiritual life wrote about spiritual exercises, they were thinking above all, and sometimes exclusively, of prayer, specifically, prayer of mediation. See Jean Lecrlecq, "Exercises spirituelles. I: Antiquité au Haut Moyen Age," *Dictionnaire de Spiritualité*, 1902–1908; André Rayez, "Exercises spirituelles. II: Au Moyen Age," *Dictionnaire de Spiritualité*, 1908–1925.

of the return from Exile, or the catechism of the New Covenant in Christ—in an act of remembering God's mighty works of love *for us*, especially the paschal mystery of Jesus Christ.

Spiritual exercises, then, both presuppose faith and serve to reinforce the "for me" dimension of revelation and thereby to deepen faith. This, in turn, reinforces the conviction that the best way to love oneself is to love God, by keeping His commandments: "If you love me, you will keep my commandments" (Jn 14:15[68]). The only way that Adam and Eve could have defeated the serpent's lie—that God did not give the commandment prohibiting them to eat the fruit of the tree of the knowledge of good and evil[69] by a motive of love—would have been to refute it by recalling all that God had done "for them," that is, all the evidence of His love. Then, based on the logic of love being evident in acts of bestowing goodness, they could have asked the serpent: "And what have you done for us?" But they did not.

In reality, Adam and Eve entrusted themselves to the groundless words of one who had done nothing to prove his love for them. Sin always entails such an unreasonable act of self-entrustment to another, even oneself, who provides no foundation to justify it. St. Paul shows that such sin elicits the jealousy of God. As Christ's apostle, Paul participates in God's own jealousy (2 Cor 11:2), which is manifest in his astonishment at the thought that his converts could give themselves over to "another Jesus," "a different spirit," or a "different gospel" (2 Cor 11:4). Only his Gospel, the Gospel of Jesus Christ, is worthy of

---

[68] See Jn 14:21 and the Old Testament precedents in Ex 20:6 and Dt 5:10.

[69] Since love consists in loving and doing what is good and detesting and avoiding what is evil, the tree of the knowledge of good and evil is a symbol for the truth about love. Moreover, since judgments of conscience are judgments about the good to be loved and done, and the evil to be shunned and not done, the prohibition against eating the fruit of the tree of the knowledge of good and evil "symbolically evokes the insurmountable limits that man, being a creature, must freely recognize and respect with trust" (*CCC*, 396).

the self-entrustment of faith for "logical worship" (Rom 12:2) of God, which is, "the kind of worship for ... sensible people" (Rom 12:1 NJB), "the rationally directed worship conformed to the *logos*,"[70] or "worship in harmony with the eternal Word and with our reason."[71] This is the "obedience of faith" (Rom 1:5; 16:26). The sin of Adam and Eve began with forgetting what God had done for them, and this led to disobeying His commandment. And so it is in all sin. The truth about God's love "for us" is the truth of faith that is our victory over the world (1 Jn 5:4) by setting us free (Jn 8:32) from every lie about God's love.

The key that unlocks the potential of spiritual exercises to deepen faith in God's love is the very faith that we bring to them. Spiritual exercises, then, exhibit the pattern established in the miracle of the multiplication of loaves. Jesus clearly desired that the apostles contribute to this miracle, but only after they expressed despair over the challenge. "Two hundred denarii would not buy enough bread for each of them to get a little," says Philip (Jn 6:7). Responding to this pragmatism, which does not take into account the power of Jesus, Andrew retorts: "There is a lad here who has five barley loaves and two fish." We know what Jesus was able to do with this humble offering of a little food and a little faith.

The faith that we bring to spiritual exercises is like this humble offering. We know that we cannot save ourselves. The arduous path of constant conversion seems beyond us. But, we also know that because of the dignity that He sees in us, Jesus desires our cooperation. He desires to make us His associates in our own redemption. In the words of St. Augustine: "God created us without us: but He did not will

---

[70] Joseph Ratzinger, *Truth and Tolerance*, trans. Henry Taylor (San Francisco: Ignatius Press, 2004), 130.

[71] Benedict XVI, Address to Representatives of Science, September 12, 2006.

to save us without us."[72] This is the operative principle in spiritual exercises. When we approach the God of love in spiritual exercises, we know in advance that He will receive our humble offering of the desire to respond to His love, bless it, and multiply it—even as He blessed Mary's act of faith at the Annunciation so that Jesus be conceived in her womb. Our offering is the desire to be true friends of Jesus who desire no longer to follow Him "at a distance" but to love Him "to the end." God desires that we desire what He desires. In spiritual exercises, these two desires meet.

Here, yet again, the Eucharist emerges as paradigmatic. In the Offertory, by offering bread and wine, and ourselves with them, we imitate St. Andrew. We do our part to prepare for the transformation in the bread and wine in the Eucharistic Anaphora and in ourselves through Holy Communion. We believe that Jesus's blessing that multiplied the morsels of food offered by Andrew anticipated His blessing that transformed the bread and wine at the Last Supper into His body and His blood given up *for us*. We believe that this same blessing transforms both the bread and wine offered by His priests and those who receive it.

A similar dynamism occurs in spiritual exercises. When we offer to God the little bit of time set aside for Him alone with our humble desire to grow in holiness, it is with hope that He will accept and bless what we have already received from Him so that we might receive them anew from Him, now multiplied to bear the fruit of being more perfectly "conformed to the image of his Son" (Rom 8:29) in our lives.

---

[72] Augustine, *Sermo* 169, 11, 13: PL 38, 923; quoted in *CCC*, 1847.

5.
A Sustainable Set of Spiritual Exercises in Response to the Call to Holiness and the Apostolate

Having examined some of the theological foundations of spiritual exercises and their role in the life of Christ's disciples and friends, we are now in a position to consider eleven particular spiritual exercises. Together these comprise a sustainable set of activities designed to live the wisdom of the saints regarding how to respond God's love for us with a love that continually grows through ongoing conversion.

The first two, prayer and examination of conscience, concern the response to God's presence within us, His dwelling in our hearts. They can be done at any time and in any place, "even in the tumult of a great city."[1] It will unfold that examination of conscience is a particular form of prayer and, in a way, the first form of prayer. For, prayer is dialogue with God, who alone can lead us to the truth of conscience. God awaits us in our hearts and consciences.[2] To meet Him there, we must turn inward. St. John of the Cross put it this way:

> Anyone who is to find a hidden treasure must enter the hiding place secretly, and once he has discovered it, he will also be hidden just as the treasure is hidden. Since, then, your beloved

---

[1] Reginald Garrigou-Lagrange, *Three Ages of the Interior Life*, vol. 1, trans. Sr. M. Timothea Doyle, O.P. (St. Louis, MO: B. Herder Book Co., 1947), 3.

[2] See Vatican II, *Gaudium et spes*, 14 and 16.

> Bridegroom is the treasure hidden in a field …
> and that field is your soul, in order to find Him
> you should forget all your possessions and all
> creatures and hide in the interior, the secret
> chamber of your spirit.[3]

The centrifugal forces at work in a culture of preoccupation with things outside of us and a corresponding activism to secure the needs and comforts of material existence should not be underestimated. On this point, the *Catechism* is profoundly pastorally realistic:

> It is important for every person to be sufficiently
> present to himself in order to hear and follow
> the voice of his conscience. This requirement of
> interiority is all the more necessary as life often
> distracts us from any reflection, self-
> examination or introspection.[4]

The centripetal force required to counteract the forces that draw us outside of ourselves "can come only from love. Against our dullness and laziness, the battle of prayer is that of humble, trusting, and persevering *love*."[5] For many Christians, it is a battle to establish a habit of turning inward and the discipline of prayer. This is why spiritual writers place great emphasis on the grace to come to the realization of the necessity of prayer. God will always provide the further graces needed to be a good steward of this realization, but these graces always require our cooperation. During the battle for prayer, the saints encourage us to commit to other spiritual exercises, such as liturgical participation, self-denial, study of the faith, and spiritual reading. These, along with establishing spiritual

---

[3] John of the Cross, *Spiritual Canticle*, Stanza 1, 9.
[4] *CCC*, 1779.
[5] *CCC*, 2742.

friendships, contribute to victory in the battle for prayer. Spiritual friendships will be discussed in the following chapter.

Every spiritual exercise that will be discussed in this chapter requires a deliberate transition from being focused on matters concerning worldly activity to being focused on God. There is, of course, a God-centered way to think about and to interact with worldly goods and to engage in worldly activities. As the Church prays: "May we work together to build up the earthly city,— with our eyes fixed on the city that lasts for ever."[6] For, the world is God's creation and His first gift to us. He commissions us to "fill the earth and subdue it; and have dominion over ... every living thing" (Gen 1:28). The spiritual life is not a flight from the world. It entails engagement with the world as a vocation received from God.

Nevertheless, when approaching the living God in spiritual exercises, we must, like Moses, remove our sandals, which symbolize engagement with the world, in order to walk unshod and thus come into contact with the Creator of the world in the holiness of His truth. The Holy One is present in many ways outside of us, for example, in Sacred Scripture, churches and shrines consecrated for this very purpose, and most especially in the Holy Eucharist. Yet all of these ways of being present are at the service of His abiding presence in our souls—our interpersonal communion, or friendship with Him. The objective, exterior modes of His presence are always a call to turn inward in order to encounter Him in our hearts and

---

[6] Liturgy of the Hours, Morning Prayer, Intercessions for the First Sunday of Lent. Similarly, Preface II of Lent: "For you have given your children a sacred time for the renewing and purifying of their hearts, that freed from disordered affections, they may so deal with the things of this passing world as to hold rather to the thing that eternally endure." These short prayers condense several pages of Vatican II's teaching on the relation between the goods and values of creation, on one hand, and faith, the kingdom of God, and the Church's mission of salvation, on the other hand.

consciences.

In this interior encounter, and thus in all spiritual exercises, reception is the order of the day. The reason is that the God whom we seek and encounter is love, and the proper act of love is to give of itself. The only thing required of us is that in our desire to receive from Him we make the effort to seek Him: like the Magi (Mt 2:1); the woman with a hemorrhage (Lk 8:43–44); the rich young man (Mk 10:17); the Canaanite woman (Mt 15:22); Jairus (Lk 8:41); and a group of Greeks (Jn 12:21).

It might come as a surprise that Jesus's first words to us will echo what He said to two blind men who came to Him: "What do you want me to do for you?" (Mt 20:32). It is the same question that Jesus put to St. Andrew and St. John, when they came to Him: "What are you looking for?" (Jn 1:38). This is Jesus's way of getting down to the business of His mission of love by requiring that we examine ourselves to ascertain our true motives. What are the true desires of our hearts? What is our "real love" and what are our "actual preferences"?[7] Are we seeking what He wants to give, what He alone is able to give?

We should always have our answer prepared. We should be ready to tell Him what we are looking for and what we want Him to do for us. St. Thomas Aquinas provides us with a most appropriate answer. When God asked what He could give to him, St. Thomas responded: "Nothing but you, Lord."

We should also be prepared to learn that spiritual exercises will entail a purification of concepts. Are we prepared to discover that while we may be using the correct words when we speak to Jesus, it is very likely that we do not fully understand them as He does? This is what happened to St. Peter. Immediately following his profession of faith in Jesus as the Messiah and Son of God, Jesus confronted him with the fact that he did not

---

[7] *CCC*, 2732.

understand the role of suffering and death in the Messiah's mission (Mt 26:21–22). The same thing happened with the apostles regarding the nature of the kingdom that Jesus taught about and came to establish. After all of their time with Him and hearing about the kingdom, their understanding still needed to be purified (Acts 1:6). Similarly, in the Parable of the Good Samaritan, Jesus clarified that to be neighbor to someone means to show mercy to those in distress (Lk 10:30–37) and that this mercy is the criterion for His final judgment (Mt 25:31–46).

The purification of concepts that spiritual exercises foster is not merely cognitional. The more perfect conformity of our thinking with God's thinking is meant to bring the whole of life into conformity with God's will. Spiritual exercises inevitably lead to a most personal confrontation with the truth that is more accurately perceived as a result of the purification of concepts. God designed the conscience for this confrontation between the way things should be in one's life and the way things are, between one's current level of conformity to the truth and the new call to conformity that comes with every new and deeper perception of the truth. For, truth is always a call to freedom, and thus to conversion. We see this in Jesus's dialogue with the Samaritan woman at the well of Sychar (Jn 4:1–42) and in His dialogue with the rich young man (Mt 19:16–29). In both cases, Jesus's partner loses control of the dialogue. Jesus leads them to a place of insight that they had not anticipated, and which makes a demand on them: the demand of conversion. We know that the Samaritan woman cooperated with the truth of her vocation while the rich young man did not.[8] The outcome is always

---

[8] May the reader permit a personal reflection here. Based on the optimism of supernatural hope, I wonder if the rich young man returned at some point. Perhaps it was the next day, or a few days later, but Jesus recognized him among the crowds around Him. Might such an eventuality be the occasion for Jesus to have conceived and delivered

a matter of our free cooperation. Spiritual exercises operate according to this dynamism of dialogue with Jesus.

Every purification of a concept of faith also purifies hope and charity because these two virtues depend on faith. Both the love of hope and the love of charity depend on what we know. More than any other concept of faith, spiritual exercises will inevitably entail the continuing purification of our concept of love.[9] Because God is love, and because, made in His image, we are made for love, the more our concept of love is purified the more accurately we grasp the truth about God and the truth about ourselves. More than anything else, this purification will concern the place of evil and suffering in God's plan of love as well as His hierarchy of good and evil, joy and suffering. Since all of these are definitively revealed in the paschal mystery of Jesus Christ, spiritual exercises are, in the end, at the service of an ever more perfect understanding of the paschal mystery and a correspondingly ever more perfect participation in it. With this, yet again, we discover that the Eucharist is the source and summit of all spiritual exercises.

1. Prayer

Prayer has many forms. It should be both personal and communal. It includes devotional prayer, such as the Rosary, the Chaplet of Divine Mercy, and novenas, and it entails petition, adoration, thanksgiving, praise, and contrition. It should also include Eucharistic adoration.

The focus here is on that form of mental, meditative

---

the short parable of the two brothers whose father instructed them to go to work in his vineyard (Mt 21:28–31)? Might the son who refused at first, but later regretted his decision and went off to do as his father had instructed, depict the return of the rich young man?

[9] Benedict XVI's first encyclical, *Deus caritas est*, is a splendid example of the apostolic teaching office in service of purifying the concept of love.

prayer that the *Catechism* has in mind when it conveys the absolute necessity of prayer by stating: "Christians owe it to themselves to develop the desire to meditate regularly, lest they come to resemble the three first kinds of soil in the parable of the sower."[10] This prayer is ordered to adhering to and responding to what the Lord is asking[11] in order "to make it [the object of meditation] our own by confronting it with ourselves,"[12] and in this way "to deepen our convictions of faith, prompt the conversion of our heart, and strengthen our will to follow Christ."[13] Such prayer is the condition for remaining with Jesus and being sent by Him, for persevering in being attached to Jesus, the Vine, and bearing fruit.

Meditation on Scripture and points of doctrine bears the fruit of discovering their spiritual-moral sense, that is, their "for me" value. This is the point at which the reading of Scripture or reflection on doctrine becomes *lectio divina*, that is, prayer that stamps an imprint on one's memory and conscience. For, the function of conscience is to assure that what we know by faith become a guiding light of truth for all decisions.[14] This form of prayer bears the fruit of an increasingly more perfect, full, conscious, and active participation in the Liturgy of the Word, which, of course, always remains ordered to the Liturgy of the Eucharist, which in turn bears fruit in daily life.[15]

The fruits of prayer are the maturing of conscience (see below), advancement in the practice of Christian virtue in

---

[10] *CCC*, 2707.

[11] See *CCC*, 2705.

[12] *CCC*, 2706.

[13] *CCC*, 2707.

[14] This helps us to understand the role of resolution(s) that spiritual masters recommend should come at the end of a time of prayer. Resolutions are a commitment to live out the moral sense of Scripture and doctrine (discussed earlier) that has become a gift of grace for the deepening of the baptismal grace of a conscience purified by the blood of Christ.

[15] See *CCC*, 1332.

daily life, and greater benefit from the practice of other spiritual exercises.

> For Saint Teresa, mental prayer—the door of the castle and the way of perfection—is less a particular exercise than the very practice of the spiritual life, being one with it, regulating and encompassing all the other elements (mortifications, readings, works of charity). Asceticism will be guided by mental prayer and will have for its aim, to purify the gaze of faith and to destroy whatever is an obstacle to more profound intimacy with God. Study will furnish food for mental prayer and will search out the best spiritual ways. Works of mercy will be the fruit of the overflowing of contemplation.[16]

As the spiritual life develops, prayer becomes more contemplative and thus simpler and more affective, with the focus being on loving God for His own sake. Here, prayer may be likened to marital union. It is engaged in as an end in itself, as an expression of love for its own sake; at the same time, it bears the fruit of new life. The fruit of particularly focused times of intense union with God is the deepening that union. St. Leo the Great expresses it thusly: "For the one who loves God it is enough to be pleasing to the One whom he loves: for no greater reward should be sought than that of love itself; charity in fact is of God in such a way that God himself is charity."[17] And, St. John of the Cross:

> The loving soul, however great her conformity to the Beloved, cannot cease longing for the wages of her love, for which she serves the Beloved. Other-

---

[16] Marie-Eugene of the Child Jesus, *I Want to See God*, 53.

[17] Leo the Great, *Sermo XCII*, Ch. III: *PL* 54, 454, quoted by St. John Paul II in *Veritatis splendor*, 10.

wise there would not be true love, because the payment for love is nothing else—neither can the soul desire anything else—than more love, until the perfection of love is reached.

Love is paid only with love itself.[18]

Some forms of prayer—such as mental prayer, spontaneous prayers, and inculturated prayers, like prayer before meals—should be a daily activity. Depending on factors like personal temperament, vocation, condition of life, and the current season of grace, some forms of prayer should be part of a weekly or even monthly discipline.[19] Spiritual directors provide a service of inestimable value by advising about: establishing a reasonable and sustainable plan or discipline for prayer; an appropriate method;[20] adjustment of the plan when needed.

Traditionally, the prayer prescribed for beginners is ordered to strengthening and purifying the commitment to follow Christ and to deepening conversion through particular confrontations with the truth. Here, the disciple of Christ is graced to be profoundly aware that he is like St. Peter prior to his full conversion: following Jesus at a distance (Mt 26:58; Mk 14:54; Lk 22:54). The preoccupation of prayer corresponds to the desire to be a good disciple by leaving all things to follow Jesus. This entails continuing formation of conscience (about which more will be said in the next section), cultivating a discipline of life in keeping with Christian virtue, and learning to rely on the infinite mercy of God, made available in the sacraments.

The prayer prescribed for those who are more advanced promotes ongoing conversion by a more intense love for God. The focus shifts from striving to be a good disciple to being a faithful friend of Jesus. The friend of

---

[18] John of the Cross, *The Spiritual Canticle*, Stanza 9, 7.

[19] For example, the First Friday devotion.

[20] For example, *lectio divina*.

Jesus sees more clearly that mercy is God's chief attribute. This is the fruit of that deep knowledge of self as a sinner. It has the effect of unifying and simplifying the understanding of God's love and the mission of Christ. The friend of Christ intensely desires to give God glory through the fruit of his own transformation through advancement in Christian virtue. At the same time, the friend of Christ is more and more motivated by a zeal for souls and the desire to give God glory through the fruits of ministry and apostolate. Love of enemies and the desire to suffer with Christ are signature fruits of this stage of prayer.

The progression from one stage to another is not necessarily as linear as we might be tempted to think. This is why it can be helpful to speak of modes of prayer. It often happens that when one mode is predominant another mode is nevertheless experienced intermittently, as a foretaste and preparation for a time when it will predominate. The value of wise spiritual direction, which draws on the wisdom of the saints, is invaluable in these matters, especially during times of transition from the predominance of one mode of prayer to the predominance of another.

2. Examination of Conscience

Examination and maturation of conscience are so closely related to prayer that the two develop together.[21]

---

[21] See Hinnebusch, *Prayer*, vi and 151. "Every judgment of conscience is rooted in love .... Practical certitude ... does not result, properly speaking, from the *number* of objective reasons, but from their 'value.' ... The highest degree of a certain conscience ... is that of the soul of prayer, in whom the successive nights [of purification] have left no other light than that which comes forth from the Beloved" (René Carpentier, "Conscience," *Dictionnaire de Spiritualité*, col. 1562). Since the effect of the dark nights is a more perfect love and because conscience entails judgments about love, the certainty of conscience corresponds to the degree to which a person participates in Christ's love.

This explains St. Alphonsus de Liguori's bold assertion that "it is impossible for him who perseveres in mental prayer to continue in sin: he will either give up meditation or renounce sin."[22]

In reality, because it is done in the light of faith, examination of conscience is a form of prayer. For St. Ignatius of Loyola, examination of conscience "springs from the prayer that surrounds it" so that "the examination constitutes a prayer."[23] Prayer and Christian life are inseparable: "We pray as we live, because we live as we pray. If we do not want to act habitually according to the Spirit of Christ, neither can we pray habitually in his name."[24] Because conscience entails judgments about the moral quality of our actions, in other words, about what love requires,[25] it is the bridge between prayer, which is about love because it is about God and man, and life, the meaning of which is love.

> Prayer and *Christian life* are *inseparable*, for they concern the same love and the same renunciation, proceeding from love; the same filial and loving conformity with the Father's plan of love; the same transforming union in the Holy Spirit who conforms us more and more to Christ Jesus; the same love for all men, the love with which Jesus has loved us. "Whatever you ask the Father in my name, he [will] give it to you. This I command you, to love one another" (Jn 15:16–17).[26]

---

[22] Alphonsus de Liguori, *The Complete Works of Saint Alphonsus de Liguori*, ed. Eugene Grimm, vol. 3: The Ascetical Works (New York: Benziger Brothers, 1886), 258.

[23] Irénée Nove, "Examen de conscience: IV. Moyen Age et Temps Modernes," *Dictionnaire de Spiritualité*, 1807–1831, at 1824.

[24] See *CCC*, 2725.

[25] See Vatican II, *Gaudium et spes*, 16.

[26] *CCC*, 2745.

To pray "in Christ's name" is more than including those words as a formula that guarantees our petitions being heard and answered. At an early stage of prayer, a disciple of Christ might understand it this way. But it will not be long before this understanding is purified. To pray "in Christ's name" means that when we bring our petitions to the Father we do so with a full awareness of the meaning of Christ's life and mission to redeem us from sin. Since sin is always a rejection of God's love, redemption in Christ is a call, a vocation to love as He has loved us (Jn 13:34). To pray "in Christ's name," then, means to beg God for the grace needed to fulfill the vocation to love. As this vocation more and more becomes one's primary concern, it brings about a maturation of conscience: "In its more mature development, conscience experiences its 'obligation' rather as 'vocation' to love; and understands sin as the refusal to love."[27] It also conduces to the further development of prayer corresponding to God's hierarchy of values. Once the disciple and friend of Christ learns that it is possible to love in any imaginable circumstances, prayer is less interested in obtaining temporal benefits because its full attention is fixed on the one thing necessary: being perfect and merciful as the heavenly Father (Mt 5:48; Lk 6:36) by loving as Christ has loved us (Jn 13:34).

The Penitential Rite at the beginning of Mass instructs us that examination of conscience is always fitting when coming into the presence of God, that is, upon becoming aware of His presence. "Brethren, let us acknowledge our sins and so prepare ourselves to celebrate the sacred mysteries." Based on this, the *Catechism* invites us to begin times of personal prayer in the same way: "Asking forgiveness is the prerequisite for both the Eucharistic

---

[27] Hinnebusch, *Prayer*, 169. Ratzinger also links prayer with the development of conscience, in the context of describing prayer as "freedom's laboratory." Man is truly free when he is free from every encumbrance to love. See Ratzinger, *Behold the Pierced One*, 42.

liturgy and personal prayer."[28] Of course, asking forgiveness presupposes awareness of sin, and thus an examination of conscience. St. Theresa of Avila bears witness to this when she instructs her spiritual daughters: "As is already known, the examination of conscience, the act of contrition, and the Sign of the Cross must come first,"[29] that is, either as preparation for prayer or as the first part of prayer. This directive is valid for all spiritual exercises, which, as we have seen, are so many ways of coming into God's presence in order to encounter His love.

Since God's love takes the form of mercy, the best way to become disposed to receive His mercy is by acknowledging our need for it. We can be assured that God will not allow us to confront the truth about our sins without at the same time reminding us of His mercy. "The verdict of the judgment of conscience remains a pledge of hope and mercy."[30] "Thus in this "convincing concerning sin" [of the Holy Spirit] we discover a double gift: the gift of the truth of conscience and the gift of the certainty of redemption."[31]

Examination of conscience is perhaps the most straightforward way to become aware of and to renew the graces of Baptism. For, Baptism is initiation into the New Covenant, which is a conscience purified by the blood of Christ.[32] This gift is the fulfillment of the prophecy of Jeremiah regarding the New Covenant, to which Jesus referred when instituting the Eucharist.[33] To examine one's

---

[28] *CCC*, 2631.

[29] Theresa of Avila, *Way of Perfection*, Ch. 26.

[30] *CCC*, 1781.

[31] John Paul II, *Dominum et Vivificantem*, 31.

[32] See especially Heb 9:9, 14; 10:2, 20–22; 1 Pt 3:21.

[33] See Jer 31:31–34, Lk 22:20, and 1 Cor 11:25. The Letter to the Hebrews quotes the passage of Jeremiah in chapter eight. Chapters nine and ten show that Jesus Christ fulfilled this prophecy. Significantly, while for Jeremiah the new covenant is written upon *hearts*, for Hebrews it entails the purification of *consciences.*

conscience in the light of faith is to become aware of the entire economy of salvation that culminates in the paschal mystery of Christ. It is to place oneself "*at the very center of that enmity*, that struggle which accompanies the history of humanity on earth and the history of salvation itself."[34] And this leads into thanksgiving and praise, which are expressed with the "for me" formulation of faith of the Blessed Virgin Mary and St. Paul.[35]

As conscience develops, it cannot fail to affect the way that Christians pray. The object or content of prayer of petition reveals the heart's desires, and thus also the understanding of God's love, mercy, and kingdom, and Christ's mission. The maturity of faith and conscience is discernable when the petitions of Christ's friends are compared to the petitions of His disciples. Disciples are inclined to appeal to God to work some kind of change regarding one or another aspect of the condition of their lives, an exterior change in the world. Friends of Christ live more fully according to His priorities. Their concern is with the change in hearts and consciences that constitutes the New Covenant. Their focus is inward. They know that "Transformation of the praying heart is the first response to our petition"[36] because "The first movement of the prayer of petition is asking forgiveness."[37]

In the Liturgy of the Hours, the psalm-prayer following Psalm 51, which is prayed on Fridays, petitions the Lord: "Look upon our contrite heart and afflicted spirit and heal our troubled conscience, so that in the joy and strength of the Holy Spirit we may proclaim your praise and glory before all the nations." In the Bible, sin is a crushing, debilitating weight or burden: "Our transgressions and our sins weigh upon us" (Ezek 33:10). "My iniquities ... weigh like a

---

[34] John Paul II, *Redemptoris Mater*, 11.

[35] See Lk 1:49 and Gal 2:20.

[36] *CCC*, 2739.

[37] *CCC*, 2631.

burden too heavy for me" (Ps 38:4). There can be no greater weight for man to bear than the burden of an accusing conscience, which insinuates what has been called the "logic of sin." This logic is premised on the fact that sin is an act of rejecting God's love by disobeying a divine commandment, which He has given out of love, and which stipulates a demand of love. The agonizing deduction is that due to having rejected God's love I am no longer worthy of being loved. For, it is an axiom "that one is punished by the very things by which one sins" (Wis 11:16).

The logic of sin is evident in the confession of the prodigal son: "*I am no longer worthy* to be called your son" (Lk 15:19). It is also the logic that the Church has the faithful make their own shortly before receiving Holy Communion: "Lord, *I am not worthy* that you should come under my roof." Only the logic of God's mercy is higher than the logic of sin. This is why the indisputable sign that awareness of sin is a grace from God is that it is always accompanied by the grace of faith and hope in God's mercy. Were it otherwise, the logic of sin can only lead to despair, as it did for Judas. This is why the confession of being unworthy to receive the Eucharistic Lord is immediately followed by: "But only say the word, and my soul will be healed." Only the word of God's mercy, fully revealed in the paschal mystery of Jesus Christ, can relieve us of bearing the burden of the unreconciled guilt of sin.

Jesus is the suffering servant, who bore the weight of our iniquities and was crushed by it (Is 53:5, 12; 1 Pt 2:24). By faith in Him, we are able to "lay aside every weight and the sin that clings so closely" (Heb 12:1) and to accept the gift of a conscience purified by His blood, that is, by His redeeming, merciful love. Examination of conscience is the practice of being a good steward of this most precious gift of Baptism. The guidance that St. Francis de Sales gives regarding the assessment of progress in the devout life can well serve as direction for the examination of conscience. He encourages us to reflect on our dispositions and our actions regarding the three loves concerning which conscience makes known what we must do and what we must avoid: love of God, love of self, and love of neighbor.[38]

Fidelity to the examination of conscience will bear the fruit of frequent celebration of the Sacrament of Penance and Reconciliation. A sustainable set of spiritual exercises is not complete without time set aside for this sacrament. This raises the question of frequency. Many spiritual directors recommend sacramental confession of sins at least monthly. There are seasons of grace during which more frequent Confession is fitting. And should a person commit a mortal sin, sacramental absolution should be sought at the earliest opportunity. The counsel of a wise and experienced spiritual director can be most helpful in setting the frequency that is best for a person at a particular juncture of the pilgrimage of faith. Penitents can also ask their confessor for a recommendation.

These brief considerations regarding the examination of conscience should make it clear that this is the spiritual exercise that is prerequisite for drawing fruit from all other spiritual exercises.

3. Liturgy and Sacraments

The liturgy and sacraments are the source and summit of the Church's life. The liturgy "is the outstanding means whereby the faithful may express in their lives, and manifest to others, the mystery of Christ and the real nature of the true Church."[39] Baptism confers the capacity, and thus the privilege, to participate in the liturgy and thereby to bear witness, with the Church, to the definitive revelation of God's love in the paschal mystery of Jesus Christ.

---

[38] See Francis de Sales, *Introduction to the Devout Life*, Bk. 5, ch. 3–7.

[39] Vatican II, *Sacrosanctum Concilium*, 2.

Daily prayer and examination of conscience are the best preparation for that full, conscious, and active participation in the liturgy that is the condition for the reception of sacramental graces.[40] Both prayer and examination of conscience, and liturgy, concern love and bear the fruit of extending love into daily life. Regular celebration of the Sacrament of Penance and Reconciliation is also an element of participation in the Church's liturgical life.

As a loving mother, the Church requires the faithful to attend Mass on all Holy Days of Obligation, which includes Sunday Mass. She highly recommends that the faithful attend daily Mass when it is compatible with their vocation and related responsibilities. She invites all the faithful to join in praying the Liturgy of the Hours. There are many opportunities to participate in particular devotions, such as devotion to the Sacred Heart of Jesus, Forty Hours, and the Novena to the Divine Mercy. Sacramentals, such as holy water and blessed objects, and devotions like the Rosary, serve to occasion acts of faith, hope, and charity and contribute to a well-rounded set of spiritual exercises. Their purpose is to dispose us both to receive the graces that come to us through the liturgy and sacraments and faithfully to live out those graces in daily life.[41]

"Christ glorified is present in the Church's liturgy, which participates in the liturgy of heaven."[42] Because the liturgy, especially the Eucharist, is a foretaste of the eternal liturgy of heavenly praise, participation in it reinforces the eschatological dimension of the pilgrimage of faith and promotes its development. "Eschatological" refers to the final realities that bring about the consummation of God's plan of love: purgatory, heaven, and hell; Christ's second coming; His judgment of the living and the dead;

---

[40] See *CCC*, 1078, 1092, 1122, 1128, 1229, 1415.

[41] See *CCC*, 1667–1673.

[42] *CCC*, headings for 1084, 1088, 1090.

resurrection of the body. The liturgy presupposes the eschatological longing to be with the glorified and ascended Lord, which characterizes the prayer of every soul that has been wounded by His love. The liturgy also most perfectly expresses and perfects this eschatological longing, especially during Advent.

Some spiritual exercises take on a liturgical rhythm in the life of Christ's disciples and friends. Lent is an opportunity to augment participation in the Church's liturgical life, for example, through more frequent sacramental Confession and attendance at Mass, and praying the Rosary or the Chaplet of Divine Mercy. Some of the faithful who do not regularly pray the Liturgy of the Hours do so during Lent. Lent is traditionally the time for the devotion of the Stations of the Cross. It is also a favorable time for increasing time for spiritual reading and for works of mercy.

4. Spiritual Reading

Spiritual exercises foster a living faith that continuously grows through ongoing conversion. Spiritual reading contributes to this by immersing us into the spiritual culture of the saints, who intercede for us and who exemplify the obedience of faith. This extra-liturgical contact with the saints enlightens our minds and dilates our hearts to reinforce our commitment to follow Christ in all things.

Spiritual reading exposes us to the divine wisdom contained in the saints' examples and their writings regarding how best to respond to the various seasons of grace and the ways that God makes Himself present to us. Since the life of every saint is a unique and unrepeatable realization of the riches of the grace of Christ, to deepen our knowledge of the saints and to imitate their virtues is to deepen our knowledge of Christ and to imitate Him according to the reflection of His grace in the saints. To follow the saints on their path of conversion into the perfection of charity is to follow Christ, whom they followed.

Spiritual reading is taken, here, as something distinct from *lectio divina*. As a method of prayer, *lectio divina* falls under that particular spiritual exercise. Spiritual reading can certainly be the occasion for prayer inspired by what is being read, but that is not its specific place in a set of sustainable spiritual exercises. Rather, its defining goal is to foster conscious immersion into the Communion of Saints with a view to appropriating their spiritual wisdom, transmitted by their example as well as their writings and writings about them. This is the same wisdom from which homilists and spiritual directors draw. The more a person is familiar with the lives of the saints and the principles that are discernable in their lives and writings, the more that person is disposed to receive and to benefit from homilies and the counsel of a spiritual director.

In addition, deepening friendship with the saints draws a person into a more perfect, full, conscious, and active participation in the sanctoral cycle of the liturgy. Moreover, communion with the saints, who are our best friends along the path of the pilgrimage of faith, greatly contributes to the development of supernatural prudence and docility to the gifts and promptings of the Holy Spirit, who is *the* spiritual director, in daily life. Particularly during times of intense suffering and purification, knowledge of the heroic virtues that the saints exercised to sanctify their suffering by participating in the suffering of Christ reinforces convictions of faith, strengthens hope, and inspires us to love "to the end."

The saints' love for us verifies the principle that when God loves us He is always intending to love others through and with us. The first mission of our own sanctification always entails the second mission of loving others. God desires to actualize the dignity of being causes in all whom

He has made in His own image and whom Christ calls His. The saints exercise this causality of love through their example, teaching, and intercession. By turning to them and opening ourselves to their love for us, we cooperate with them in giving glory to God: "The saints are called the witnesses of God because in word and deed God is glorified by them."[43]

For those who pray, examine their consciences, and participate in the liturgy and sacraments, the doctrine of the communion of saints becomes more than a revealed truth to which faith assents. Mature faith discovers and embraces its "for me" dimension so that it becomes a lived experience. Spiritual reading opens the doors of our imagination, intellect, and memory to what we can learn from the saints, while prayer, examination of conscience, and participation in the liturgy and sacraments work to assure that what is learned be written on our hearts. In this way, what we learn through spiritual reading becomes integrated into how we understand ourselves and our vocation (our self-consciousness), which we project into daily life through actions that conform to the dictates of conscience (the obedience of faith).

While not every saint has left us something in writing, many have, in which case we have direct access to their own accounts of their lives, their experience of God's mercy, their path of continual conversion, and their guidance for the spiritual life. Access to those who did not personally write anything often comes to us through their friends and other contemporaries on whom they had an unforgettable impact. This is the case for Jesus Himself, whose life and teachings we know through Matthew, Mark, Luke, and John. It is also true for saints like St. Anthony of the Desert and St. Francis of Assisi.

Among the saints who did write, the authors of the

---

[43] Aquinas, *Commentary on the Letter to the Hebrews*, Ch. 12, lect. 1 (Marietti, 657).

sacred scriptures have a place of primacy when it comes to spiritual reading. The bible is the word of God in the words of men. It is the foundational witness to the place of saints in God's plan, and within the bible, the gospels should have a certain primacy, even as they do in the Church's liturgy. For, all holiness is a participation in the fullness of the holiness of Christ. It was saints who received the gifts of revelation and inspiration. In the Old Testament, we encounter the witness to the impact of God on Moses, David, Jeremiah, and the other prophets. In the New Testament, we encounter the witness to the impact of Jesus on the apostles and their close associates, like St. Mark and St. Luke.

The Church's saints bear witness to the efficacy of God's word and grace. God speaks to us through His saints. The saints are the true interpreters of God's word because they lived it.[44] Reading what they have written, accounts of their lives, and theological studies of their lives and teaching both informs and inspires us. By establishing a discipline of spiritual reading, we take advantage of the gift that they are to the Church, open ourselves to God who is present in them, and cooperate with them in their mission of intercession in our behalf, which complements their first mission of having opened themselves to God's transforming power.

In addition to gaining knowledge, one of the benefits of spiritual reading is that the examples and exhortations of the saints inspire us and reinforce our commitment to follow Jesus. The saints' examples and spiritual doctrine convince us anew that Jesus truly is the pearl of great price and the treasure hidden in a field, and that it is wise to dispossess ourselves of everything else in order to obtain Him. The heroic sacrifices of the saints inspire us to scale the summit of perfect generosity in the gift we make of ourselves to God. The saints are our truest friends.

---

[44] See Benedict XVI, *Verbum Domini*, 48–49.

There are three basic kinds of literature that lend themselves to spiritual reading.[45] The first is works that exhort and inspire Christ's disciples and friends to strive for the perfection of the beatitudes and the perfect imitation of Christ. *The Imitation of Christ* by Thomas à Kempis is a well-known example of this first category. The second kind are works that bring together and describe the saints' experience of God's love and their response to it. Vernon Johnson's *Spiritual Childhood*, which sets forth the major themes in the life and writings of St. Thérèse of Lisieux, is a splendid example of this category. Works of spiritual theology comprise the third kind. These systematically set forth the nature of Christian perfection and the means to attain it. Jordan Aumann's *Spiritual Theology* is an example of this third.

Spiritual directors, parents, catechists, and theologians render a great service by recommending spiritual reading that corresponds to a person's vocation, temperament, and educational background. To the extent that they are qualified, they should also take into account the current season of grace that can be discerned in a person's life. Online sources abound in our times, and parish libraries provide a most valuable service by making the classics of spirituality available.

5. Study

There is no lack of resources available for the systematic study our faith: Scripture, Bible studies, the *Catechism of the Catholic Church*, histories of the Church, papal documents, works of doctors of the Church and theologians. Study entails extending knowledge of faith in breadth (learning), in depth (analysis), and in ordering

---

[45] See Jordan Aumann, *Spiritual Theology* (Westminster, MD: Christian Classics, 1987), 18–19.

wisdom (synthesis). These cannot fail to take place, to some extent, in spiritual reading, for our minds are at work there as well, and it is the very nature of our minds to work this way. Nevertheless, the defining purpose of study is to expand, to deepen, and to order our knowledge of the faith according to the mind of the Church.

In spiritual reading, we place ourselves in the presence of the Christian experiences and virtues of the saints with the primary purpose of recreating for ourselves their personal cultures of holiness by imitating them. Of course, this entails effort to understand, especially when one encounters something new, or when the historical context of a statement or action is required accurately to grasp it, or when one perceives for the first time how one virtue, vocation, or spiritual exercise is related to others. Still, the focus is on the goodness of the saints' lives as examples to be imitated and the soundness of their wisdom to take as direction. In study, the focus is on fulfilling the desire *better to know God and all that He has revealed.*

> "Faith *seeks understanding*" (St. Anselm): it is intrinsic to faith that a believer desires to know better the One in whom he has put his faith and to understand better what He has revealed; a more penetrating knowledge will in turn call forth a greater faith, increasingly set afire by love. The grace of faith opens "the eyes of your hearts" (Eph 1:18) to a lively understanding of the contents of Revelation: that is, of the totality of God's plan and the mysteries of faith, of their connection with each other and with Christ, the center of the revealed mystery.[46]

The study of faith can include the study of the spiritual life, but it will not be limited to it. In order for the spiritual

---

[46] *CCC*, 158.

life to be dogma in action, Christ's disciples and friends must know and accurately understand that dogma. The broader study of faith helps to place the spiritual life within the entirety of what God has revealed. And this, in turn, can be very helpful in preventing certain erroneous interpretations of personal experience and unwarranted conclusions being drawn from a first but superficial understanding of doctrine. At the same time, a comprehensive understanding of faith enhances the dialogue of prayer. It is rather difficult to carry on a conversation with someone about whom one knows little. Study that includes the entirety of what God has revealed and what the Church teaches expands the possible subjects for meditation. It also allows a person better to cooperate with graces received during prayer, or outside of prayer, when God takes the initiative to propose a given subject for consideration.

We have seen that faith entails remembering what God has revealed. Dogmas are so many distillations of divine revelation. They are landmarks of divinely revealed truth that has been more precisely understood along the way of the Church's pilgrimage of faith. They are the fruit of the action of the Holy Spirit, who is the Church's living memory. Study deepens a friend of Christ's participation in the Church's living memory so that the Holy Spirit is able to call to mind the particular truths of faith that, at any given moment, inform a purified conscience so that we are set us free from dead works of sin (Heb 9:14) in order love in the truth (Eph 4:15; 1 Pt 1:22).

Sometimes the Holy Spirit indicates a particular doctrine to be studied. This may come about in one of two ways. First, regarding the first mission of personal holiness and prayer, grace draws attention to a particular doctrine. There may be various reasons for this, but very often they cannot be readily discerned. Nevertheless, it is important to be a good steward of such lights of faith, and further study of the particular doctrine is the most obvious way to exercise such stewardship. Second, a particular doctrine might come into focus as a result of the second mission of loving others. It frequently happens that when discussing the faith with friends, when catechizing, and when evangelizing a disciple and friend of Christ confronts the limits of his understanding of a certain doctrine. This can be considered a gentle and humbling nudge of the Holy Spirit to make the effort better to understand the doctrine in question.

6. Development of Virtue

Spiritual exercises bear the fruit of intensifying the desire to be a true friend of Jesus by following Him into His paschal mystery and no longer at a distance, and to give glory to God by producing the fruit of Christian virtue in one's life. They safeguard and expand the freedom of the sons and daughters of God (Rom 8:21): freedom *from sin*, which is rejection of God's love, and freedom *for love* in every thought, word, and deed. Every decision is a call to love, an opportunity to obey God's law of love by following the dictate of the baptismal gift of a conscience purified by the blood of Christ. In this way, the disciple and friend of Christ is able to say, with St. Paul: "I always take pains to have a clear conscience toward God and toward men" (Acts 24:16).

Christian conscience bears upon all that is required to fulfill the new commandment of the New Covenant, to love as one has been loved by Christ (Jn 13:34). It "translates" the desire to be a disciple and friend of Christ into concrete imperatives concerning love. In this way, conscience assures a perfect continuity between the commitment *to be* a friend of Jesus and *acting* like a friend of Jesus. Conscience is like the director of a theatrical production, assuring that each scene corresponds precisely to its place in the whole. Every life, and every action in every life, is a personal drama within the great "dramatic struggle between good and evil."[47] God directs this drama through the dictates of conscience, which "always summons man to love good and avoid evil" and "reveals that law which is fulfilled by love of God and neighbor."[48]

To conceive the desire to strive for the perfection of charity is to enroll in the school of humility. St. Thomas Aquinas tells us that humility is the disposition by which a person submits to the gifts of God in others.[49] The clear reason for this that a person has come to the realization that he needs those gifts, not as a kind of optional adornment of a complete spiritual life, but for the very survival and development of that life. Thus, he also says that the humble person restrains himself from striving to attain that which is beyond him. "He must know his disproportion to that which surpasses his capacity. Hence knowledge of one's own deficiency belongs to humility."[50] For the Carmelites, this is knowledge of self.[51]

The wise man's exhortation extends to anyone who would embark upon placing his life in service to the Lord:

> My son, if you aspire to serve the Lord, prepare your-self for an ordeal.... Whatever happens to you, accept it, and in the uncertainties of your humble state, be patient, since gold is tested in the fire, and the chosen in the furnace of humiliation. (Sirach 2:1, 4–5 NJB)[52]

---

[47] Vatican II, *Gaudium et spes*, 13.

[48] Vatican II, *Gaudium et spes*, 16.

[49] See Aquinas, *ST* II-II, Q. 161, a. 3.

[50] Aquinas, *ST* II-II, Q. 161, a. 2.

[51] See Marie-Eugene of the Child Jesus, *I Want to See God*, 33–48.

[52] For the first verse, in place of "ordeal" other English versions have: trials, testing, temptation. The Greek word, *peirasmos*, alludes to the testing of Israel in the desert (Ps 95:8), the essence of which every disciple of Christ must confront and can hope to overcome only with the help of God's grace (Mt 6:13). On the petition of the Our Father, "and lead us not into temptation," see Douglas Bushman, "Lead Us Not Into

To embrace the call to holiness is to learn what Jesus meant when He said, "apart from me you can do nothing" (Jn 15:5). It is to live the spirituality of "I do not understand my own actions. For I do not do what I want, but I do the very thing I hate" (Rom 7:15). It is to enter into the school of humility in self-knowledge, which is knowledge of the misery of sin. St. John of the Cross says that this knowledge of self is the chief benefit of the dark night.[53]

It is for good reason, then, that the *Catechism* refers to Christian life as a battle thirty-five times. Nearly three-quarters of these come in the fourth part on prayer. Prayer itself is a battle, but because we pray as we live and live as we pray, this is inseparable from the battle of life: the battle to conform every thought, word, and deed to the high standard of imitating Christ's virtues.[54] For, "Christ enables us to live in Him all that He Himself lived, and he lives it is us."[55]

It is no small benefit to be able to identify the virtues by their proper names and to know their characteristic actions. Of course, the law that more will be required of the one to whom more is given accompanies this knowledge. The zealous disciple and friend of Christ does not view this law as an imposition from without. It is seen, rather, as a logical corollary of the privilege of being entrusted by Christ with the mission of bearing fruit. The very life of Christ's disciples and friends is the field into which He sends them to work: "You go into the vineyard too" (Mt 20:7). With eyes fixed on Jesus, even as Peter's were when he stepped out of a boat onto the water in order to approach Him, the zealous disciple and friend of Christ is eager to cultivate all of the virtues by which he responds to Jesus's bidding: "Come" (Mt 14:29).

Temptation." *Homiletic and Pastoral Review Online*, February 21, 2017.
53 John of the Cross, *Dark Night*, Bk. I, ch. 12, 2.
54 See *CCC*, 407 and 2725.
55 *CCC*, 521.

St. Thérèse of Lisieux reassures us that God inspires within us the desire for holiness because He intends to fulfill that desire.

> I have always wanted to be a saint. Alas! I have always noticed that when I compared myself to the saints, there is between them and me the same difference that exists between a mountain whose summit is lost in the clouds and the obscure grain of sand trampled underfoot by the passers–by. Instead of becoming discouraged, I said to myself: God cannot inspire unrealizable desires. I can, then, in spite of my littleness, aspire to holiness.[56]

The proof of God's intention to fulfill the desire to imitate Christ's virtues is the price of love that Christ paid in the paschal mystery. The story of St. Thérèse's pilgrimage of faith illustrates the extent to which the God-given desire to be a saint will be tested and purified regarding the right understanding of holiness (faith) and an ever more perfect reliance on God's grace and mercy (hope). These are purified above all through suffering.

St. Thérèse learned the place of suffering in the progress that Christ's disciples and friends make in reproducing in themselves the virtues of Christ.

> Later on, when perfection was set before me, I understood that to become *a saint* one had to suffer much, seek out always the more perfect thing to do, and forget self. I understood, too, that there were many degrees of perfection and each soul was free to respond to the advances of Our Lord, to do little or much for Him.... Then ... I

---

[56] Thérèse of Lisieux, *Story of a Soul. The Autobiography of St. Thérèse of Lisieux*, trans. John Clarke (Washington, D.C.: Institute of Carmelite Studies, 1996 [3rd edition]), 207.

cried out: "My God, *I choose all!*" I don't want to be a *saint by halves*, I'm not afraid to suffer for You, I fear only one thing: to keep my *own will*; so take it, for 'I *choose all*' that You will!"[57]

The high standard of holiness, which is the perfection of charity, cannot fail to result in a conscience that denounces every act that falls short of that perfection. This is why St. Thérèse's spiritual doctrine is built on the foundation of God's mercy. "To me He has given His *infinite Mercy*, and *through it* I contemplate and adore the other attributes."[58] She approaches her heavenly Father with the "humble boldness" that comes from the "certainty of being loved."[59] Drawing on her knowledge of Scripture, she writes:

> I repeat, filled with confidence, the publican's humble prayer. Most of all I imitate the conduct of Magdalene; her astonishing or rather her loving audacity which charms the Heart of Jesus also attracts my own. Yes, I feel it; even though I had on my conscience all the sins that can be committed, I would go, my heart broken with sorrow, and throw myself into Jesus' arms, for I know how much He loves the prodigal child who returns to Him.[60]

A conscience purified by the blood of Christ, informed by doctrine and the examples and teaching of the saints, and kept alert through prayer and daily examination—such a Christian conscience is a most sensitive alarm when thoughts, words, and deeds contradict the truth about love.

---

[57] Thérèse of Lisieux, *Story of a Soul*, Clarke translation, 27.

[58] Thérèse of Lisieux, *Story of a Soul*, Clarke translation, 180.

[59] *CCC*, 2778.

[60] Thérèse of Lisieux, *Story of a Soul*, Clarke translation, 258–259.

For, dictates of conscience concern the truth about what constitutes an act of love, either what is essential to love and thus must be done, or what is opposed to love and thus must not be done. Christ's true disciples and friends view such moments of truth as acts of divine mercy, as the necessary first step in coming to live more fully in the truth that sets us free (Jn 8:32). Conscience is truth that sets free for love. When conscience is disregarded, it does not cease to function. Rather, it denounces the violation of truth's right to guide every single action. Through conscience, "Like a physician who probes the wound before treating it, God, by his Word and by his Spirit, casts a living light on sin."[61] For, conversion into more perfect virtue *"requires convincing of sin*; it includes the interior judgment of conscience, and this, being a proof of the action of the Spirit of truth in man's inmost being, becomes at the same time the start of a new grant of grace and love."[62]

Daily examination of conscience and frequent celebration of the Sacrament of Penance and Reconciliation make it possible for a person (and his spiritual director or confessor) to discover certain patterns regarding particular weaknesses, temptations, and sins. Spiritual authors write about a person's predominant fault, and the saints, through their writings but also through confessors and spiritual directors, provide a most important service by giving guidance with respect to disciplines ordered to address it. This can include: direction regarding material for spiritual reading and study; developing a devotion to a saint associated with a particular virtue; particular forms of asceticism (the discipline of self-denial) ordered to avoiding the near occasion of sin; direction regarding actions corresponding to the virtue in question.

The Sacrament of Penance and Reconciliation is an invaluable source of healing and strengthening grace.

---

[61] *CCC*, 1848.

[62] John Paul II, *Dominum et Vivificantem*, 31.

Confessors provide one of the greatest of all consolations in the spiritual life. When a disciple and friend of Christ struggles over months and even years to overcome a particular sin, the temptation to despair is great. A confessor's serene and joyful welcoming introduces the penitent to God's own joy over the conversion of sinners,[63] and his gentle patience in listening, prudent advice, and repeated exhortations contribute to the penitent's experience of Christ's mercy and its transforming power.

It should not be assumed, however, that at any given moment a predominant fault can be identified, or that to identify it is a straightforward matter. It is better to be patient and to wait until it becomes obvious than to grasp at one that, while identified with good intention, might prove to be a distraction that blinds a person to a deeper, underlying fault. Perseverance in hope and in generous efforts to address the issue are the keys.

Balance is the watchword if one is to avoid two extremes. The first is an overly zealous and ultimately unsustainable attempt to root out a sin according to the person's own schedule rather than God's. God's schedule nearly always tests our patience. But, in this way, it serves to strengthen our hope. The second is lassitude, or a form of acedia, which can be a sign of waning hope. The first is rooted in presumption and the second in despair. And it matters a great deal whether the recurring sin is against an acquired virtue or a supernatural virtue. As is so often the case, the guidance of a wise spiritual director is invaluable in this matter.

The development of other virtues also contributes to the battle with a predominant fault. As an athlete rehabs an injured muscle in part by strengthening the muscles around it, so in the spiritual battle, other spiritual exercises, spiritual reading, penitential self-denial, and fidelity to the duties of one's vocation, contribute to the development of

---

[63] See Lk 15:6–7, 9–10, 23–24, 27, 32.

virtue. By including these in the overall discipline of Christian life, the various spiritual exercises reinforce one another, extending the balance of virtue more and more into every part of life. This reinforces conscience and the habit of subjecting all of life to the rule of reason, which, when illumined by faith, constitutes our spiritual sacrifice in the obedience of faith.

Among aids to the development of virtue, strong friendships grounded in faith and the pursuit of holiness deserve special mention in our culture of widespread isolation. A community of friends who are also dedicated to the practice of spiritual exercises and to the development of Christian virtues is the normal context in which we are called to live as Christ's disciples and friends. This begins in the Christian family, in which parenting is the first form of discipleship for children. It is extended to the community life of parishes and various kinds of associations of the faithful. A culture of Christian virtue is the normal context in which virtue develops.

Strictly speaking, Christ-centered friendships are not means to an end but goods to be sought for their own sake. The same is true of a culture of virtue and of love. Nevertheless, such friendships and such a culture bear advantageous fruits. Friends are in a unique position to support and to encourage one another, thereby reinforcing each friend's commitment to grow in human and Christian virtues. Especially when one friend has sinned, the experience of God's mercy through being forgiven by and reconciled to Christian friends prompts conversion and restores the supernatural hope that motivates all spiritual exercises. Furthermore, a culture of Christian virtue is above all a culture of divine mercy and the joy of conversion. Finally, it should never be forgotten that the saints are our best friends. Their accounts of humility and persevering hope in God's mercy during their own struggles reinforce our own humility and hope, and their intercession reassures us that we are not alone in the battle for virtue.

7. Fidelity to the Duties of One's Vocation

Fidelity to vocational duties is the principal element of "the obedience of faith" (Rom 1:5; 15:26). It is imitation of Christ in accomplishing the Father's will: Thy will be done, on earth, in me, as You, Father, have decreed in heaven. It is an incessant *fiat* to everything that pertains to the two missions of love of self and love of others. Fidelity to the duties of one's vocation is not included among the traditionally acknowledged spiritual exercises. It is typically either presupposed or considered the *fruit* of spiritual exercises, but not a spiritual exercise in its own right. There are good reasons to reconsider this view. For, solicitously fulfilling vocational duties is also a source of grace and growth in holiness. For this reason, it is included in these reflections on spiritual exercises.

In its teaching on the universal call to holiness,[64] the Second Vatican Council placed a particular emphasis on fidelity to the duties of one's vocation. For most Christians, this constitutes by far the greater part of each day, with explicit spiritual exercises being limited to no more than ninety minutes. For these disciples and friends of Christ, God is present above all through the awareness that the duties and events of the day are manifestations of His will because they are related to their vocation. It is one thing to muster the discipline and attention to focus on God and His love for the duration of daily Mass, a Rosary, a half an hour dedicated to mental prayer, and time for some spiritual reading. It is quite another thing to cultivate the habit of constant awareness of the essential meaning of life that comes with faith.[65] That essential meaning is love. It is one thing to have this awareness and actually to love during spiritual exercises. It is quite another thing to love

---

[64] See Vatican II, *Lumen gentium*, 41.

[65] See 1 Thes 5:16–18; Eph 6:18; Phil 4:4–7; Col 4:2–4. See also Anonymous, *The Way of a Pilgrim and The Pilgrim Continues His Way*, trans. Helen Bacovcin (New York: Image Books, 1992).

in all things and at all times. There is all the difference between a short sprint and a marathon.

The saints were intensely committed, even fixated, on accomplishing *everything* they did with the fullest measure of charity. And, this charity depends on faith that perceives every event, no matter how apparently insignificant, as a manifestation of God's will. Nothing in God's plan of love is insignificant. The Council's teaching on sanctifying daily duties and events recapitulates the best of the spiritual treatises on the doctrine of divine providence. Faith perceives the mystery of God's plan of love in everything, so that each moment has the character of being a sacrament of God's presence and self-gift to us, and our response in faith.

We need only consider the life of Jesus to realize that relatively few hours of His days were spent in explicit spiritual exercises, such as prayer, services in synagogues, and pilgrimages. Rather, He spent His days doing the Father's will, first during the hidden years in the home of the Holy Family in Nazareth. Then, once His public ministry began, He fulfilled the Father's will by teaching, healing, forming His disciples, and reacting to the people around Him: "For I have come down from heaven, not to do my own will, but the will of him who sent me" (Jn 6:38). Every act of His was an act of love, and since God is love, His every act fulfilled the Father's plan of love for Him and, through Him, for us.

Doing God's will is not limited to obeying His commandments and to those times when explicit spiritual exercises are being performed. That would result in a split between faith and life—the very error that Vatican II denounced. For the vast majority of Christ's disciples, the laity, explicit spiritual exercises—daily Mass, prayer, examination of conscience, spiritual reading, and study—typically do not amount to more than ninety minutes per day. But that is more than enough time for God to bless and to multiply what is offered to Him, in order to nourish us with the graces that we need to carry out His will in all things. As we have seen, one of the great fruits of daily spiritual exercises is the development of the baptismal gift of a conscience purified by the blood of Christ. For, God speaks to us in the rightly formed judgments of conscience, which bear upon fulfilling the demands of justice and love in accordance with one's vocational duties and the circumstances of life. To do God's will in all things is to love Him, oneself, and others in all things.

To reprise the previous discussion of being with Christ and being sent by Him (Mk 3:14), spiritual exercises are times set aside for being especially intent on being with Christ, while the fulfillment of vocational duties constitutes the greatest part of being sent by Him. The wonderful thing about believing that vocational duties specify God's will is that in reality we do not leave Christ behind when He sends us to live out our vocation. Rather, it is another way of being with Him. And, given that this is His will for us, to fail to execute those duties would in fact diminish being with Him. This is why Vatican II insists: "Every person must walk unhesitatingly according to his own personal gifts and duties in the path of living faith, which arouses hope and works through charity."[66]

Exercising one's personal gifts in order to fulfill vocational duties glorifies God by building up the Church in faith, hope, and charity. Still, we must keep in mind that every vocation is bipolar by reason of entailing *exterior* expressions of the *interior* mystery of communion with God in Christ. Just as for Christ interior communion with the Father precedes and gives life to exterior mission, so for His disciples and friends, *being with Him* interiorly is the life-giving source for all exterior aspects of *being sent by Him*. For, "religion, of its very nature, consists before all else in those internal, voluntary and free acts whereby man sets the course of his life directly toward God."[67]

---

[66] Vatican II, *Lumen gentium*, 41.

[67] Vatican II, *Dignitatis humanae*, 3.

The heart and conscience constitute the domain of what God "sees in secret" (Mt 6:4, 6, 18). Whether exterior compliance with God's will be truly sanctifying depends on a person's interior disposition. For this reason, Vatican II concludes its teaching on fidelity to vocational duties by stressing that "all Christ's faithful ... will daily increase in holiness *if* they receive all things with faith from the hand of their heavenly Father and *if* they cooperate with the divine will."[68] Similarly, what the Council says about the lay faithful is valid for all Christ's disciples and friends:

> For all their works, prayers and apostolic endeavors, their ordinary married and family life, daily occupations, and physical and mental relaxation, *if* carried out in the Spirit, and even the hardships of life, *if* patiently borne—all these become "spiritual sacrifices acceptable to God through Jesus Christ" (1 Pt 2:5).[69]

Just as the efficacy of the sacraments depends on the faith of those who receive them, so the sanctifying potential of the sacrament of each moment can only be actualized by faith. That is the meaning of the conditional "ifs" in the preceding texts.

Furthermore, as the text indicates, conforming to God's will in all things includes the hardships of life, that is, suffering. By its nature suffering reduces our capacity to act, and severe suffering does so severely. At such times the primacy of the interior activity of faith, hope, and charity is on full display. More will be said about suffering in the next chapter.

The purpose of spiritual exercises is to "strengthen the inner man"[70] so that Christ's disciples and friends are able

---

[68] Vatican II, *Lumen gentium*, 41, my emphasis.

[69] Vatican II, *Lumen gentium*, 34, my emphasis.

[70] See Eph 3:16 and John Paul II, *Dominum et Vivificantem*, 58–60.

to grow in holiness as they fulfill their vocational duties. This is why the diligent and faith-filled fulfillment of vocational duties is not just the fruit of spiritual exercises. It is also fruit-bearing, bringing an increase in holiness and transforming even the most seemingly mundane actions into spiritual sacrifices acceptable to God. In this way, the fulfillment of vocational duties also strengthens the inner man. This is why fulfillment of vocational duties is included among spiritual exercises.

It should be mentioned that often it is a greater demand on faith to believe in the presence of God in, and the value of fidelity to, daily duties in His plan of love than it is to believe in His presence in explicit spiritual exercises. The spiritual exercises by which a person removes his sandals in order to step outside the daily routine—prayer, study, liturgy, retreat, pilgrimage—will bear more fruit to the extent that a disciple and friend of Christ is a good steward of their fruits. Fidelity to vocational duties is such a fruit. The more explicit spiritual exercises should never diminish awareness of the value that God sees in fulfilling the demands of justice and love as these are made known in the duties, events, and circumstances that specify His will for us.

These considerations show how important it is to develop a clear sense of one's vocation, and to inform oneself regarding it. This includes the examples of the saints who precede us in our vocations. They also show how helpful a *horarium* can be. A *horarium* is a daily schedule of activities, an hour-by-hour layout of what a day of following Christ and living out one's vocation should look like. Many, perhaps most of the lay faithful do not think of their days in terms of a *horarium*. Yet, this is simply another way to convey what it means to go through each day with a vivid awareness of the duties of one's vocation. To adapt terminology traditionally used for religious: work, family, citizenship, cultural participation, spiritual exercises, and, when it comes, suffering, are the rule of life for the lay faithful. The routine of daily life that these establish is their *horarium*. Since most of the day is taken up with fulfilling the tasks and duties relating to family and work, a *horarium* for the lay faithful concerns setting aside time for the daily spiritual exercises of prayer, liturgy, examination of conscience, spiritual reading, study, time with friends, and wholesome recreation.

Establishing a *horarium* requires prudent discernment. Simply because many saints have lived by and recommend a *horarium* does not mean that a formal one is necessary in everyone's life. Often, a lay person's duties regarding family, work, parish membership, and citizenship, as well as a commitment to a plan for spiritual exercises, so fill and order their days that for all practical purposes they are living according to a *horarium*. In the case of many devout lay men and women, such a *horarium* is clearly not a preconceived ideal plan to be enacted. Rather, it is the fruit of a love so strong that it has in fact ordered a person's days according to the priorities of Christian charity.

It is possible to apply to the *horarium* the distinction between the effective and the affective practice of the evangelical counsels of poverty, chastity, and obedience. Many of the faithful, as just described, live according to an affective practice of an *horarium*. For them, "the love of Christ impels" them to pray, to study, to read the saints, to exercise the virtue of Christian service, and to enjoy the company of other disciples of Christ so that these completely fill the "free" time remaining after fulfillment their duties. In effect, love has created a *horarium* by filling each day with activities ordered to responding to the many ways that God makes Himself present. A life ordered entirely by love is the goal of every *horarium*. Many of the lay faithful live such a life, even if they do not think of it in terms of a *horarium*.

Fidelity to vocational duties is "the obedience of faith" (Rom 1:5; 15:26). Understood in this way, fidelity to vocational duties is especially related to conscience. The more clearly and penetratingly Christ's disciples and friends understand their vocation, the more clearly conscience perceives what love requires in all things. A mature conscience shines the light of the truth about love on every action, while fidelity to that truth, especially when it entails some difficulty or suffering, contributes to the continuing maturation of conscience. In this way, Christ's disciples and friends "excel *in everything*" (2 Cor 8:7), "are obedient *in everything*" (2 Cor 2:9), act with "a clear conscience ... to act honorably *in all things*" (Heb 13:18), and observe the commandment of "love, which binds *everything* together" (Col 3:14), "in order that *in everything* God may be glorified through Jesus Christ" (1 Pt 4:11).

8. Penance

"Penance is an essential constituent of the patrimony in the ecclesial life of the baptized."[71] It is entirely ordered to full reconciliation with God and more perfect participation in Christ's life and mission. By it, Christ's disciples and friends seek to deepen friendship with Him by participating in His suffering.[72] In this way, the virtue of penance reinforces the centrality of Christ's paschal mystery so that, while living in the world His disciples and friends are not of the world. In this way, they put into practice St. Paul's exhortation that "those who deal with the world [act] as though they had no dealings with it. For the present form of this world is passing away" (1 Cor 7:31). Accordingly, the Church prays: "For you have given your children a sacred time for the renewing and purifying of their hearts, that, freed from disordered affections, they may so deal with the

---

[71] Congregation for Clergy, *The Priest and the Third Christian Millennium*, March 19, 1999, ch. 3, 3

[72] See Aquinas, *ST* III, Q. 90, a. 2.

things of this passing world as to hold rather to the things that eternally endure."[73]

Acts of penance are acts of denying oneself the enjoyment of some earthly good that it is permissible to enjoy in order to intensify detestation of sin and to atone for it. Such acts are "a participation in the suffering and death of Christ."[74] St. John Paul II gives us a comprehensive description of Christian penance:

> But *doing penance* is something authentic and effective only if it is translated into *deeds and acts of penance*. In this sense *penance* means, in the Christian theological and spiritual vocabulary, *asceticism*, that is to say, the *concrete daily effort* of a person, supported by God's grace, to lose his or her own life for Christ as the only means of gaining it;[75] an effort to put off the *old man* and put on the *new*;[76] an effort to overcome in oneself what is *of the flesh* in order that what is *spiritual*[77] may prevail; a continual effort to rise from the things of *here below* to the things of *above*, where Christ is.[78] Penance is therefore *a conversion that passes from the heart to deeds* and then to the Christian's whole life.[79]

That two liturgical seasons that are penitential in nature shows the importance of penance in the life of Christ's Church. During the forty days of Lent, we embrace fasting,

---

[73] Preface II for Lent.

[74] International Theological Commission, *Penance and Reconciliation*, 1982, II, 3.

[75] Cf. Mt 16:24–26; Mk 8:34–36; Lk 9:23–25.

[76] Cf. Eph 4:23.

[77] Cf. 1 Cor 3:1–20.

[78] Cf. Col 3:1f.

[79] John Paul II, *Reconciliatio et paenitentia*, 4.

almsgiving, and prayer, which are also appropriate for Advent. Both of these seasons prepare the faithful for a momentous encounter with God by focusing attention on what only He can give: "salvation ... in the forgiveness of our sins" (Lk 1:77). Christ's disciples and friends are also called to make Friday a day of penance, thereby deepening the faith-awareness of sin and the depths of the mystery of God's merciful love, fully revealed in Jesus Christ, who took upon Himself all of the punishment for sin in order to transform it by His redeeming love.

Prayer becomes penitential especially by reason of its content. For example, during Lent it is fitting to participate in the Stations of the Cross, to meditate on the gospel narratives of Christ's passion, and to pray the penitential psalms, especially Psalm 51. Prayer also takes on a penitential dimension when more time is set aside for it, especially during Advent and Lent. In this, prayer as penance differs from fasting, which does not require the commitment of a greater amount of time. The same is true for almsgiving, which generally does not require a significant increase in time.

During Advent and Lent it is appropriate to allocate more time for prayer. For example, those who don't habitually pray the Liturgy of the Hours or engage in Eucharistic adoration can add these to their regular routine of prayer. Thus, complementing the subject matter that makes prayer penitential, setting aside more time for prayer is also penitential because that time could be used for any number of other legitimate activities. This is what Christians mean when they say that they are fasting from screen time (television, computer, phone) or from other activities in order to make more time for God. This time for God can be used for any of the spiritual exercises, such as the Christian service of corporal and spiritual works of mercy, or more extensive spiritual reading and study.

There is an important place for personalized penance outside of the Advent and Lent, and apart from Fridays.

This can be connected with efforts to grow in particular virtues, and to address one's predominant fault, discussed earlier. A personal discipline of penitential self-denial contributes to preventing future sins and keeping consciences alert to every new coming of Christ in our lives. For, He comes to us in the truthful judgments of conscience, in the needs of our neighbors, and in the tasks and duties of our vocation. In this way, we maintain a state readiness, like the wise virgins (Mt 25:1–13), to respond to the many ways that God continues to come to us during our earthly pilgrimage. Penance similarly contributes to awareness of the eschatological dimension of faith and hope, keeping us in a state of readiness for Christ's second coming.

Like all spiritual exercises, penance must be balanced in order to be sustainable. Never can penances interfere with the fulfillment of the duties of life. Further, it is mistake to be overly zealous in taking on penances that are either too severe or too frequent, or both. If St. Augustine might call them "good mistakes," this does not mean that he would approve of the excesses. It only means that he was able to glimpse something of the enthusiasm and generosity of a disciple and friend of Christ who would do so. But it is, nonetheless, a mistake, as is its counterpart of penance being underdeveloped. Because of the interrelationships among the spiritual exercises, excess or defect in penance inevitably affects the whole of the spiritual life. The wisdom of a spiritual director is just as helpful here as it is for the practice of other spiritual exercises.

As a personal spiritual exercise, penance can also entail the practice of the evangelical counsels of poverty, chastity, and obedience. While many people associate these counsels with religious and consecrated life, they have their place in the life of every disciple and friend of

Christ.[80] For, everyone is called to the perfection of charity, and charity cannot be perfect unless it is accompanied by poverty, chastity, and obedience.

The practice of these counsels serves to overcome various attachments. "Attachment" refers to an inordinate desire or love. It may concern grave as well as light matters. St. John of the Cross assures us that even in light matters, an attachment prevents the perfection of charity. For, charity is perfectly ordered love because it is a participation in God's own love. Christ calls His disciples and friends to live in a way that accords the highest priority to relationships with God and with one another. Because attachments are inordinate love, they reduce our freedom always to be ready to do the truly most loving thing. They weaken responsiveness to the dictates of conscience, which are always about love. In the end, they diminish the very relationships that Christ's disciples and friends have pledged themselves to make the highest priority. It is inherent in our dignity and vocation to love that we gain self-mastery over the pleasures that accompany the acquisition of possessions (poverty), the functions of the body (chastity), and willfulness (obedience) for the sake of that freedom of the sons and daughters of God in the Holy Spirit to respond to whatever love requires.

A plan for living the evangelical counsels must be motivated solely by the desire for the perfection of charity. Other motives attempt to impersonate this desire, but they do not pass the test of balance and sustainability. Such are an enthusiasm to become perfect overnight and the desire to show God how much you love Him. Both err by doing things for God that He does not ask. Conversely, it is necessary to avoid the self-delusion that one is fully detached from possessions, pleasures, and one's own will by convincing yourself that you are living the spirit of the

---

[80] See Vatican II, *Lumen gentium*, 42 and *CCC*, 915, 1973, 1974, 2053, 2545.

counsels apart from any actual practice of them. In such matters, the wisdom of the saints, to which we have access through a spiritual director, is invaluable.

The *horarium* or its practical equivalent is very helpful in achieving the kind of detachment that increases with the development of charity. By filling one's days with the good things that give glory to God there is no room left for things that are rooted in self-indulgence.

> The effort at detachment must be persevering and will go hand in hand with progress towards union.... It needs to be sustained by a certain organization of the exterior life. The spiritual person in the world will have to find it normally in a rule of life, a plan that is stable, yet flexible, which will fix precisely the obligations of his state and his times for prayerful converse with God. This will safeguard him not only from solicitude for external things and the stubborn violence of his passions, but also from the whims of his own fancy and excessive preoccupation.[81]

A most important fruit of practicing various forms of penance is being able to respond to suffering, which we do not choose but nevertheless comes our way, by making it the occasion to participate in the suffering of Christ. It is no use to offer to God the penances that we choose for ourselves as if these could replace the penances that God chooses for us.

> ... it is the most ordinary penance that gives the greatest glory to God and most surely advances the soul in perfection. By "ordinary" is meant actual, chosen by God. The "ordinary" penance

---

[81] Marie-Eugene of the Child Jesus, *I Want to See God*, 170.

of living in a state of constant surrender to the divine will may well be accompanied ... by works of active voluntary penance, but always it must be borne in mind that no penance can substitute for abandonment into God's hands....
In accepting whatever happens, whether pleasurable or painful or indifferent, the soul is in no danger of getting caught up in the niceties of active penance.... Constantly to accommodate oneself, always to remain flexible and uncomplaining, never to assert what one conceives to be one's rights, patiently to wait upon God's will: penance finds its highest expression in such an attitude. Only when a man can assure himself that he is able to face with equanimity the work, the people, the climate, the food, the leisure, the recognition, the devotion—in fact every mortal contingency—which God sends *and recognize it as sent by God* can he begin to talk about penance. Penance begins and ends with this attitude of mind; whatever penances there are in between are thrown in for good measure, are tokens of generosity.[82]

9. Retreats and Pilgrimages

Retreats and pilgrimages are extended times dedicated to being with the Lord. Thus, they are occasions for more concentrated and prolonged prayer, listening to the word of God, liturgy and sacraments (Penance and Reconciliation, Eucharist, Eucharistic devotion, Divine Office), spiritual direction, and spiritual reading. "Francis [de Sales] attached such great importance to retreats ... that in his

---

[82] Hubert Van Zeller, *Approach to Penance* (New York: Sheed & Ward, 1958), 97.

Treatise he described them as a 'holy method, familiar to the ancient Christians, but lapsed into disuse until the great servant of God, Ignatius of Loyola, again put them into practice a generation ago.'"[83]

Often, retreats are prescribed prior to the beginning of a new mission. This is the case, for example, for men preparing to be ordained and for novices prior to vows. Retreats are offered also for engaged couples preparing for their exchange of vows, and confirmands preparing to celebrate the sacrament of Confirmation. This custom of arranging retreats in close proximity to a new mission reflects what we see in Sacred Scripture. Moses's mission was preceded by forty years of purification and preparation as a shepherd (Ex 7:30), and again he spent forty days alone with God atop the mountain (Ex 24:18; 34:28). Prior to the beginning of His public ministry, Jesus similarly spent forty days in the desert (Mt 4:1–11), and before several major initiatives, He withdrew to be alone in conversation with the Father.[84]

Retreats are not only recommended as preparation for a new mission or significant event within one's vocation. They also serve the purpose of renewing the perspective, zeal, and commitment to fulfilling God's will in the obedience of faith. Retreats reinforce the precedence of being with Christ over being sent by Him. Thus, the dynamism of retreats is essentially the same as prayer and examination of conscience, which renew the conversion of Baptism: "Separation from others to be alone with God facilitates the soul's concentration and fosters the rising of one's true desires in order to confront them in the light of

---

[83] François Charmot, *Ignatius of Loyola and Francis de Sales. Two Masters—One Spirituality*, trans. Sr. M. Renelle (St. Louis and London: B. Herder Book Co. 1966), 46.

[84] See Mt 26:36; Mk 6:46; Lk 6:12; 9:18, 39. On this theme of Jesus's prayer preceding the major events of His mission, see Joseph Ratzinger, *Behold the Pierced One*, 15–22.

Christ and the divine call."[85]

Unless specified by some authority, there is no fixed formula for the frequency, duration, and kind of retreat. For some, an annual retreat might be a week long. For others, an annual retreat or semi-annual retreats might go from Friday through Sunday. Evenings of recollection offered in parishes or by various apostolates fall into this category of a more prolonged time set aside for spiritual exercises. Retreats can be silent, or they can entail some God-centered exchanges among retreatants. The ratio of silent time for prayer and spiritual reading to time for preaching by a retreat master and/or suitable theologically rich teaching can vary greatly.

"To go on pilgrimage really means to step out of ourselves in order to encounter God where he has revealed himself, where His grace has shone with particular splendor and produced rich fruits of conversion and holiness among those who believe."[86] The typical destination of a pilgrimage is a place revered as holy because of an event in which God has manifested His power and love. While the sites of the great events of Christ's life, in the Holy Land, are unequaled in this regard, the very efficacy of Christ's mission of redeeming love results in many other sites bearing witness to Him. Such are the places of the martyrdom of saints, especially Peter and Paul in Rome, and places where the Mother of God has appeared with important messages for the Church. Shrines have been erected in these places to perpetuate acts of remembrance. Since all acts of Christian remembering point toward and culminate in the remembrance of faith regarding the paschal mystery of Christ and the Eucharist, it is highly fitting that celebration of Mass should be the crowning act of a pilgrimage.

---

[85] Manuel Ruiz Jurado, "Retraite," *Dictionnaire de Spiritualité*, 426.

[86] Benedict XVI, Address at the Cathedral of Santiago de Compostela, November 6, 2010.

Outward acts of seeking Jesus in holy places both flow from and express the inner search for God and foster the purification and intensification of that search. Pilgrimages particularly accent the eschatological dimension of the life of Christ's disciples and friends. They "evoke our earthly journey toward heaven and are traditionally very special occasions for renewal in prayer. For pilgrims seeking living water, shrines are special places for living the forms of Christian prayer 'in Church.'"[87] The pilgrim people of God know, in faith, that "here we have no lasting city," and in hope "we seek the city that is to come" (Heb 13:14).[88]

Faith, prayer, and conversion make the physical pilgrimage a journey of the heart to God. We relive the faith-journeys of Abraham, Israel, the Magi, and Mary. Every pilgrimage of faith is participation in the great pilgrimage of our Lord, Jesus Christ, to the Father. For, "The whole of the Christian life is like a great pilgrimage to the house of the Father, whose unconditional love for every human creature, and in particular for the 'prodigal son' (cf. Lk 15:11–32), we discover anew each day. This pilgrimage takes place in the heart of each person, extends to the believing community and then reaches to the whole of humanity."[89]

Pilgrimages can be local and short, for example, a walk or drive to a nearby shrine or cathedral. They often entail several days, thereby affording pilgrims more opportunities for prayer, examination of conscience, spiritual reading, and celebration of the sacraments.

---

[87] *CCC*, 2691.

[88] A theology of pilgrimages can be found in the document of the Pontifical Council for the Pastoral Care of Migrants and Itinerant People, The Pilgrimage in the Great Jubilee, April 25, 1998.

[89] John Paul II, *Tertio millennio adveniente*, 49.

10. Service

Service is distinct from the daily exercise of one's charism(s) or gift(s) in the fulfillment of the duties of vocation. No doubt, this also merits being called service, but it falls under the heading of fidelity to obeying God in the concrete obligations that accompany one's vocation. This is not what is meant by service here. Nor are we considering those unscheduled acts of kindness shown to those whom we meet and who need to be loved. Every disciple and friend of Christ should be prepared to act like the Good Samaritan when coming across someone who has in one way or another been beaten and robbed, not necessarily by someone else, by some event, even when that event is a very poor choice of the person in need of being loved.

The kind of service of which it is a question here concerns the use of one's time that is not determined by duties of vocation or a random encounter. It is something scheduled as a priority of the spiritual life. For many, for whom virtually every hour of most days is filled with the demands of justice, this kind of service may be relatively infrequent. Nevertheless, it says a great deal about the actual priorities of Christ's disciples and friends that they should set some time aside to serve those who are less fortunate than they are.

Typically, parishes and apostolates dedicated to serving the poor and needy do a good job of publicizing opportunities for volunteer service. A culture of Christian love and service can do much to form children in families that annually contribute to organized efforts to feed the hungry, for example, at Thanksgiving, or to provide clothing for those in need and to bring some of the joy of Christmas to children by providing presents. What a powerful witness it is to set aside time for others in this way!

When service is a group activity and entails interacting

with others, it can be the occasion for deepening the bond of unity among members of the family and with friends. It is profoundly edifying to observe the generosity, creativity, and sacrifice in one's family and friends. Communal service is often an occasion for common prayer and the celebration of Mass.

Service very often takes the form of one or another of the corporal or spiritual works of mercy, by which the exhortation of St. Paul is fulfilled: "Bear one another's burdens, and so fulfill the law of Christ" (Gal 6:2). As Christ has loved us in the misery of our poverty, so we are called to love others in their poverty. Thus, the test of our love for Him is our love for the poor and unloved: "as you did it to one of the least of these my brethren, you did it to me" (Mt 25:40).

St. Paul also exhorts us: "do not use your freedom as an opportunity for the flesh, but through love be servants of one another" (Gal 5:13). Service conforms us to Christ: "whoever would be great among you must be your servant, and whoever would be first among you must be your slave; even as the Son of Man came not to be served but to serve, and to give his life as a ransom for many" (Mt 20:26–28). It gives God great glory when Christ's disciples and friends use their free time to serve others rather than to pursue any number of activities that they might find satisfying for themselves. For, it bears witness to how His love has transformed them and to the new hierarchy of values—the values of the kingdom of God—that comes with the renewal of our minds by faith.

11. Spiritual Direction

Spiritual direction is a charism that I think falls under the heading of what St. Thomas Aquinas calls the "grace of the word."[90] As a charism, it is a means to the end of growing in holiness. The director draws on the wisdom of the saints in order to guide the directee about how best to respond to God's many ways of being present, always with a view to the directee's vocation and in consideration of particular and personal seasons of grace.

Spiritual direction has also been called the direction of conscience.[91] This should not be surprising, given the unique place of conscience in Christian anthropology,[92] morality, and the spiritual life, as we have seen. There is no progress in holiness apart from the development of conscience. A spiritual director, or director of conscience, does not impose his own judgments of conscience for those of their directees. Rather, a spiritual director is more like a midwife, who cooperates with and aides the natural dynamism of giving birth. In the case at hand, it is the word of God passing through the birth canal of conscience.

Christ has conferred on the disclosing of conscience to another the dignity of being a sacrament when a person confesses his sins to a priest or bishop. The Sacrament of Penance and Reconciliation is the natural context for the direction of conscience. This may happen within the actual celebration of the Sacrament, in which case it often takes the form of some brief encouragement and direction from the confessor. Those who are fortunate to have a holy and wise priest for a spiritual director know from experience how closely the direction of conscience is associated with this sacrament. Those whose director is not a priest often discover that there is an advantage to coordinating sessions of spiritual direction with the celebration of Penance and Reconciliation and communicating what they experienced in the confessional. This is a great aid for the spiritual

---

[90] See Aquinas, *ST* II-II, Q. 177.

[91] See, for example, the 1983 *Code of Canon Law*, c. 630 §1 and c. 246 §4.

[92] Because "'soul' signifies the *spiritual principle in man*" (*CCC*, 363), "direction of souls" is a synonym for spiritual direction and the direction of conscience.

director's role in conscience midwifery.

Like submission to the power of the keys exercised by a priest in Penance and Reconciliation, spiritual direction is premised on the virtue of humility. The humble person submits to God by submitting to His gifts in others.[93] The charism of wisdom in directing others certainly qualifies as such a gift. As the Holy Spirit, Inspirer of Scripture, advises:

> Attend the gathering of elders; if there is a wise man there, attach yourself to him. Listen willingly to any discourse coming from God, do not let wise proverbs escape you. If you see a man of understanding, visit him early, let your feet wear out his doorstep. (Sirach 6:34–36 NJB)

> But stay constantly with a godly man, whom you know to be a keeper of the commandments, whose soul is in accord with your soul, and who will sorrow with you if you fail. And establish the counsel of your own heart, for no one is more faithful to you than it is. For a man's soul sometimes keeps him better informed than seven watchmen sitting high on a watchtower. And besides all pray to the Most High that he may direct your way in truth. (Sirach 37:12–15)

One of the great services a spiritual director provides is to assist a person in establishing a balanced and sustainable set of spiritual exercises, and in adjusting it according to the discernment of the directee's vocational duties, personal temperament, and season of grace. Fidelity to a plan of spiritual exercises is ordered directly, or immediately, to the encounter with God's love and thus to the ongoing conversion that is the fruit of this encounter. A spiritual director will have an in-depth understanding of the

---

[93] See Aquinas, *ST* II-II, Q. 161, a. 3.

goal of the spiritual life, namely, holiness or the perfection of charity, the means to holiness, the fruits or signs of holiness, and the stages of conversion leading to the purification of faith and hope and the perfection of charity. For, the sustainable set of spiritual exercises is both established and adjusted precisely to promote holiness through conversion.

It is not uncommon, however, for people to think that the purpose of spiritual direction is to assist a person in discerning God's will with respect to one's vocation or major decisions. In a way, this is true. For, by guiding a person in applying the wisdom of the saints about how to respond to God's love, the spiritual director does what is possible to guide a person through the various stages of conversion. Conversion, or death to sinful self in order to put on the mind of Christ and to come to know the movements of the Holy Spirit, is necessary in order to have moral certitude about the outcome of discerning God's will. Still, life does not consist in making major decisions, but in living out the commitments resulting from them. And spiritual direction is about life, and life is about love.

In the periodic adjustment of spiritual exercises, a director must be vigilant against overreacting to more superficial indications in a directee's life, especially various forms of suffering. For, suffering is "that hermeneutical vantage point where real and unreal [can] be distinguished, and communion with God [comes] to light as the locus of true life."[94] The aim of the spiritual life is an ever-greater participation in the paschal charity of Jesus Christ and thus in His paschal suffering. The director's mission is not to remove suffering but to assist in sanctifying it.

A certain kind of consolation comes with knowing that the same spiritual exercises through which God has worked

---

[94] Joseph Ratzinger, *Dogmatic Theology: Eschatology and Eternal Life*, trans. Michael Waldstein (Washington, D.C.: Catholic University of America Press, 1988), 91.

to bring a person to a particular season of grace or stage in spiritual growth will also carry him through that season of grace and into the next one. This is especially important when the season of grace is one of darkness and desolation, as well as a prolonged season of what appears to be spiritual stagnation. At the same time, one should not underestimate the possibility of imprudent reactions to sometimes intense and/or prolonged consolations. In all these cases, the virtue of hope is being purified, and the temptation to think that one needs to adjust spiritual exercises or to find new ones is very real. It is a grace and thus a consolation to know, at the level of one's conscience, that one has been faithful to the spiritual exercises that have been established with the help of a spiritual director.

6.
Complementary Exercises of Faith and Reason

The following considerations complement the preceding theology of spiritual exercises and overview of a sustainable set of spiritual exercises. They are presented here either because they are important complements to spiritual exercises (recreation, friendship) or because misunderstandings that contribute to serious errors and practical mistakes in the spiritual life make clarity about them especially important.

1. On Spiritual Direction, Discernment of Vocation, and Prudential Decisions

The commitment to engage in spiritual exercises presupposes a commitment to respond to the call to holiness, which includes a call to participate in Christ's mission in the Church and for the world. It presupposes, then, a commitment to the first mission of following Christ along the path of Christian perfection. Often, especially for Christ's younger disciples and friends, this commitment of faith is accompanied by a desire to discover their personal vocation within the Church.[1] One of the great services of a spiritual director is to assist in the discernment of a person's charism(s) or gifts and vocation, and to adapt spiritual exercises to that person's vocation and personal gifts, temperament, and circumstances.

What is to be avoided at all costs is to confuse what it means to make a prudential decision, on one hand, and to

---

[1] See Germain Grisez and Russell Shaw, *Personal Vocation. God Calls Everyone By Name* (Huntington, IN: Our Sunday Visitor, 2003).

receive and to act on the advice of a spiritual director, on the other hand. The sincere desire to do God's will requires that a person know what it is. So, it is understandable that a person would turn to a director for guidance in ascertaining His will. The director's role is to guide a person through the *process* of discernment so that the directee can discover God's will for himself. The director knows that it is fidelity to this *process* that removes doubts and confers assurance that the outcome is God's will for the person.

A spiritual director serves a directee well by recalling that Christ died in order to rectify our wills, not to provide us with infallible certitude about every prudential decision, even the greatest of them, such as the choice of vocation. In other words, apart from the foundational moral precepts, Christ does not dictate to us what we must do, concretely, to fulfill the Father's will. He does not do this because this is not how He experienced His communion with the Father. By revealing the Father's love, Christ creates the perfect setting for the flourishing of our freedom and responsibility. If He is not afraid of our freedom, then we must learn to trust Him and to overcome any fears that we have of our freedom.

There would be no room for the virtue of prudence in the spiritual life if it were otherwise. This is why spiritual directors must keep a respectful distance out of regard for the mystery of the other, that is, in order to safeguard the directee's dignity, freedom, and responsibility. It is, notwithstanding, no small service for a director to train a directee to subject a potential prudential decision to a checklist of questions ordered to a directee being as transparent to himself as possible. Questions such as: Are you aware of the influence of pride, or fear, or vanity, or impatience, or anything else that is incompatible with faith and trust in God? Are you being honest about your personal aptitudes, gifts, aspirations, and woundedness?

Put another way, a spiritual director must never interfere with or act in any way to influence the prudential decisions of a directee that would in effect, to one degree or another, substitute the director's prudence for that of the directee. That is the role proper to parents, until a child gradually matures into adulthood, during which time parents gradually reduce their child's dependence on their own prudence.

The province of a director's prudence has two spheres: interpreting the movements of grace in the life of the directee and the best way to respond to it, and the configuration of the most apt set of spiritual exercises. For, spiritual exercises have the effect of forming the directee's conscience, expanding, through ongoing conversion, his freedom and responsibility for his own life and prudential decisions, and making him docile to the promptings of the Holy Spirit.

2. On the Eucharist as Source and Summit of the Spiritual Life

Those who take seriously the call to holiness know that the Eucharist is the source and summit of the Church's life and of their own life of faith. From this they not infrequently conclude that attending daily Mass should be the highest priority among their spiritual exercises. The answer whether this is a valid conclusion and if so how it should be understood depends on understanding the interrelatedness of spiritual exercises.

To be convinced that the benefits of daily reception of Holy Communion depends upon the disposition of faith with which it is received, it suffices to read the *Catechism*: "These dispositions are the precondition both for the reception of other graces conferred in the celebration itself and the fruits of new life which the celebration is intended to produce afterward."[2] This disposition is fostered by

---

[2] *CCC*, 1098. This principle is so important that the *CCC* repeats it several

fidelity to other spiritual exercises—especially mental prayer, examination of conscience, regular sacramental confession, fidelity to one's daily duties of vocation through the obedience of faith, penance, spiritual reading, and uniting suffering with the paschal suffering of Christ.

The disposition of faith required for the fruitful celebration of the sacraments cannot be summoned at a moment's notice. It presupposes the life of faith and especially the deepening of baptismal conversion through the spiritual exercises just mentioned. This assures the continuity between liturgy and life. For, while it is true that we believe, live, and pray as we worship in the liturgy, it is also true that we worship in the liturgy as we believe, live, and pray.[3]

Holy Communion presupposes Baptism (first conversion) and the living faith that motivates ongoing conversion (second conversion). This faith is nourished by the various spiritual exercises, among which mental prayer is especially important. In the prayer of meditation, a person "confronts" the divine model(s) of holiness with his own life in order to foster ongoing conversion, which is a deepening and extension to all of life of baptismal conversion. This is what motivated St. Teresa of Avila to write: "meditation is the basis for acquiring all the virtues, and to undertake it is a matter of life and death for all Christians."[4] Complementing this, the *Catechism* forcefully declares: "Christians owe it to themselves to develop the desire to meditate regularly, lest they come to resemble the three first kinds of soil in the parable of the sower."[5]

Mental prayer entails a dialogue in the most personal depths of one's being, the conscience. Its foundation is baptism: the triumph of the logic of mercy over the logic of sin. The logic of sin: because I have rejected God's love by

---

times: 1072, 1122, 1123, 1128, 1129, 1248, 1423, 1426, 1430.

[3] See On the Unity of Faith, Liturgy, Prayer, and Life, below.

[4] Teresa of Avila, *Way of Perfection*, 16, 3.

[5] *CCC*, 2707.

sinning I do not deserve to be loved. The logic of mercy: God is faithful to His love for me and is always ready for forgive and to reconcile. Christ instituted the Eucharist and suffered and died so that I can live in the certainty of God's love "for me."

The fruit of such prayer is to desire to make all of life a return of love and a sacrifice of praise and thanksgiving in the obedience of faith. And while it seems logical to conclude that the first and highest priority should be daily Holy Communion, a text of St. Thomas Aquinas invites us to examine that conclusion. Focusing on the disposition that is presupposed for the fruitful reception of Holy Communion (like the *Catechism*), he held that the faithful are "required to approach this sacrament with great reverence and devotion. Consequently, if anyone finds that he has these dispositions every day, he will do well to receive it daily." Yet, because this devotion is subject to vacillation, "it is not expedient for all to approach this sacrament every day; but they should do so as often as they find themselves properly disposed."[6]

Since devotion is the fruit of prayer, it is understandable that a respected theologian and disciple of St. Thomas would echo this wisdom and insist on the inseparability and mutual complementarity of daily Communion and mental prayer:

> Those who aspire to sanctity by giving themselves completely to the active life while neglecting the life of prayer may just as well forget about Christian perfection. Experience proves that there is absolutely nothing that can supply for the life of prayer, not even the daily reception of the Eucharist. There are many persons who receive Communion every day, yet

---

[6] Aquinas, *ST* III, Q. 80, a. 10. St. Thomas is elaborating on texts of St. Augustine.

their spiritual life is mediocre and lukewarm. The reason is none other than the lack of mental prayer, either because they omit it entirely or they practice it in a mechanical and routine fashion. We repeat that without prayer it is impossible to attain Christian perfection, no matter what our state of life or the occupation to which we dedicate ourselves.[7]

The insistence of Aquinas and Aumann on the proper disposition for the fruitful reception of Holy Communion corresponds to the conviction that "the fruits of the sacraments also depend on the disposition of the one who receives them."[8] Vatican II took this as the guiding principle for promoting what it termed "full, conscious, and active participation in the liturgy."[9]

With the same pastoral concern, Joseph Ratzinger asked, "Do we not often take the reception of the Blessed Sacrament too lightly?" He considers the advantages of a principled and thus balanced Eucharistic fast: "Might not this kind of spiritual fasting be of service, or even necessary, to deepen and renew our relationship to the Body of Christ?" He goes on to discuss the issue in light to the liturgical tradition of fasting from the Eucharist on Good Friday. "A fasting of this kind," he writes, "could lead to a deepening of personal relationship with the Lord in the sacrament. It could also be an act of solidarity with all those who yearn for the sacrament but cannot receive it."[10]

The thought of a fast from the Eucharist raises the practical issue of making a judgment about one own's fervor of love and reverence. Having already seen that spiritual exercises bear the fruit of Christian virtue in daily

---

[7] Aumann, *Spiritual Theology*, 232–33.

[8] *CCC*, 1128.

[9] Vatican II, *Sacrosanctum Concilium*, 14.

[10] Ratzinger, *Behold the Pierced One*, 97–98.

life, it appears that the measure of the fervor of love and reverence is a faith-based awareness of God's mercy and one's status as a forgiven and reconciled sinner.

Daily mental prayer, complemented by the other spiritual exercises, is the normal way that this disposition (Aquinas's "devotion") develops. We have seen that prayer exercises and develops the baptismal grace of a conscience purified by the blood of Christ. Thus, the foundation of the ardent desire of charity for Holy Communion consists in a fully conscious, intentional participation in the Penitential Rite, in the "for me" meaning of faith that corresponds to the Liturgy of the Word, in how "right and just, always and everywhere, to give God thanks," in the twofold "for you" of Christ's words of institution of the Eucharist, in the humble confession of being unworthy just before receiving Holy Communion, and in reception of the final blessing with the pledge of a conscience resolved to live the whole of one's life in the obedience of faith.

The essential content of mental prayer is the very heart of the Gospel itself, namely, God's mercy. Prayer being a dialogue with God, the one who prays exercises the biblical virtue of hospitality by allowing Him to speak about what is important to Him. God's favorite subject is the event with which He brings the economy of revelation to completion, namely, the paschal mystery of Jesus Christ, in which he definitively reveals the mystery of sin and the mystery of divine mercy. Since God is love and to love is to bestow gifts, prayer as conscious attentiveness to God is always an encounter with His merciful love and His desire to make a gift of Himself—as this is fully revealed in the paschal mystery. This reality makes us aware of the obstacles to our reception of his self-gift, that is, our sins. This is why personal prayer should begin the same way that the liturgy of the Mass begins, that is, with a penitential rite.[11] With this, the truth about God and about

---

[11] "Asking forgiveness is the prerequisite for both the Eucharistic liturgy

man—man's sin and God's mercy—becomes the foundation for the ensuing dialogue.

One can see, then, how closely related the Eucharist is to daily examination of conscience and prayer. One can also see how mental prayer serves to deepen authentic love of self as rooted in being loved by God in Christ, as was mentioned in the introduction. With this, personal prayer and liturgy both become the praise of God above all for his mercy (St. Augustine), His greatest attribute in relation to us.

The vital lesson in all of this is the interdependence of the spiritual exercises. This is especially important during periods when vocational duties and circumstances combine to reduce the time available for spiritual exercises to a bare minimum. At such times, it should be not assumed that daily reception of Holy Communion is the highest priority. While spiritual direction is very helpful in this matter, not everyone has access to a spiritual director. One practical solution is to pray for at least a few minutes before or after Mass. Another is to alternate the daily half an hour between Mass and mental prayer. In the end, the question remains whether the choice between mental prayer and Mass is due to circumstances beyond one's control, or if it should be interpreted as a call from God to reexamine one's priorities in order to make more time for spiritual exercises.

3. On the Balancing Effect of the Eucharist and Conscience

It does not require many years of pastoral experience to discover how common certain exaggerations in the spiritual life are. Four of these are superstition, a certain preoccupation with spiritual warfare, an excessive concern regarding the end times and divine chastisement, and a disproportionate emphasis on a particular apostolate or one

---

and personal prayer" (*CCC*, 2631).

or another charism, or charisms in general. Each of these introduces an imbalance in the life of faith[12] that impedes ongoing conversion into the holiness of the perfection of charity.

Still, it is the life of faith onto which such exaggerations have been grafted. In my experience, those who exhibit them do so precisely because they see them as a way to take their faith seriously. This makes correcting them both difficult and delicate. For, if it is rather easy for others—family, friends, teachers, pastors, spiritual directors—to spot exaggerations, it is not so easy for those who live with them. This is why theological balance and pastoral prudence must be exercised in addressing them, lest the good seed of faith be uprooted in efforts to remove the weeds of excess.[13]

It is doubtful that many who exhibit such distortions do so purposefully. It is more likely that exaggerations have crept in, as if to compensate for a sense that something is missing. Imbalances in the spiritual life may well be rooted in the conviction that faith should permeate every aspect of life. If the claims made about Jesus Christ and His Church are true, then one quite rightly concludes that they ought to explain and give meaning to everything that Christians experience. The challenge is to receive in faith the explanation and meaning that God assigns to life's events. If faith-formation has been defective, is it a wonder that people will attempt to fill the perceived void as best they can?

To complement solid catechesis regarding the spiritual life, a good set of spiritual exercises can contribute to attaining an equilibrium in the spiritual life that corresponds to God's will. This is why the theology of spiritual exercises exposited here has taken God's jealous love, the many ways that He makes Himself present to us, the primacy of holiness as the perfection of charity, divine

---

[12] Superstition is "a perverse excess of religion" (*CCC*, 2110).

[13] See Mt 13:29 and *CCC*, 1676.

mercy, conversion, and conscience as theological foundations. Knowing the many ways that Christ is present and following the wisdom of the saints about how to respond to Him is the remedy for the malady of overemphasizing just one of those ways He is present or distorting the essential purpose for which He makes Himself present.

That essential purpose is love. As we have seen, love is God's favorite subject. He Himself is love, and the entire history of salvation is revelation of His love for us and the love to which we, made in His image, are called. The passion, death, and resurrection of Jesus Christ is the summit of all of salvation history and revelation of love. In one way or another, all spiritual exercises are ordered to the ever more perfect reception and living of God's love in the obedience of faith following the dictates of a conscience purified by the blood of Christ. By sanctifying grace, God abides within us, and He constantly speaks to us through the memory of faith and the dictates of conscience. Those who know this and live it are not easily distracted by exaggerations about His presence and activity outside the soul, which is precisely what is common to the aforementioned distortions.

This is why this book has defined the call to holiness as the call to the perfection of charity (the first mission) and has discussed other spiritual exercises in terms of this love. Love is the highest meaning of life and of every event in life. This why conscience and fidelity to the duties of vocation have received a special attention in this theology of spiritual exercises. Other spiritual exercises, including reception and adoration of the Eucharist, are punctuated moments in the course of life. These might be extended by retreats and pilgrimages, but all spiritual exercises are ordered to the observance of the great commandments of love in the obedience of faith, so that charity more perfectly permeate every aspect of life. Those who understand this and are able to see the presence of Love in this way perceive the exaggerations discussed here as distractions that divert attention away from the one thing necessary.

It is a serious mistake, for example, virtually to equate one's mission or apostolate with one's relationship with Jesus. Yet, this is not an uncommon reality. After all, the thinking goes, Jesus entrusted the mission-apostolate to me. It is because I love Him that I take it with utmost seriousness and pour myself into it. I owe it to Him to give it my very best and to give Him glory by succeeding in it. This is, of course, logical and true, as far as it goes. But if and when unflagging dedication to a mission apostolate results in neglecting other spiritual exercises, proper balance is forfeited. Nor is it healthy to speak only about one's apostolate and to exaggerate its importance, as if the Church could not survive or thrive without it: What's good for my apostolate is good for the Church, and what's good for the Church is good for my apostolate. Proper perspective is also lost when a person measures relationships with others only in terms of their potential contribution to his apostolate. Such excesses can hardly fail to create an unhealthy culture within an apostolate. How many of the faithful who have been invited to work for an ecclesiastical institution or apostolate have been scandalized by the way they and others are treated? When the second mission of the apostolate eclipses the first mission of holiness, Jesus is no longer present in the apostolate as He desires to be present.

Those who wholeheartedly embrace the call to the perfection of charity see Christ where He truly is. As their charity increases so does their thinking with the Church (*sentire cum Ecclesia, sensus fidei*), so that they can discern what is authentic and balanced from what is a distortion. Their fundamental criterion for measuring all things is ongoing conversion on the foundation of the orthodox faith, with God's mercy at the center. They cannot be fooled into getting too excited about the latest program and movement that promises a renewal of the

Church but omits speaking about the death-to-sin and to self of conversion. They realize that one need not exaggerate the way that Christ is present and at work in an apostolate or in charisms because of His unsurpassable and stable presence in the Eucharist and His abiding presence in the heart and conscience. They realize that one need not see the devil everywhere—which, by the way, virtually assures that he will not be seen where he really is—in order to live with an all-pervading consciousness of Christ's victory over him and one's freedom in the Holy Spirit to love. They realize that one need not interpret every event as an indication that the end times have come because one knows that every moment of truth in conscience is invested with eschatological meaning, since every such moment is a judgment of truth and we will be judged by the Truth.

Distorted theologies and claims about prayer itself deserve special mention here. They are on display virtually everywhere, and the internet makes them readily available—just a click away. Billed as the answer to people's thirst for God, yet lacking a solid doctrinal foundation and only selectively drawing from the saints, these methods of prayer are "broken cisterns" that cannot hold the real water of God's truth and love (Jer 2:13). The reason is that they do not address the fundamental issue of sin and the confrontation with it and the ensuing battle of prayer and life, as the *Catechism* does. Only the prayer that does not evade suffering but adheres to its meaning in God's plan of love, only the prayer that embraces suffering with Christ for victory over sin nurtures the faith that is "hermeneutical vantage point where real and unreal [can] be distinguished, and communion with God [comes] to light as the locus of true life."[14]

A theology of spiritual exercises, such as the one presented here, has great pastoral potential to address numerous exaggerations in the spiritual lives of many of

---

[14] Ratzinger, *Dogmatic Theology: Eschatology and Eternal Life*, 91.

the faithful. It must be built on the solid theological foundation of the primacy of love, the drama of the interior battle, and the many ways that God makes Himself present to His people. These bedrock principles must be transmitted through a kerygmatic catechesis and preaching, which take the revelation of God's love in Jesus Christ and the purification of consciences for the sake of fulfilling the commandments of love as primary in a pastoral hierarchy of truths. Such a focus on love, conversion, and the purification of conscience to live in the obedience of faith is, essentially, the little way of spiritual childhood of St. Thérèse of Lisieux. Such a focus does not eliminate or diminish any of the ways that Christ is present. It does, however, keep them in proper perspective and prevents spiritual exercises and their fruits, including the Eucharist, from being diminished by superstition, a neurotic preoccupation, or a distorted valuation of some particular aspect of faith.

4. On the Unity of Faith, Liturgy, Prayer, and Life

One of the main goals of this book has been to show that considerations pertaining directly to Christian life (conversion into the perfection of charity) and others pertaining more directly to spiritual exercises are inseparable. This was the foundation for the discussion, above, of finding the proper balance in living out the truth of faith that the Eucharist is the source and summit of the Church's life and of the life of every disciple and friend of Christ. The principle is contained in a few lines of the *Catechism*:

> We pray as we live, because we live as we pray.
> If we do not want to act habitually according to
> the Spirit of Christ, neither can we pray

> habitually in his name. The "spiritual battle" of the Christian's new life is inseparable from the battle of prayer.[15]

This can be expanded to include all four parts of the *Catechism*: We believe as we worship, live, and pray; We worship in the liturgy as we believe, live, and pray; We live as we believe, worship, and pray; We pray as we believe, worship, and live.

With these assertions, we perceive how profoundly the *Catechism* corresponds to the central pastoral concern of the Second Vatican Council, namely, to overcome the split between the faith that Christians profess and celebrate, and their daily lives.[16] The *Catechism* conveys this unity by showing that the essential subject or content of each of its four parts is the mystery of Christ. Catholic spirituality concerns the mystery of Christ inasmuch as by participating in it the pilgrimage of faith of Christ's disciples and friends entails ongoing conversion into more and more perfect charity and participation in His life and mission. Spirituality cannot be separated from the doctrine of faith, which expounds various aspects of the meaning of the mystery of Christ. Nor can it be separated from the Church's liturgical life, since the mystery of Christ is made present and operative in the liturgy.

The unity of the four aspects of the mystery of Christ gives rise to several important insights contained in the wisdom of the saints. We have already seen one such insight in the counsel of St. Augustine and St. Thomas Aquinas regarding daily reception of Holy Communion. Another derives from the unity of prayer and life: the life of Christian virtue is a reliable commentary on prayer, and prayer is a helpful commentary on life. For example, St. Teresa of Avila judged the perfection of prayer based on the influence

---

[15] *CCC*, 2725.

[16] Vatican II, *Gaudium et spes*, 43.

of charity not only in prayer but also in virtue.[17] Progress in humility and virtue are indications that one is praying according to the graces of prayer that God is giving.[18] This is a most helpful principle for spiritual directors in discerning various seasons of grace in the lives of directees and in adjusting spiritual exercises accordingly.

This theology of spiritual exercises has drawn particular attention to the examination of conscience. The fundamental reason is that the entire spiritual life is the unfolding of the graces received in Baptism, which confers the gift of a conscience purified by the blood of Christ.[19] The function of conscience is to assure the unity of faith (the mystery of Christ believed) and worship (the mystery of Christ celebrated) with life (the mystery of Christ lived). Judgments of conscience presuppose the assent of faith to God's revelation in Christ regarding what constitutes human fulfillment or happiness. For, He is the perfect man,[20] Who reveals what it means for those whom God has made in His image to fulfill their vocation to love. Judgments of conscience are, in the end, judgments about what love demands.[21] To conform oneself to the truth dictated by conscience and determined by prudence constitutes what St. Paul calls the "obedience of faith" (Rom 1:5; 16:26),[22] and in another place a Christian life of "truth in love" (Eph 4:15). The truth about God's love and man's vocation to participate in it, fully revealed in Jesus

---

[17] "It is on this quality of friendship, that is, on the quality of supernatural love and its effects in virtue and in union, that she is going to judge the perfection of prayer itself" (Marie-Eugene of the Child Jesus, *I Want to See God*, 60).

[18] "If one finds in a soul signs of the action of God, namely, humility and progress in virtue, one must not disturb it in its modes of prayer; it has a right to its liberty, and all have a duty to respect this" (Marie-Eugene of the Child Jesus, *I Want to See God*, 58).

[19] See Heb 9:9, 14:10:2, 20–22; 1 Pt 3:21.

[20] See Vatican II, *Gaudium et spes*, 22, 38, 41, 45.

[21] See Vatican II, *Gaudium et spes*, 16.

[22] See Vatican II, *Dei Verbum*, 5.

Christ, "needs to be sought, found and expressed within the 'economy' of charity, but charity in its turn needs to be understood, confirmed and practised in the light of truth."[23]

On this, we can turn to Hinnebusch once more. He shows that in order for faith to penetrate into the daily life of believers, and thus to make the whole of their lives a prayer, that is, a spiritual sacrifice or logical worship, it must work through the judgment of conscience.

> Addressed to the conscience and received by the conscience, the word of faith should ever be alive in the conscience as a source of life in response to God's love: "Hold the mystery of faith with a clear conscience" (1 Tim 3:9). Conscience is called faith (Rom 14:23) inasmuch as it holds onto the word of faith and acts according to it. For faith is its light, and the word of God received in faith gives it direction. Man must ever direct his life according to the Gospel of Christ; his conscience, perfected by faith, judges how the Gospel ought to be applied in life's particular actions.
>
> For conscience is in vain unless through faith it reaches God in all of life's action. And faith is in vain unless it is operative through conscience in every life-situation. Only each man's personal conscience can judge, in the light of faith, what is good or evil for him personally in this or that precise situation. "Whoever knows what is right to do, and fails to do it, for him it is sin" (Jas 4:17).
>
> Conscience is therefore immature unless it lives constantly by faith. For only through a conscience fully enlightened by faith can the faith become operative in the whole of life. Only through a conscience expert in "practicing the

---

[23] Benedict XVI, *Caritas in veritate*, 2.

truth in love" does the grace of God received in faith flow into all of life (Eph 4:15).

For every grace brings a responsibility. Grace is fully effective only through responsible action carried out in this grace. Thus the grace we receive from God in faith becomes our responsibility in conscience. Through the workings of right conscience, grace effectively passes into one's whole life. Faith and conscience thus work as one.

When conscience thus makes the grace of faith operative in the whole of life, the whole of life is a prayer, a communion with God, a response in grace to God and His grace.[24]

Hinnebusch's comment on the identity of faith and conscience in Romans 14:23 could very well have been taken from St. Thomas's commentary on that verse:

Here faith can be taken in two ways: in one way of faith as a virtue; in another way, so that conscience is called faith. These two meanings differ only as particular and universal. For what we hold by faith universally, for example, that the use of foods is lawful or unlawful, conscience applies to a deed performed or to be performed.[25]

The obedience of faith is the Christian's submission of obedience to God as He makes His will known in judgments of conscience. How else could one's whole life be a spiritual sacrifice pleasing to God, and thus be called

---

[24] Hinnebusch, *Prayer*, 179–180.
[25] Aquinas, *Commentary on St. Paul's Letter to the Romans*, Ch. 14, lect. 3 (Marietti, 1140).

logical worship?[26] The obedience of faith is participation in Christ's obedience, of which the Virgin Mary is the most perfect realization: "let it be with me according to your word" (Lk 1:38). By her faith, God's eternal Word and Mary become one. By her faith, God's words about her vocation to be the mother of the Messiah and Son of God become fully hers by informing her conscience. As the meaning of these words unfold throughout her pilgrimage of faith and reveal to her all that she must do in order to be faithful to her vocation, and thus to God, Mary lives as "the handmaid of the Lord" in the obedience of faith.

5. On the Order of Reason and the Order of Faith

The unity of truth is a fundamental principle of Catholic faith and spirituality. By "unity of truth" is understood the complementarity between what we can know by reason alone, without faith, and what we know by faith.[27] In the spiritual life, this corresponds to two sets of virtues: the natural virtues, acquired by discipline and repetition, and the supernatural virtues, especially faith, hope, and charity, received as gifts of grace.

Christ's disciples and friends can, at times, neglect how God makes His will known through what we know by reason. Although it may be due to defective catechesis, it is nonetheless a practical contempt for the first gift of creation. The result can be called an exaggerated supernaturalization of Christian life based on unfounded

---

[26] "I appeal to you therefore, brothers and sisters, by the mercies of God, to present your bodies as a living sacrifice, holy and acceptable to God, which is your spiritual worship" (Rom 12:1). The Greek translated here as "spiritual worship" is, literally, worship according to the *logos*, that is: "worship in harmony with the eternal Word and with our reason" (Benedict XVI, Address to Representatives of Science at the University of Regensburg, September 12, 2006).

[27] See John Paul II, *Fides et ratio*, 34.

assumptions about how God's graces actually work. For example, a person neglects the arduous discipline required to cultivate acquired virtues, like temperance and prudence, while praying that God grant what would amount to a miraculous mastering of the passions regulated by temperance, or infused knowledge to guide certain decisions that should be directed by prudence.

Moreover, it is obvious that a great many acts of daily love concern basic human goods related to the development of the mind and body, and that the effective imparting of these goods requires a great deal of practical wisdom acquired by experience and transmitted through culture. Thus, parents need to be well-informed regarding an expansive number of issues regarding their children's physical, psychic, and intellectual well-being. The Gospel commands that we love by desiring the good for those whom we love, but regarding goods of nature it leaves us to acquire the knowledge by which we can effectively impart those goods.

The distinction between the natural and the supernatural orders was one of Vatican II's principal themes. Their harmonious integration in the lives of Christ's disciples and friends was perhaps the Council's principal pastoral concern. This is one reason why conscience receives the attention it does in the Conciliar texts. For, the function of the Christian conscience is precisely to bring about this harmonious integration.

> Because of the very economy of salvation the faithful should learn how to distinguish carefully between those rights and duties which are theirs as members of the Church, and those which they have as members of human society. Let them strive to reconcile the two, remembering that in every temporal affair they must be guided by a Christian conscience, since even in secular business there is no human activity which can be

withdrawn from God's dominion. In our own time, however, it is most urgent that this distinction and also this harmony should shine forth more clearly than ever in the lives of the faithful, so that the mission of the Church may correspond more fully to the special conditions of the world today. For it must be admitted that the temporal sphere is governed by its own principles, since it is rightly concerned with the interests of this world. But that ominous doctrine which attempts to build a society with no regard whatever for religion, and which attacks and destroys the religious liberty of its citizens, is rightly to be rejected.[28]

Because God is the Author of both the created, natural order and the supernaturally revealed order of faith, this integration of conscience is necessary to be faithful to Him in all things by living out the "obedience of faith" (Rom 1:5) so that the whole of a believer's life be a "spiritual sacrifice" (1 Pt 2:5) and "spiritual worship" (Rom 12:1).

6. On Recreation and Enjoyment of the Goods of Creation and Culture

"For all things are yours ...; and you are Christ's, and Christ is God's" (1 Cor 3:21–23). Among the things that belong to God because they belong to Christ and yet are entrusted to us is time. How we use our time depends on our priorities, our hierarchy of values, and these ultimately depend on our definition of happiness, our vision for a

---

[28] Vatican II, *Lumen gentium*, 36. See also *Gaudium et spes*, 43. The function of conscience to integrate the truth known by natural reason and by faith is a foundational principle in the Council's documents on education (*Gravissimum educationis*) and religious liberty (*Dignitatis humanae*).

fully meaningful and happy life. We have seen how responsibility for the use of time, informed by faith, results in making spiritual exercises a priority. While recreation is not a spiritual exercise, it is nevertheless an important consideration for anyone who desires to be faithful to a sustainable set of spiritual exercises. Like eating well and exercising, discipline regarding recreation is an element of living reasonably, and thus, virtuously. Such activities are ordered to the supernatural end of friendship with Christ and the call to holiness and to mission.

In their wisdom, the saints warn us against the kind of presumption that does not take into consideration the need for relaxation and recreation (or amusement). This is all the greater an issue when a person experiences the dynamism of charity that empowers a generous gift of oneself: "the love of Christ urges us on" (2 Cor 5:14). Charity desires to pour itself out for the sake of others. While charity itself in indefatigable, since it is a participation in God's own love, the subject of charity, the human person, must humbly accept the limitations that come with the human condition. This is where recreation has its place.

Closely associated with recreation is the enjoyment of the goods of creation and culture. The good of friendship will be considered in a moment. Here the focus is on time set aside for participation in cultural events and goods, such as concerts, museums, and anniversaries, marveling at God's creation, and enjoying works of art and the fruits of the earth and the work of human hands. Weekends, holidays, and vacations reflect the rhythm of daily meals with family and friends, when the fruits of preceding work are enjoyed. Similarly, periods of relaxation and enjoyment of goods are preceded by work. They are more than mere respites from work. They are the opportunity to enjoy the blessings of creation and thus of the Creator and in a way to rest in Him. In essence, we are dealing with a spirituality rooted in the theology of the Sabbath.

For recreation and enjoyment of earthly goods to be

authentically Christian they must be morally upright, subordinated to overall personal well-being, which includes the life of faith, and willed for the sake of fulfilling the vocation to give God glory by bearing witness to His love. In other words, Christ's disciples and friends recreate because it is God's will to do so. Moral integrity concerns both the nature or object of the recreational activity as well as its duration and frequency. Not all activities pass the test of moral integrity, and if recreation is used to avoid responsibilities concerning justice and charity then it is no longer good. It is possible to recreate too often and for too long, but it is also possible not to recreate often enough.

Productive hobbies and the cultivation of related skills (such as gardening, writing letters or poetry, fishing, photography, wood-working, knitting, reading, cooking and baking, walking and other forms of exercise) can fill hours of recreation without the moral risks involved in watching programmed television and surfing the internet. When it is done with others, recreation is also an opportunity to build and to deepen friendships.

Recreation can be an element of a *horarium*, whether communal or personal. If it is part of a personal *horarium*, it can be either formal in the sense of having been worked out, perhaps with a spiritual director, or it can be a *de facto horarium* resulting from the ordering of daily and weekly life in view of following Christ as closely as possible. A *horarium* is made for the spiritual life, not the spiritual life for the *horarium*.

Like all spiritual exercises, recreation is subject to adjustment. Flexibility in recreation is especially important for those whose lives are subject to significant vicissitudes, whether due to health, age, work, or family. For example, a family vacation might have to be postponed due to some unforeseen circumstances. It might be wise to schedule it earlier than usual when a family has been through some significant, stress-producing event, and is need of some relaxation. Or, it might be wise to schedule it prior to some important event.

As the fruit of fidelity to spiritual exercises, an alert conscience will guide decisions about recreation that are moral in nature, that is, decisions regarding love. Christ's disciples and friends do not blindly follow societal and cultural standards. Regarding vacations, for example, the standard of Christian faith and love determines things like the kinds of activities and reasonable affordability. That standard also determines the necessary adjustment of spiritual exercises during a vacation. There is no such thing as a vacation from daily prayer and attendance at Sunday Mass! For some, the development of the "love of Christ that impels" leads to using some of their annual vacation time for one or another form of charitable work, like a medical mission. For them, and others, love has so transformed them that service has become a form of recreation. This is a profoundly edifying witness to the great reversal of values brought about by faith in Jesus Christ. Still, one should not be naïve about the need for regular relaxation, recreation, and enjoyment of the good of creation.

The desire for the perfection of love in all things can lead a person to seek the advice of others regarding the right balance of recreation. For example, it is not uncommon for friends of Christ to examine themselves regarding how much money to spend on a house, car, vacation, or hobby. In such cases, consulting a wise friend, pastor, or spiritual director can contribute to arriving at the right prudential decision.

7. On the Importance of Friendship in the Spiritual Life

Strictly speaking, friendship or community is not a

spiritual exercise. Like fidelity to vocational tasks and duties, it is the fruit of Baptism and the spiritual exercises ordered to the full development of baptismal grace. At the same time, it is incontestable that, again, like fidelity to vocational duties, spiritual friendships also bear fruit. This is why many Christians, especially young adults, who lack meaningful friendships and community grounded in the common commitment to strive for holiness,[29] know they are missing something profoundly important.

For one thing, we observe how spontaneously Christ's disciples and friends who have the same vocation and related gifts associate with one another. For another, as the family of God, the Church's unity takes the relationships within families as a foundational point of reference. The members of a family live in an all-embracing solidarity. They go through life together, support one another, and share in one another's joys and accomplishments as well as their sorrows and struggles.[30] The hunger for Christian friendship is all the stronger in a culture experiencing the breakdown of the family and social solidarity.

It is extremely difficult to sustain spiritual exercises and a life of Christian virtue in isolation. In His plan of wisdom and love, God did not intend that we do.[31] Friendship and community—the ecclesial dimension of the spiritual life—are the normal context in which disciples and friends of Christ grow in holiness. Moreover, how can one be a true disciple and friend of Christ without

---

[29] Programs for young adults attempt to address the transition from a time when the family meets the needs of children, teens, and to some extent, young adults, to college and the world of work (e.g., Young Catholic Professionals, FOCUS, campus ministries).

[30] "If one member suffers, all suffer together; if one member is honored, all rejoice together" (1 Cor 12:26).

[31] "God, however, does not make men holy and save them merely as individuals, without bond or link between one another. Rather has it pleased Him to bring men together as one people, a people which acknowledges Him in truth and serves Him in holiness" (Vatican II, *Lumen gentium*, 9).

associating with His other disciples and friends?

St. Teresa of Avila bears witness to the wisdom of the saints regarding the value of spiritual friendships:

> A great evil it is for a soul to be alone in the midst of so many dangers. It seems to me that if I should have had someone to talk all this over with it would have helped me, at least out of shame, not to fall again since I did not have any shame before God. For this reason I would counsel those who practice prayer to seek, at least in the beginning, friendship and association with other persons having the same interest. This is something most important even though the association may be only to help one another with prayers.... Since friends are sought out for conversations and human attachments, even though these latter may not be good, so as to relax and better enjoy telling about vain pleasures, I don't know why it is not permitted that persons beginning truly to love and to serve God talk with some others about their joys and trials, which all who practice prayer undergo.... Since this spiritual friendship is so extremely important for souls not yet fortified in virtue—since they have so many opponents and friends to incite them to evil—I don't know how to urge it enough.[32]

This text is a splendid example of the unity of the natural and supernatural orders, briefly discussed, above. St. Teresa observes that it is natural for people to form friendships. She might have added, and perhaps this is

---

[32] Teresa of Avila, *Life*, 7, 20–21 (*The Collected Works of St. Teresa of Avila*, vol. 1, trans. Kieran Kavanaugh and Otilio Rodriguez [Washington, D.C.: ICS Publications, 2nd edition, 1987], 92–93).

implicit for her, that friendships develop as a result of common interests. So, she thinks it is natural—we might say supernaturally natural—for those who are serious about living their faith to form friendships centered on Jesus Christ and His Church. For St. Teresa, friendship in the Lord is so indispensable an element of the Christian vocation that she cannot imagine how she could have persevered in faith and avoided hell without it.

> But a good means to having God is to speak with His friends, for one always gains very much from this. I know through experience. After the Lord, it is because of persons like these that I am not in hell, for I was always very attached to their praying for me, and so I strove to get them to do this.
>
> This spiritual love is the kind of love I would desire us to have. Even though in the beginning it is not so perfect, the Lord will gradually perfect it.[33]

She relates that she learned this lesson the hard way. Based on this experience, she exhorts parents to be solicitous in assuring that their children keep company with other children of virtuous character: "If I were to give advice, I would tell parents that when their children are this age they ought to be very careful about whom their children associate with."[34] She continues:

> It frightens me sometimes to think of the harm a bad companion can do, and if I hadn't experienced it I wouldn't believe it. Especially during adolescence the harm done must be

---

[33] Teresa of Avila, *Way of Perfection*, 7, 4–5 (*The Collected Works of St. Teresa of Avila*, vol. 2, trans. Kieran Kavanaugh and Otilio Rodriguez [Washington, D.C.: ICS Publications, 1980], 67–68).

[34] Teresa of Avila, *Life*, 2, 3 (*The Collected Works of St. Teresa of Avila*, vol. 1, 58).

greater. I should like parents to learn from my experience to be very watchful in this matter. And indeed this conversation so changed me that hardly any virtue remained to my naturally virtuous soul. And I think she and another girl friend of the same type impressed their own traits upon me.

From such experience I understand the great profit that comes from good companionship. And I am certain that if at that age I had gone around with virtuous persons, I would have remained whole in virtue. For should I have had when that age someone to teach me to fear God, my soul would have gained strength not to fall. Afterward, having lost this fear of God completely, I only had the fear of losing my reputation, and such fear brought me torment in everything I did. With the thought that my deeds would not be known, I dared to do many things truly against my honor and against God.[35]

St. Teresa's advice about friendship, given to parents and to the sisters of her community, confirms her title as *Mater Spiritualium*—Mother of those aspiring to the heights of the spiritual life. It is equally valuable for pastors, those engaged in an apostolate for youth, and spiritual directors.

How many promising starts in the spiritual life end up resembling the second or third kinds of seed in the parable of the sower because the disciple did not break away from prior relationships? This points to the importance of meaningful integration into the community of believers as a normal condition for spiritual growth. To neglect the importance of Christ-centered friendships would be to have contempt for the way that God made us, namely, with a

---

[35] Teresa of Avila, *Life*, 2, 4–5 (*The Collected Works of St. Teresa of Avila*, vol. 1, 58–59).

social nature. If Christ's disciples do not satisfy their need for friendship with holy friendships in the Lord, they will be tempted to associate with others whose values do not align with the values of Christ's kingdom.

> And it is a kind of humility not to trust in oneself but to believe that through those with whom one converses God will help and increase charity while it is being shared. And there are a thousand graces I would not dare speak of if I did not have powerful experience of the benefit that comes from this sharing. It is true that I am the weakest and most wicked of all human beings. But I believe they will not be lost who, humbling themselves, even though they be strong, do not believe by themselves but believe this one who has experience. Of myself I know and say that if the Lord had not revealed this truth to me and given me the means by which I could ordinarily talk with persons who practice prayer, I, falling and rising, would have ended by throwing myself straight into hell. For in falling I had many friends to help me; but in rising I found myself so alone that I am now amazed I did not remain ever fallen. And I praise the mercy of God, for it was He alone who gave me His hand. May He be blessed forever and ever.[36]

In our days, we are witnessing a profound breakdown of the family, which is the first school of moral and social virtue, and thus of love and formation of conscience. The ability to make friends derives from the experience of

---

[36] Teresa of Avila, *Life*, 2, 8 (*The Collected Works of St. Teresa of Avila*, vol. 1, 60).

being loved by one's parents, who are the first representatives of God to their children.[37] The family's mission is to reproduce the mercy and joy of conversion that typify the household of the father of the prodigal son. Only when people know that their sins cannot eradicate the love of family and friends can they face their sins and benefit from the development of conscience.

Today we hear much about evangelization through beauty. Might an element of this be the beauty of friendship? Doesn't friendship correspond to the human person's deepest longings? It is no accident that St. Thomas Aquinas defined charity as supernatural friendship. There being no more perfect a form of human association than friendship, he constructed his theology of charity on the concept of friendship. Charity is the supernatural realization of man's longing for friendship with God, and with others. As we have seen, at the end of His mission of discipling the apostles, Jesus revealed that His mission, including His passion, death, and resurrection, was entirely ordered to their becoming His friends (Jn 15:13–15).

A fascinating aspect of the friendship of charity is that while it is an end in itself, it bears fruits that have an important place in the spiritual life, as St. Teresa of Avila testifies. Friends support one another, first and foremost, by each one's fidelity to God, to His Church, and to the call to holiness. Friends exercise their charisms or gifts to serve one another and, together, to serve others. Friends forgive one another. Friends multiply the joy of living in the certainty of being loved by God.

8. On Suffering

Suffering is not a spiritual exercise but the occasion for spiritual exercises. Faith, hope, and charity can and must be

---

[37] See *CCC*, 239.

exercised as occasioned by and in suffering. Spiritual suffering (the dark nights) strengthens these theological virtues so that they may more perfectly extend their influence in all things. Temporal, or physical suffering also purifies them by driving home that because of sin all of "creation was subjected to futility" (Rom 8:20) and thrust into a state of "groaning with labor pains" (Rom 8:22), so that "the form of this world is passing away" (1 Cor 7:31). For people of faith, suffering is the reminder that "here we have no lasting city, but we are looking for the city that is to come" (Heb 13:14). Suffering elicits the eschatological dimension of faith, hope, and charity.

Spiritual exercises should bear the fruit of having a positive effect on how Christ's disciples and friends suffer, on the quality of suffering. Christ-like suffering confirms that the profession and celebration of the mystery of Christ, as well as prayer based on the mystery of Christ, has penetrated into daily life.

One of the greatest purifications of the faith of the apostles concerned the place of suffering and death in the life and mission of the Messiah.[38] They could not grasp how God could save us *from* suffering and death *through* suffering and death. Only the resurrection is able to convince that God has fulfilled His promise to bring about a definitive liberation from suffering. While we believe that the promise of the resurrection will bring about definitive liberation from temporal, physical and bodily suffering, we also believe that Christ has instituted His Church, with her sacraments, in order to free us from the greatest of all suffering, that of a remorseful conscience. In God's plan, all suffering is a catalyst for turning to Him in prayer in order to present to Him our questions regarding suffering.[39] Already here on earth, we have access to the fruits of His victory over the spiritual suffering of a

---

[38] See: Mt 16:21; Lk 24:7, 26, 46; Acts 3:18; 17:3; 26:23; 1 Pt 1:11.

[39] See *CCC*, 309 and 164.

troubled, remorseful conscience.

It gives great glory to God to continue to believe in His love even when the evidence for that love is so greatly reduced by suffering that it seems as if God has abandoned us. It is easy to believe and to hope once the crucified Lord has risen. But the reluctance of St. Thomas the Apostle to believe and the haunting words of the disciples from Emmaus, "we *had hoped* that he was the one to redeem Israel" (Lk 24:21), should serve to keep us humble regarding our ability to remain faithful even in the darkness of suffering and death—when God *seems* to have abandoned us.

Faith prompts us to see all suffering in the light of Easter and to will it as a participation in Christ's suffering and death on Good Friday, about which the Letter to the Hebrews teaches: "for the sake of the joy that was set before him [He] endured the cross, disregarding its shame" (Heb 12:2 RSV). When God's grace empowers us to be strong and faithful through suffering, we receive the spiritual consolation of knowing that our faith and hope are not based on consolations but only on the motive of God's truthfulness, goodness, and mercy.

In a culture like ours, which prizes the power to influence and to control and therefore cannot see any value in suffering, Christians who unite their suffering and death to Christ's are truly signs of contradiction. For, suffering reduces us, to one degree or another, to a state of passivity. As suffering increases, our ability to exercise the causality of love, which constitutes our very dignity as image of God,[40] seems also to decrease. When it is severe, suffering can make it impossible to fulfill the exterior tasks and duties of our vocation and mission. Precisely at such a time, Christ's disciples and friends remember that their first mission of holiness takes precedence over the second mission of active apostolate. Suffering does not interfere

---

[40] See *CCC*, 306–307.

with the first mission of being with Christ. Rather, it is the occasion to be with Christ in the suffering of His passion and death. When offered in faith as a sacrifice to God, united with Christ's sacrifice, suffering becomes efficacious atonement and intercession.

Faith perceives that the power of Christ to transform a sinful world reached its zenith in the passivity of His passion and death on the cross. It is not one of His displays of great power, such as the calming of a storm, the multiplication of fish and bread to feed thousands, the healing of lepers, the power of His teaching to bring people to faith, or even the raising of His friend Lazarus, the daughter of Jairus, and the son of the widow from Nain—it is not any of these that has pride of place among Christian symbols. Rather, it is the crucifix, where it appears that Jesus is entirely stripped of the dignity of being a cause.

It is, of course, only an apparent stripping. Faith sees beyond the exterior sacrifice to perceive the Son of God's interior sacrifice of love. We believe that Christ's power for the redemption of the world lies in His paschal charity, by which He loves His Father and us "to the end" (Jn 13:1). Jesus goes before us all in revealing what St. Paul put into words: "for when I am weak, then I am strong" (2 Cor 12:10). The paschal mystery is the definitive revelation of the human dignity of being a cause because it is the definitive revelation, in Christ, of God's merciful love. The spiritual exercises considered in this book, which are so many ways of encountering the merciful love of God fully revealed in the mystery of Christ, are necessary if Christ's disciples and friends are to unite their sufferings with His redemptive suffering and death. In this way, Christ's friends can make St. Paul's words their own: "Now I rejoice in my sufferings for your sake, and in my flesh I complete what is lacking in Christ's afflictions for the sake of his body, that is, the Church" (Col 1:24).

To unite our sufferings with those of Christ in this way fulfills our vocation, our first mission, to love ourselves by turning to God to receive His love that conforms us to Christ. Conformity to Christ, even in His suffering, is the goal and joy for His disciples. In the words of Benedict XVI:

> I would like to add here another brief comment with some relevance for everyday living. There used to be a form of devotion—perhaps less practiced today but quite widespread not long ago—that included the idea of "offering up" the minor daily hardships that continually strike at us like irritating "jabs", thereby giving them a meaning.... What does it mean to offer something up? Those who did so were convinced that they could insert these little annoyances into Christ's great "com-passion" so that they somehow became part of the treasury of compassion so greatly needed by the human race. In this way, even the small inconveniences of daily life could acquire meaning and contribute to the economy of good and of human love. Maybe we should consider whether it might be judicious to revive this practice ourselves.[41]

To be conformed to Christ, even "to the end" (Jn 13:1) of His revelation of God's mercy makes us "associate[s] in His compassion."[42] To bear witness to God in suffering is one of the most important ways to fulfill the second mission of loving others, that is, to evangelize through witness. So much so that Christ instituted the Sacrament of the Anointing of the Sick, by which His disciples and friends with serious ailments are "consecrated to bear fruit by configuration to the Savior's redemptive Passion."[43] This sacrament unleashes the love of the sick so that they

---

[41] Benedict XVI, *Spe salvi*, 40.

[42] *CCC*, 2575.

[43] *CCC*, 1521.

can "contribute to the sanctification of the Church and to the good of all men for whom the Church suffers and offers herself through Christ to God the Father."[44]

Suffering, then, is no obstacle to the fulfillment of the human vocation to be a cause by loving. Rather, suffering can be the occasion for the unleashing of love: "we could say that suffering, which is present under so many different forms in our human world, is also present in order *to unleash love in the human person,* that unselfish gift of one's 'I' on behalf of other people, especially those who suffer."[45] Can there be any better way to prepare for this sacrament than by daily offering our suffering to God? Here, again, we encounter the unity of faith, liturgy, and life.

We know that it is one thing to manifest devotion during times of consolation and relative ease in following Jesus, and quite another to be faithful in times of suffering. In Eucharistic terms: "And there is a friend who is a table companion, but will not stand by you in your day of trouble" (Sir 6:10). We know that this applies to Peter and the other apostles who celebrated the Last Supper with Jesus and yet did not stand by Him through His paschal mystery. Is this not the common experience of Christ's disciples and friends who share in the breaking of the bread with Him at Mass and yet find themselves denying Him by their actions—often, to avoid some kind of suffering, and especially the suffering of death to self?

Yet, faith assures us that "the sufferings of this present time are not worth comparing with the glory that is to be revealed to us" (Rom 8:18)—revealed, not only in heaven, but already here on earth, in the Eucharist. Awareness of the yet imperfect harmony between faith, liturgy, and life, then, is no reason to withdraw from celebrating the Eucharist. Rather, it gives rise to that "godly grief into repenting" (2 Cor 7:9) that corresponds to the contrition

---

[44] *CCC*, 1522.
[45] John Paul II, *Salvifici doloris*, 29.

expressed in the Penitential Rite. Such godly grief, or compunction of the heart,[46] humbles us—like the tax collector who beat his breast when confessing his sins[47]—and humility is the foundational disposition that we should bring to the celebration of Mass. Complementing, prepared by, and bringing other spiritual exercises to perfection, the Eucharist confers the grace of a deeper participation in Christ's mission as suffering Messiah so that, just as He left the upper room to embrace the cross of the Father's plan of love for Him, we might leave every celebration of the Eucharist strengthened in love to embrace the crosses of the Father's plan of love for us.

Bearing witness to God's wisdom, love, and power while suffering gives Him great glory. Was it not the quality of Jesus' suffering and death, revealed precisely in His final words of trust in the heavenly Father and forgiveness for those who tortured Him and put Him to death, that caused a centurion to say: "Truly this man was the Son of God!" (Mk 15:39).[48] Let us recall the principle that "Christ enables us to live in Him all that He Himself lived, and He lives it in us."[49] By faith, we enter into His mission of witness to the Father in suffering with the same effect, so that those who see how His disciples and friends suffer can say: "Truly, they are disciples and friends of the Son of God!"

---

[46] See *CCC*, 1431.

[47] "But the tax collector, standing far off, would not even lift up his eyes to heaven, but beat his breast, saying, 'God, be merciful to me a sinner!'" (Lk 18:13).

[48] In Matthew, an earthquake prompts the centurion to make this confession of faith (Mt 27:54). But that, all by itself, cannot account for his assertion that Jesus is the Son of God.

[49] *CCC*, 521.

Conclusion

To situate the place of spiritual exercises in the life of Christ's disciples and friends, this book began with the biblical question, "What, then, must we do?" Looking back, we can see that there are two answers to this question because there are two ways of understanding the question.

The first takes the question to inquire about what constitutes the uniqueness of Christian life. Here, "What, then, must we do?" means: What is the goal that we should strive to attain? What acts correspond to the essence of what it means to be a disciple of Christ? Jesus Himself answers this question by quoting Deuteronomy 6:5 and Leviticus 19:18: "You shall love the Lord your God with all your heart, and with all your soul, and with all your mind. This is the great and first commandment. And a second is like it: You shall love your neighbor as yourself'" (Mt 22:37–39).

Jesus fully reveals what it means to observe these two commandments. In His revelation of God's love for man and man's love for God, He is the definitive interpretation of the Old Testament. He fulfills the Old Covenant by establishing the New Covenant. For this reason, He recapitulates the text just quoted with a new commandment: "A new commandment I give to you, that you love one another; even as I have loved you, that you also love one another" (Jn 13:34). This is Jesus's answer to the question, "What, then, must I do?"

The "as I have loved you" has all the force of inviting us to be one with Him in His love. He calls us not only to imitate His love but to participate in it, to become one with Him and to live in Him (what we have called the first mission) in order to be sent by Him to witness to God's love (second mission). To love with the love that is a participation in the very love of Christ is the defining action of His disciples: "By this all men will know that you are my disciples, if you have love for one another" (Jn 13:35).

Jesus defined friendship with Him in terms of obeying His new commandment of love: "You are my friends if you do what I command you" (Jn 15:14). It is a great grace to desire to be a friend of Christ. It is a blessing of God's mercy, a grace won for us by Christ's self-sacrifice, to define one's happiness in terms of being one with Him in His relation to the Father and His mission to reveal love. He gives this grace in response to the question, "What, then, must I do?"

The question admits of a second understanding. This takes the question to inquire about what must be done in order to keep Christ's commandment of love. Knowing now what the goal is, what must I do live up to this high calling of loving even as Christ has loved me? What must I do to be a good steward of the grace to be His friend, so that I can say, with St. Paul: "I have been crucified with Christ; it is no longer I who live, but Christ who lives in me" (Gal 2:20). This too is a grace. So, the question is: What must I do to receive this grace to be a good steward of grace? Since only Jesus can give this grace, the question comes down to: Where is Jesus, and what must I do to encounter Him to receive this grace? The answer is: practice the spiritual exercises recommended by the saints.

The reason why Christ has made Himself present in numerous ways is because He has fulfilled and definitively revealed what it means for God to be jealous. His jealousy reveals that He wants us all—every one of us, and all of every one of us—for Himself, not because He needs us but because He is our only happiness. It is a great grace, therefore, to be baptized into Christ's apostolic Church, which preserves the memory of Christ and of His saints and their wisdom regarding spiritual exercises. It is a great grace to be instructed in this wisdom. The hope that motivated the writing of this theology of spiritual exercises is that it will introduce readers to this wisdom so that they can cooperate with the grace of being called to holiness and to the apostolate—the grace of being with Christ and sent by Him. The Church's veneration of the saints assures us that their lives and teachings, and the spiritual exercises that they practiced and recommend for others, are a sure path for following Christ by observing the commandment to love as we have been loved. Regarding these exercises, we can end by quoting St. Peter: "if you do this you will never fall" (2 Pt 1:10); and our Lord: "do this, and you will live" (Lk 10:28).

About the Author

Douglas Bushman's teaching and writing in theology has been shaped especially by the Church Fathers' spiritual reading of Scripture, the theological methodology of St. Thomas Aquinas, and the pastoral orientation of the Second Vatican Council, as interpreted and implemented by St. John Paul II and Benedict XVI. He has exercised the gift of theology in service to the Church at virtually every level of the Church's life: parish, diocese (including programs of formation and courses for adults, catechists, permanent deacons, Catholic educators, and seminarians), Catholic schools, RCIA, and undergraduate and graduate degree programs.

Bushman has served as Lay Theologian for the parish of St. Charles Borromeo (Minneapolis), Director of Parish Mission for the Church of St. Joseph (West St. Paul), Director of Education (Diocese of Duluth), Director of the Institute for Religious and Pastoral Studies (University of Dallas), and Director of the Institute for Pastoral Theology (Ave Maria University). His last academic position was with the Augustine Institute (Denver), where he was St. John Paul II Professor of Theology for the New Evangelization. Currently Prof. Bushman's research and publishing focuses on the pastoral theology of the Second Vatican Council, the New Evangelization, and Catholic Spirituality.

Following his B.A. in Aristotelian and Thomistic philosophy (College of St. Thomas, St. Paul), he studied under the Dominican Pontifical Faculty of Theology at the University of Fribourg, Switzerland, who imparted a vibrant Thomism incorporating the study of Scripture, the Church Fathers, the best of the *ressourcement* theologians of the 20th century, Vatican II, and the best among post-Conciliar theologians.

Bushman is the author of *The Theology of Renewal for His Church: The Logic of Vatican II's Renewal in Paul VI's Encyclical* Ecclesiam Suam, *and Its Reception in John Paul II and Benedict XVI* (Wipf and Stock, 2024), and *A Kingdom Within: The Conversion of King David* (Draft2Digital, 2024). He contributed to the English translation of the *Catechism of the Catholic Church*, and his articles have appeared in numerous Catholic publications including *Nova et Vetera*, *Homiletic and Pastoral Review*, *Lay Witness*, *Magnificat*, *Catholic World Report*, *Catholic Faith*, *Catholic Dossier*, and *The Catholic Servant.*

www.ingramcontent.com/pod-product-compliance
Lightning Source LLC
Chambersburg PA
CBHW031312150426
43191CB00005B/187